NEWSCATCHER

Newscatcher

JOHN PALMER

KCM Publishing

Cover Design: Deena Warner Design
Editorial Production: India Amos and Peter Costanzo
Publisher: Michael Fabiano

All photos provided by the Palmer family
Additional photos courtesy of NBC News
Back cover photo courtesy of Diana Walker

ISBN 978-1-939961-13-6
ISBN 978-1-939961-11-2 (ePub)
ISBN 978-1-939961-12-9 (Mobi)

PUBLISHER'S NOTE

This memoir has been published posthumously and therefore every effort has been made to preserve the author's personality and intent. The text has been modified and edited slightly to maintain the integrity of how John Palmer told stories, whether reported on-air or to friends and family. These memories should be read with that spirit in mind.

KCM Publishing is a division of KCM Digital Media, LLC, that publishes books in all formats, specializing in eBooks, video-enhanced eBooks and print-on-demand paper books. We have a digital-first mentality looking to partner with outside authors and publishers to explore innovative, interactive approaches to cross-media products. KCM Publishing creates original books, converts existing material, and can create e-single publications based on current events, trends, profiles, lifestyles, historical events and more.

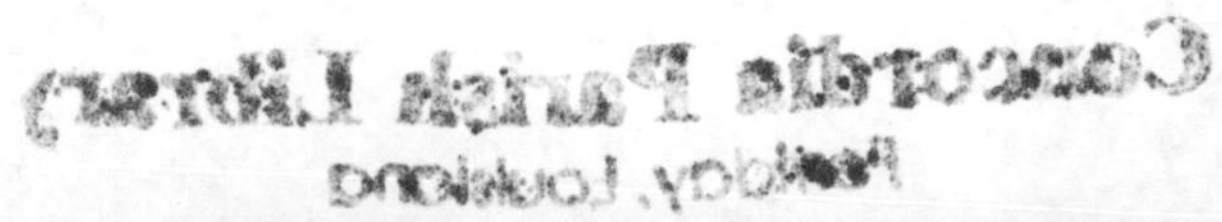

"I have laid aside business,
and gone a-fishing."

—IZAAK WALTON,
The Compleat Angler (1653–1655)

PRAISE FOR *NEWSCATCHER*

"John Palmer was the quintessential newsman—a dashing foreign correspondent and great storyteller who also has great tales from his years in Washington and as a star anchor on the Today show newsdesk at 30 Rock. His memoir is a gripping account from the trenches covering wars and terrorism in the Middle East to the political wars as a White House correspondent, all leavened with the wit and humor of a true Southern gentleman. Read this book and understand broadcast news at its best."

—ANDREA MITCHELL,
Chief Foreign Affairs Correspondent, NBC News

"I can't think of anyone but John Palmer who really had it all (and deserved it); a glamorous career as a Paris-based foreign correspondent, White House correspondent, and network anchor. And then he had his family. There's a great story here."

—JANE PAULEY,
former co-anchor for NBC's *Today*

"John Palmer's example shows us you can be a great reporter and, despite the intense pressures of journalism, a great human being at the same time. What a man of dignity and grace."

—ANN CURRY,
NBC News National and International Correspondent

"To read John Palmer's memoir is to be reminded of the kind of person it takes to be a truly great network correspondent. His tales are told with the charm that became a signature of his reporting. It's dignified, insightful, at times heartfelt, and funny. He was a wonderful mentor to me long before I became his son-in-law. He loved being a journalist, almost as much as he loved coming home to his wife and three girls. The TV news business needs more John Palmers. Life needs more John Palmers too."

—LEE COWAN,
CBS *Sunday Morning*

CONTENTS

FOREWORD
by Brian Williams

Arriving at the NBC News Washington Bureau was, for a young reporter, a bit like arriving at the Supreme Court as a rookie lawyer. Past the plaque where President Eisenhower dedicated the building—past the newsroom where you suddenly realize the "NBC NEWS WASHINGTON" banner on the back wall is something you've seen on TV all your adult life—you come to a narrow hallway lined with offices.

The names on the doors read like a hall of fame: Tim Russert, Andrea Mitchell, Irving R. Levine and Tom Pettit. Pausing at the last one, seeing him at his desk, I can hear him saying over and over, "Oswald's been shot!" the exact moment in the Dallas Police station when Tom's voice became part of our national record.

The nameplate that was most meaningful to me read John Palmer. Someone broke my stare by saying, "He's not in—he's at the White House." He was indeed. For many years. And journalism was all the better for it.

He did what he did for 40 years. He reported from postings in Chicago and Paris and the Middle East (they were fighting each other back then, and they still are now), but mostly he was a Washington guy. As good as he was at the anchor desk (where Today viewers got to see his very best every morning and early-risers got to enjoy his light touch on *NBC News at Sunrise*), Washington always called him home. In the corridors of power, especially the West Wing, John was like an old shoe in a sea of polished cordovan loafers. He was affable and self-deprecating. He got along well with everyone. His Tennessee roots came out when he was telling a story—his eyes would crinkle up, he'd add a little salt to his language, and most exchanges usually ended in laughter. Closer to deadline, it was a different story. John was all business.

Never a slave to fashion, never one to hobnob, he was the "good guy" everyone always talked about, the good reporter you dreamed of working with, the good friend you'd give anything to have back with us.

John died too soon. After a career chasing deadlines, it turns out his was approaching and none of us knew it. To paraphrase the obits he learned how to write as a young journalist: he is survived by his family—and the love and respect he gained by being invited into living rooms and kitchens each day throughout this country. This story . . . the story of John Palmer . . . is great. So was every John Palmer story, from start to finish.

PREFACE

I never gave much thought to writing a book about my 40-plus years in broadcast journalism until my last assignment as White House correspondent for NBC News. While waiting for the president at some boring stakeout or on long flights aboard Air Force One, my colleagues and I often passed the time reminiscing about people we'd met and stories we'd covered during our years in the business. After some months of this, I was about to launch into another of my "war stories" when my astute cameraman, friend and colleague Leroy Johnson interrupted.

"John, hold off. Save this one for the book. Put this stuff on paper, man."

So I started making a list:

- My teenage telephone impersonation of radio host Art Linkletter caused a minor local sensation, brought in the FBI and led to my first job in broadcasting.

- A novice reporter in Nashville covering my first civil-rights demonstration, I was hell-bent on joining the marchers until a cooler head prevailed.
- The greatest fighter of all time, Muhammad Ali, played a practical joke on me in Chicago that brought me to my knees.
- My bizarre rendezvous with a "General Camillo" led to a secret filmed interview in the Illinois woods and, eventually, a $10 million lawsuit.
- Kidnapped by PLO militants in Beirut and facing certain execution, I remembered something in my wallet that saved my life.
- In Cairo, my wild gamble won an exclusive series of private interviews with Egypt's President Sadat.
- Midway through my first day as an NBC *Today* show news anchor, unexpected kind words from Joe Garagiola's mom gave me a needed shot of courage.
- An errant email that wound up in Bryant Gumbel's computer could have cost me my job.
- A coveted lifetime scoop during the Iran hostage crisis, the highlight of my years covering four U.S. presidents, found me in the right place at the right time to break the news of the Carter administration's failed rescue attempt.

Listing these experiences prompted me to recall hundreds more. Maybe Leroy was right. All the same, the prospect of the labor involved in translating all these stories to paper drove me to make excuses. I was a newsman, not an author. I didn't have time.

Then came a step-up in invitations for public speaking dates, as my career at NBC News neared a close. In my hometown of Kingsport, Tennessee, a new high school auditorium was to be named for Nancy Necessary Pridemore, the debate coach who first saw some spark of promise in me. Honored to speak on that occasion, I found my remarks well received, as were other talks that followed. I discovered how eager audiences were to hear about what goes on behind the television screen, how the networks gather and edit the news, and especially the private side of the personalities involved.

The final push for the book came in June 2004, again back home in Tennessee, when my Dobyns-Bennett High School classmates asked me to speak at our 50th reunion banquet. The invitation came as a surprise. I hadn't been class valedictorian, salutatorian, or even close. On the other hand, I had just covered President George W. Bush's Yale graduation address, in which he confessed to being a mere C student. If he could rise to that significant occasion at his alma mater, surely I could come up with a decent speech for ours.

I spent more time preparing those remarks to my former classmates than I had on any other speech, recalling events large and small that had taken place before and after we were handed those diplomas. As babies born at the tail end of the Great Depression as our country began its inexorable slide into war, we had seen a memorable century out and another one in. As children we didn't hear about World War II by way of the television set, because no household had one. We heard about it from neighbors whose sons and brothers and dads fought it, and from the radio, weekly newsreels at the movies and newspapers that eventually blared Allied victory in letters four inches high.

After television became a household fixture we saw from our own living rooms the rise of the civil rights movement, the assassinations of admired leaders, the turbulent '60s and '70s and wars in Korea, Vietnam and the Middle East. We witnessed the fall of world communism. Then, just as we hoped to settle into our so-called golden years, terrorism and the ultimate assault of Sept. 11, 2001, burned unthinkable images into our brains. Wars in Afghanistan and Iraq followed.

Throughout those many years we faced dramatic world changes on an almost daily basis. We also made light-years of progress beyond box cameras and phone calls that began with an operator saying, "Number, please," as we adapted to computers, video tape, fax machines, cell phones, the Internet, digital cameras, Blackberrys, iPods, and every other conceivable electronic marvel.

In the pleasant afterglow of my remarks at the high school reunion, editor and writer Betsy Tice White, a friend and classmate, urged me to make that speech the starting point for a book about the fascinating people I've met and far-flung places to which the front lines of journalism have carried me. As you can see by the pages that follow, she made her case.

In writing, then, I've tried to cover two parallel themes: the fast-moving global events of my generation, and the technological changes that brought these happenings quickly and very personally into the lives of all Americans.

For decades I was often on the move and kept no journal or diary, something I now fervently wish I had done. My sources do, however, include boxes containing thousands of my scripts, scores of videotaped reports, hundreds of dated press passes from summit conferences and wars and natural disasters, letters home to parents and friends from Europe and the Middle East and more memories than this book can hold.

Although I began my book project with a hope of seeing the result in print, I quickly resolved to complete it if only for my daughters, their future grandchildren, and my nieces and nephews, to let them know what I was doing during all those momentous years. Blessings be on my patient wife, who, encouraging and supportive though she may be, has heard every story far more times than she cares to count.

—JOHN S. PALMER
Washington, D.C., 2012

1

A TENNESSEE BOY

I WASN'T SURE WHAT it meant—only that it was bad and that life would be different from then on, probably for a long time. It was Sunday afternoon, Dec. 7, 1941. Just 6 years old, I ran through our quiet neighborhood shouting to anyone and everyone who would listen: "The radio says Japanese planes bombed someplace called Pearl Harbor! Our country's at war!"

It was the first major news event I can recall, and I well remember how excited I felt to be first to report the news—at least within the small scope of our neighborhood. My lifelong fascination with news, its gathering and reporting—that's how it began.

During the next four years I followed the course of the war through newsreels at the movies, combat pictures in *Life* magazine, and, in a more personal way, at our neighbors the Conklins' house, where I followed the thumbtacks on their wall map that traced the progress of Mr. Conklin's military unit across Europe liberating towns and villages on the way to Berlin in the final months of the war.

People in our town got most of their war news by listening to the local radio station WKPT, an NBC affiliate, which twice a day carried direct reports from the war zones. The NBC commentators and war correspondents of that era were household names, and heroes to me: people like Robert McCormick, H. V. Kaltenborn, John Vandercook, Robert St. John, W. W. Chaplin, Morgan Beatty and Paul Archinard. Their impressive voices coming over our small radio beside the breakfast table planted powerful ambitions in my young mind. I wanted to grow up to be just like them.

The adults in my family, like most others in town, did their part for the war effort on the home front. From time to time, always without warning, shrill sirens would sound to signal an air-raid drill and, if dark had fallen, the mandatory blackout. Every time it happened I felt both scared and stirred. If the drill came at night Dad would put on his air-raid warden's helmet, grab his five-cell flashlight, and head out into the neighborhood to make sure no lights were visible, while Mom, my sisters and I hurried down to a windowless basement storage room to wait for the siren signaling "all clear."

Exciting though those air-raid drills were, I couldn't imagine why enemy bombers would target Kingsport, our modest-sized East Tennessee town. Not until several years after the war did I learn that the local ordnance factory had been manufacturing RDX, the explosive used to detonate the atomic bomb then being assembled a hundred miles away at Oak Ridge. We hadn't known what they were making down at Oak Ridge, either. Incidentally, that ordnance plant was also the proving ground for another life-changing product, because before his Kentucky Fried Chicken became world famous, "Colonel" Harland Saunders held down a cafeteria job at the facility.

Like all youngsters my age, I was affected by World War II in many ways large and small—everything from minor inconveniences at home to the shock of learning that one neighbor, Ben Brown, had been seriously wounded, and Tommy Peters, another neighbor's son, had been killed in the war. Compared to such terrible news as that, our mere inconveniences hardly counted.

We had shoe rationing, with Mom's frequent admonition: "Don't scuff your shoes. We don't have enough coupons yet to buy new ones." Rationing of gasoline and tires meant limited use of the family car, walking home from school, and no more vacation trips to Myrtle Beach "for the duration." Sugar rationing meant no more pies or cakes for dessert, except on birthdays or some other special occasion. Butter, bubble gum and Hershey Bars went away.

In response to drives at school, we saved coins to go toward war bonds, collected old newspapers and scrap metal, and peeled the foil from chewing-gum wrappers for the war effort. I do wonder what military use was ever made of those satisfying crumpled balls! My neighbor and buddy, Charles "Frog" Wiley, and I figured we had a fine excuse for being three hours late to school when we scoured the neighborhood for two coaster-wagon loads of old newspapers. When we walked into the classroom, however, our fourth-grade teacher promptly doused our patriotic pride.

"Boys and girls, lay down your pencils and listen to me. We must all do our best to support the war effort, but *your* main job"—she glared at us two latecomers—"and *especially* Charles and John, is being in school to *learn*. So, collecting old newspapers is no excuse for absence!"

On our town's main shopping street, a big billboard on a vacant lot between Fuller & Hillman's clothing store and S. H. Kress usually advertised current or upcoming movies. Anybody who went downtown passed by that spot, and on Saturdays country preachers often stood in front of the billboard to deliver an impromptu fire-and-brimstone rant. Once the war got into full swing and defense plants needed aluminum to build warplanes, huge evil-looking portraits of Japan's Hirohito, Germany's Hitler and Italy's Mussolini replaced the movie posters as targets for discarded aluminum pots and pans. I loved hurling pots and pans at those villains and would have wiped out my mother's entire supply had she not ordered a halt to our billboard sorties. Another wartime project was the victory garden in our back yard that produced corn, carrots, lettuce, tomatoes, rhubarb and green beans. We made do with less meat than before the war, but we never lacked for veggies.

As for Mom, she knitted dozens of sweaters for servicemen and rolled bandages for the Red Cross. The summer I was 7 years old, she completed Red Cross training to become a nurse's aide and left us for three months to volunteer at an Army hospital in White Sulphur Springs, West Virginia. With Dad busy at work or doing air-raid duty and my older sisters involved in their own pursuits, that summer still stands out in memory as the loneliest time of my life.

Just as many people my age remember where they were and what they were doing when World War II began, I remember the war's end every bit as well. In August of 1945 I was spending two weeks at Camp Dixie for Boys in the mountains of north Georgia. We slept in open cabins, our days filled with archery, tennis, swimming, canoeing, boxing and crafts. On Aug. 6, our counselor Walter hiked out with me and the seven other boys from our cabin for a sleepover in the woods. The next morning on our way back we were paused on a ridge overlooking the camp when we heard a man's voice blaring over loudspeakers. After listening for a few minutes we recognized the familiar Missouri twang of Harry Truman, President of the United States, announcing that something called an atomic bomb had been dropped on the city of Hiroshima, Japan.

"What's an atomic bomb?" we asked Walter.

"I'm not sure," he said, "but I think it's really, really big."

We rushed down the mountain to join our fellow campers in celebrating. At the end of the week when camp closed and Mom and Dad came to pick me up, they told me a second A-bomb had been dropped on Nagasaki, Japan had surrendered, and the war was over. We drove home to Kingsport in an atmosphere of sheer joy. Mom was especially happy, knowing she could soon have that new washing machine, and maybe even a new car. Life would surely be better for us all.

When I was growing up, my hometown had fewer than 20,000 residents, but it never seemed small to me. Nestled as it was between the Appalachian and Great Smoky Mountains, their timeless beauty provided a breathtaking backdrop for a place where I've always felt very much at home. Kingsport is a unique planned community, developed in the early 1920s around several large manufacturing companies. The largest, Tennessee Eastman Corporation, then a division of Eastman Kodak, had lured my dad south from New Jersey in the fall of 1931, to be joined a year later by Mom and my sisters, Audrey and Pat.

I arrived on Sept. 10, 1935, the second baby born at the new Holston Valley Community Hospital a few hours after it opened. Mom often complained that I would have been the first child born in the new hospital and received loads of gifts from local merchants, were it not for a secretive young unwed mother who came down from the mountains during the night, gave birth to a baby girl, and quickly left without revealing her name. Thus I began life settling for a consolation prize—free diaper service for a month.

I'm a "hillbilly," at least that's what some of my fraternity brothers called me years later during my time at Northwestern University when they learned I was from the hills of East Tennessee. I read somewhere that the term "hillbilly" first appeared in a New York newspaper around 1900, listing the definition as "a white person from Alabama without visible means of support, ambition or much of anything else." I guess over the years the definition was expanded to include Tennesseans and other mountain folk from the South. I actually liked the moniker and took pride in it but took great exception to the definition given by that New York newspaper. Once, while speeding to get my date home just minutes before her curfew at Northwestern, I was stopped by a Chicago motorcycle cop who added an unwelcome prefix to the "hillbilly" label. When he looked at my Tennessee driver's license, he turned to me and said, "Son, you don't look like a "shit-kicking hillbilly." I glared at him. He apologized and let me off with a warning ticket.

*

Mom grew up in New York City. After two years of college she appeared in several off-Broadway musicals and taught school in Brooklyn. After marrying Dad and moving to Tennessee she no longer pursued a career outside the home, but nobody could ever have labeled her a stay-at-home mom. While raising three children she served as Girl Scout Commissioner, volunteered as a nurse's aide at our local hospital two days each week, appeared in local theater productions, and put in endless hours at the Kingsport Vocational School teaching women to knit. At Mom's funeral in 1979 dozens of women I didn't know came up to me to say how lovingly and patiently she'd taught them to knit sweaters, scarves and socks for their families.

Also a voracious reader, Mom went through about two books a week, and at home when she wasn't reading or knitting she was working on a jigsaw puzzle. She played the piano and insisted that I take lessons until, frustrated by my failure to progress beyond the "Marine Hymn," she and my music teacher Miss Duncan gave up. I was greatly relieved.

A great many things happened the year that I was 7. I was very fond of my grandfather Herbert Palmer, who lived next door to us, and when he died I wanted to go with my parents to his funeral. They decided I was too young to attend, which left me feeling hurt and angry. In an alternative plan that nearly led to my own premature end, they arranged for me to spend the day of the funeral with my friend Margaret Rose Brashear, whose family lived in a lovely house on the outskirts of town near a large, deep stream.

Despite the freezing temperatures, Margaret Rose and I were playing outdoors. We had climbed high into a tree directly over the stream when suddenly I lost my grip and fell in. Weighted down in a thick wool jacket, corduroy pants and heavy boots, I hadn't a chance of swimming and went straight to the bottom in water so icy cold it burned my face. I opened my eyes and watched in a strange detached way through the bubbles as my hands clawed futilely for the hard clay bank.

Then came a big splash and lots more bubbles right beside me. A robust youngster, Margaret Rose had jumped from the tree into the water and grabbed me by the jacket, pulled my head above water, and screamed for her mother, who fortunately heard her and came running to haul me out of the drink. Back at their house I felt embarrassed to have Margaret Rose perch on the edge of the tub while her mother gave me a hot bath. I guess she was entitled, since she had saved my life.

My sister Audrey, nine years older than me, was what people used to call a tomboy. She loved horseback riding, played a fine golf game, loved basketball, and starred on a local softball team with her childhood friend Lib Dudney. A popular, fun-loving blonde, Audrey also played clarinet in the high-school band, acted in school plays, and had numerous boyfriends, chosen mostly, it seemed, for their car-repair skills. They put in many hours under the hood of Audrey's old A-Model Ford roadster, which was always in need of repair. That rattletrap had no ignition key, so to make sure nobody stole it while she was in school or at the movies, Aud would unscrew the wing nut that held the steering wheel to the shaft and take the steering wheel with her. After college and a stint with a Boston insurance company, she married and went to live with her husband on Cape Cod, where they raised three wonderful children—Annie, Amy, and Anson—before breast cancer took her life, far too early for such a vital person.

My other sister Pat, two years older than me, shared Audrey's love of horses and had one of her own that she rode after school and on weekends, winning several ribbons at area horse shows. She was also the best student in the family. I remember coming home once with a D in algebra on my report card, accompanied by two unsightly C's. I knew that at the dinner table Pat would present her report card to our parents and be praised and congratulated, but if I produced mine there'd be hell to pay. Before we left school I decided on a preemptive strike.

"I'll make a deal with you," I told Pat. "I'll clean out your horse's stall for a solid month if you promise not to show Mom and Dad your report card." Pat agreed, and both of us forged our parents' signatures when it was time to return the cards to school. The rest of the semester passed as I had hoped, with no parental questions about report cards. Months later I felt considerably less clever when Pat confessed, to my amazement, that she'd had not one but two C's on her own report card and had welcomed my offer of a deal.

In adulthood Pat became a respected clinical psychologist before retiring from practice, at age 70, to join the Peace Corps. Of her four adult children—Spencer, Peter, Jennifer, and David—one lives in Florida and the other three in California, while Pat herself has now settled in Tucson, Arizona and facilitates mind-body retreat programs in the U.S, Europe and South Africa.

Our hometown, Kingsport, was and is a marvelous place to live. The city's thriving chemical, glass, paper, printing and textile industries and their progressive management brought us excellent public schools, a community orchestra, a fine public library, a large public auditorium and recreation facilities including swimming pools and tennis courts, plus other civic and cultural benefits far beyond what most small cities in the region could afford.

Yet with so many pluses there had to be a downside. The Tennessee Eastman plant, which provided the Palmer family with a comfortable lifestyle and me and my sisters with college educations, also gave us pollution. It was not the only local industry contributing to the toxic miasma, but it was upwind of our house. Often at dawn on Saturday as Dad and I walked out to his car, ready for a day's fishing at Cherokee Lake, we found soot coating the windshield and our eyes burned from pollution in the air.

When I complained, Dad would always say, "Son, that's your college education you're smelling," then repeat one of his favorite sayings: "'Tis a poor bird that fouls its own nest." Obviously he didn't consider it much justification.

Dad died of cancer, as did my mom, my grandparents who lived next door, and my oldest sister. My sister Pat is a cancer survivor. I have no proof, but family history notwithstanding, I've always been suspicious about the role those smokestacks may have played in the health of my family.

East Tennessee is blessed with an early spring, a long summer and late fall. Winters often meant snow, with no school and plenty of sledding, but summers were the best. I enjoyed days spent with friends at the American Legion Pool, fishing in Reedy Creek, frog-gigging at the city reservoir on Bays Mountain, and boating and picnics at several nearby TVA lakes. Some outings were family events, a Fourth of July favorite being picnics to Stony Creek, where a natural rock slide and fast-rushing water combined for what we called "shoot-the-chutes." After Mom's friend Mrs. Horsley shot the chutes and lost the top of her bathing suit in the process, we never let her forget it.

Pets always had a special place in the Palmer family. At one time or another my sisters and I owned horses, a pony, a goat, hamsters, white mice, a baby alligator that I ordered from Florida, canaries and numerous cats and dogs. When the poor little foot-long 'gator arrived in something like a shoebox with holes along the side, I went to work digging a backyard "swamp" for him, complete with one of Mom's baking pans where he could "swim." He loved having the top of his head stroked, and I loved sitting beside his "swamp" stroking it. But children rarely care for their pets as assiduously as they promise to, and when the weather turned cold I forgot about my little pet. By the time I remembered and went down in the yard to see about him, he still had his head above water, but the rest of him was a solid block of ice. He got a proper burial in the rapidly growing animal graveyard out back.

As for dogs, we had one after another. Mom loved the Pekingese breed, so we had four of those. We called our favorite Chiang after the Chinese leader Chiang Kai-Shek, despite the American Kennel Club's refusal to register a dog named for a prominent living person. Then there was Hugo, a 250-pound St. Bernard, whose time with us was cut short after he bit Audrey's boyfriend on the cheek and was sent away to live on a farm.

My favorite was Robin, a long-legged mutt, part shepherd, part collie, who loved to lie in front of the fireplace on winter nights after a day of roughhousing with me. Once while playing softball in the empty lot across from our house I dove for the ball just as a younger boy, Fritz Pilgrim, got his hands on it. Robin, ever loyal, rushed into the game and bit Fritz on the hand. The injury wasn't that bad, but Fritz ran home in tears, so my parents decided to exile Robin, too, to a farm about five miles out of town. To my delight, good old Robin, just like Lassie, found his way back home not once but three times. The first two times Dad took him back to the farm, but when Robin showed up at our back door for the third time Dad put him in the car and drove him to the police station. I didn't know what happened to Robin until a fishing trip several years later. When Dad told me the troubling story I tried to think positively.

"I'll bet some policeman took Robin to live with him, and maybe he's still alive!"

Dad's next words cut like a knife. "No, son, I heard the shot before I drove away."

It took me a long time to forget that. I guess Dad just got tired of being the dog warden.

*

East Tennessee's population was and still is fairly homogeneous. Early settlers worked small farms, unlike the big plantations in other areas of the South. There were relatively few "colored" or

"Negro" residents, as we were taught to call them. During the War Between the States many East Tennessee freeholders were Union sympathizers, as evidenced by the Monument to the Union Soldier on historic Greeneville's courthouse lawn, and the Underground Railroad had stops nearby. Ours was not a stereotypical Southern town.

For more than 20 years my parents employed Henrietta Long as our cook and live-in housekeeper. Mom taught her to read and write, and she returned the favor with her gift of delicious Southern cooking such as cornbread, all-day green beans seasoned with fatback, and country ham. Most of the African-American people I knew when I was growing up were maids, yard workers or janitors, although the big manufacturing plants employed some in more responsible jobs.

Maybe it was the upbringing and lessons taught by my Yankee parents, but I remember being perplexed at how blacks were treated in our town and elsewhere in the South. The local newspaper carried a column titled "Activities of Kingsport Negroes" and I was amazed to discover that most of my school friends believed black people were very different and had lower morals and limited life expectations, yet were happy and content. But even I didn't recognize the injustice of "separate but equal" in our school system until my senior year in high school, when the Supreme Court handed down its ruling in Brown v. Board of Education of Topeka, Kansas. Twelve more years would pass before Dobyns-Bennett High School's desegregation.

With one memorable exception, I had no black friends my age, because they attended separate schools on the other side of the railroad tracks. That exception was Marcella, our housekeeper's niece, who came from the North to stay with Henrietta in her basement apartment in our house during the winter of 1949, when Marcella and I were both 14. Marcella had long black hair with penetrating dark eyes and a warm, brown complexion. She smiled and laughed a lot, and we had great fun together in the afternoons when I came home from school. That year it snowed a lot, and we often went out sledding together until dark.

Then, for some reason not explained to me, Marcella became less and less available for our afternoon fun. Henrietta always seemed to be making up excuses—"Marcella is busy," or "She can't play now." Or, more perplexing, "She has already played too much this week." In this sophisticated age it seems odd to think of 14-year-olds talking about playing, but that's how we saw it.

It was an early spring afternoon when I came home from school as usual and went to Henrietta's apartment door, knocked, and asked if Marcella could come out to join me and the other neighborhood youngsters.

"No," Henrietta said through the door. "Marcella's gone. She went back up North to live with her uncle."

I was crushed. There had been no goodbye, no hint she might be leaving. Even now as I write about what happened that day more than 50 years ago, my eyes fill with tears.

Sometime later my mother confessed to me that she had "had to speak to Henrietta about Marcella" because that nice girl and I "had gotten too close." It seems that someone had seen me kiss Marcella on the cheek. It was another time, and that was another place.

*

Junior high school meant new friends—including some very amusing ones—and the beginnings of a boy-girl social life. It was around this time that I first saw television—this new invention we had heard so much about that was to have such an impact around the world and on my life in particular. The TV set, with its tiny 6-inch screen, was on display in a downtown store window with the addition of an outside speaker so passers-by could listen to what was being said. Each evening for several weeks, people would crowd around the window to watch the likes of Milton Berle, Howdy Doody, Championship Wrestling, or Arthur Smith and the Crackerjacks, through what appeared to be a perpetual snowstorm. The signal was weak by the time it reached our town, since it came from a TV station several hundred miles away in Charlotte, North Carolina. But that didn't seem to bother the onlookers gathering to see this new electronic marvel for themselves, even if it meant staring at a stationary test pattern through the "snow." Dad said it was prudent to wait until this new gadget was perfected, so our family did without a television set for the next five more years. At the time, I had no idea then what an impact this new marvel would make on my life.

The war's end had brought a calmer time, except for a new worry—the Big Bomb. Sure, nuclear war was a scary thought, but even as a 15-year-old I saw the humor any time a teacher read out our school's instructions in case of nuclear attack:

> Get away from windows.
> Go to an inner hallway if possible.
> Otherwise, crouch under your desk and cover your eyes.

Someone in our class always added, *sotto voce*, "And kiss your ass goodbye!"

2

CATCHING THE NEWS BUG

A PAIR OF WIRE cutters, borrowed from my father's desk, provided my introduction to journalism. I used them to break open the 40-pound bundle of newspapers dumped each morning at 5 a.m. outside Kabool's Grocery for my delivery route. One snip, and the bundle tied with baling wire burst open with a bang to reveal the day's headlines. And during my two years as a paperboy in the early 1950s there were some big ones:

TRUMAN FIRES MACARTHUR

SINGER AL JOLSON DIES

SPIES ETHEL AND JULIUS ROSENBERG
SENTENCED TO DEATH

WAR WITH NORTH KOREA

EISENHOWER DEFEATS STEVENSON

JOE DIMAGGIO RETIRES FROM BASEBALL

I was among the first to know, which always excited me.

Seven days a week during my freshman and sophomore years in high school I delivered The Kingsport News, our local morning paper, to 120 homes and apartments. Many of my customers, especially working-class families, were up early, often waiting impatiently on their front porches for the paper as I roared up on my motorbike.

If there was a very big story I'd shout the headline as I tossed the paper in the customer's direction. Back then very few homes had a television set yet, and for those of my customers who didn't rely on the radio I was often their first source of news. Heady stuff! In awe of the reporters who traveled to all those places, had all those experiences, met all those people, and wrote all the stories, I knew I wanted to do that.

Dad had insisted that I take on the paper route—not to promote any interest in journalism, but as a way for me to learn the value of work and money and a sense of responsibility. When he sweetened the deal with promise of a motorbike I agreed. Only when I was really sick was I allowed to sleep in. On those occasions, Dad, dressed in a suit and tie for work and wearing his fedora as other white-collar types did back then, got in his car, picked up and folded the papers, and delivered them himself.

I usually finished my paper route by 8 a.m. in time to join my mother at the breakfast table, where we listened to NBC's *World News Roundup* blaring from the little radio on the windowsill. Those correspondents broadcasting their own news reports from around the country and the world made a huge impression on me. By age 16, I was hooked.

*

Money from the paper route paid for a microphone and tape recorder, which I used to emulate the news broadcasters I'd heard on the radio. Much creativity was involved, sometimes with comic results. For the dramatic but imaginary rescue of a man swept out to sea during a hurricane, I locked myself in the bathroom, closed the shower curtain, stood fully dressed outside it, turned the shower on full blast, and flushed the toilet. Water hitting the shower curtain and the gurgling toilet made a fine background for my narration as I ad-libbed into my tape recorder. At other times I sat in the family car gunning the engine while covering a fantasy Indianapolis 500.

Soon, as a "reporter" broadcasting from some faraway place, I discovered that speaking into a water glass held next to the microphone produced an echo, and rocking the glass back and forth in front of my mouth as I spoke made my recorded voice fade in and out like the voices of those foreign correspondents whose broadcasts reached us by transatlantic telephone cable.

Our poor housekeeper Henrietta. When she happened to overhear one of my broadcasting sessions, she shouted downstairs to my mother, "Mrs. Palmer, come quick! John's in his room calling for help, and I think something's on fire!"

It was just me, reporting the rescue of a family from the roof of a burning building while crunching a newspaper to simulate the sound of crackling flames.

Then came the Sunday afternoon when my imaginary broadcasting got me into big trouble. Idle and with nothing interesting to do, I rode my motorbike up the street to see my good buddy Charles "Frog" Wiley. Frog's physician dad was out, probably seeing patients at the hospital as he often did, and for once his mom and sisters were away from home as well—nobody around but Frog and me.

After an hour or so of one-on-one basketball we got bored, and I came up with the bright idea of making a random phone call to some unsuspecting person claiming to be calling from a national radio quiz program. We both thought it was a fine idea, so into the house we went.

Since our local telephone company had recently brought in dial phones, placing a call no longer involved an operator saying, "Number, please?" The new system's relative anonymity held a certain fascination for us kids. By this time we considered ourselves far too sophisticated for the old routine of: "Have you got Prince Albert in a can? Well, you better let him out!"

Frog picked a number at random from the phone book, and I dialed the call as he picked up an extension phone in the adjoining room. After a few rings a woman answered. To protect the lady from further embarrassment and save me from further legal problems, I shall refer to her only as Mrs. John Doe.

"Hello there!" I said, using my water-glass technique. "Am I speaking with Mrs. John Doe, in Kings Point, Tennessee?"

I hoped mispronouncing our town's name might add extra authenticity. Frog could see me through the doorway, and with a hand over the mouthpiece and a thumbs-up he laughed and egged me on.

"Well, yes, it is," the woman said, "except it's Kings*port*, Tennessee."

Another thumbs-up from Frog.

"Thank you, ma'am, for correcting that. Well, Mrs. Doe, I'm calling you from Hollywood, California, from the *Art Linkletter Show*."

"You are? Oh, my goodness! From Hollywood? How did you happen to call *me*?"

Our ruse was going so well that it took superhuman effort to keep my voice level and my face straight. Frog didn't even try. He doubled over laughing, his phone muffled in a sofa pillow.

"We're calling you, Mrs. Doe, because your number was the lucky one selected. Now, we'd like you to stand by, because two hours from now when the radio program comes on the air, Mr. Linkletter will call and speak with you himself."

"Art Linkletter calling *me*? Good gracious, I'll be so nervous I won't know what to say!"

Water glass at the ready, I said, "All you have to do is answer the phone when it rings, then listen carefully to Mr. Linkletter's question and give the right answer if you can. If your answer is correct, you'll win hundreds of dollars worth of valuable prizes! Mrs. Doe, will you stand by for Mr. Linkletter's call?"

"Oh, my, yes, I certainly will! Two hours, did you say?"

"That's right. We'll call you back in two hours. Good luck, Mrs. Doe, and thanks so much."

After hanging up, Frog and I had a good laugh, went outside to shoot a few more baskets, and came back in to grab a snack. I'd forgotten about the call until Frog said, "Hey, Palmer, it's been about two hours, let's don't keep that lady waiting."

I grinned. "Oh no, we can't do that."

We reopened the phone book and found Frog's pencil mark by the number we'd called. This time he made the call and, in the deepest voice he could muster, told the woman to stand by for five minutes, then signaled that the rest was up to me. On the other end of the line we could hear excited conversation, with Mrs. Doe telling people to shush so she could hear Art Linkletter when he came on. We watched the minutes tick by on Dr. Wiley's desk clock, and after five I launched into my best Linkletter voice.

"Mrs. Doe?"

"Yes, this is Mrs. Doe."

"Hello, there, Mrs. Doe! This is Art Linkletter calling from Hollywood, and you're on the air coast to coast!"

"Gracious me, this is so exciting! I can't believe I'm actually talking to Art Linkletter!"

At this point Frog began clapping, whistling and cheering in the background.

I went on. "It certainly is Art Linkletter, Mrs. Doe. Now if you can answer our jackpot question correctly, we have thousands of dollars' worth of valuable prizes just waiting for you."

Mrs. Doe screamed with excitement. "I'm ready! Go ahead!"

"Very well," I said, "Here is the question. Give me the name of the detective program that is heard every Sunday on the NBC radio network. I'll give you a hint: it's the name of a fictitious person, and his initials are S.S."

"Oh, I know I know this! S.S.—oh, my goodness—what fictitious person could it be—Mr. Linkletter, give me a minute to think of it, please!"

When she couldn't come up with the answer, I helped her out. "I'll give you another hint. The last name is the same as an everyday garden implement."

"An everyday garden implement—a hoe, a shovel?" After a few seconds she got it. "I KNOW! IT'S SAM SPADE!"

"RIGHT YOU ARE, MRS. DOE!" I shouted back. "Now let me tell you about all the prizes you've won!" Frog quickly put down the extension phone, grabbed a Spiegel catalogue from the coffee table, and handed it to me with an impish grin. He turned the pages as I read off an impressive list of merchandise: a washing machine, a clothes dryer, an upright freezer, a bicycle, a set of fine china, twelve place settings of silverware, camping equipment, and on and on—a total of about $20,000 worth in prizes. Mrs. Doe was ecstatic, thanking me over and over before I ended the call.

We collapsed into the Wileys' chairs with laughter, and when Mom called me home for supper Frog and I shook hands, greatly pleased with our coup.

*

My first inkling that something had gone terribly wrong came early the next morning when I opened my bundle of newspapers to see a front-page article with the headline "LOCAL WOMAN WINS

PRIZES ON NATIONAL QUIZ SHOW." Hurriedly I scanned it to find that Mrs. Doe had made good use of her two hours of standby time. I also saw, with dismay, that Frog and I had the misfortune of unwittingly having picked a prominent attorney's wife as our quiz-show victim. While she waited for "Art" to call, she'd phoned the newspaper as well as a contingent of neighbors and friends to report her impending good fortune, and I soon discovered that someone at the radio station got word of the call as well. Our little triumph was taking on a disturbing life of its own.

At breakfast Mom mentioned the matter, saying she'd heard it on WKPT. I left the second piece of toast on my plate and quickly excused myself to make an urgent call to Frog.

"Meet me by the brick wall on the way to school," I whispered, "and don't talk to anybody about yesterday's phone call, or we'll both be in big trouble."

"Don't worry," Frog said. "I won't say a word."

Foolishly, I figured we were in the clear.

Two days later "Dutch" Coward, the patient policeman who taught us high school students how to drive, walked into my biology class wearing his blue uniform, cap and badge. He spoke to the teacher, who motioned for me to accompany him into the hall. Most of the time Dutch was a friendly, easy-going fellow with a ready smile, but on this occasion there was no smile.

"Mr. Kinnick wants to see you right away in his office," he said.

Not good news. Our principal, Roy Kinnick, was a tall, stern, sometimes frightening figure who ran the school with an iron hand. I was filled with dread as Dutch walked me down the long hall and upstairs to the principal's office. Mr. Kinnick met us at the door, thanked Dutch for his help, and after ushering me into his office indicated a chair for me, assumed his usual seat of authority, and laced his fingers together atop his desk. He fixed me with his stony gaze for what seemed like a very long time, then said, in a tone more akin to an order than a question: "John, what's this telephone call business all about? I want the unvarnished truth."

Roy Kinnick was not a man to be trifled with. Not bold enough to take the Fifth Amendment, I promptly confessed all—without mentioning Frog. Nor did Mr. Kinnick mention Frog to me. I waited, sweating, for the axe to fall.

The principal pressed his palms together as he pondered my revelation, then finally said: "John, I'm expelling you from school for two days. However, this really is not a school matter. You've committed fraud on the telephone, which is a federal offense, and unjustly held up to public ridicule the innocent person you victimized on the phone. The police tell me you can expect to hear from the FBI, as well as from this lady's lawyer."

After Mr. Kinnick stood up to see me out the door, my heart sank to my shoes as I left to retrieve my books. I was one frightened kid as I walked home from school mid-morning with dozens of thoughts racing through my head, none of them good. At that very moment one of J. Edgar Hoover's G-Men might be hot on my trail. My parents' reaction, especially Dad's, didn't bear thinking about, and my dream of a broadcasting career vanished down the drain.

"Why, John!" Mom said. "What are you doing back home?"

"You won't like this," I began, then explained all. Just as I'd feared, she called Dad, who rushed home from work and after hearing my story was furious with me. Furthermore, he was deeply worried. Mrs. Doe's husband was a very successful trial lawyer, and Dad quickly put in a call to our own family attorney, Lynn Minter, and a second call to Val Edwards, our family friend and insurance agent. The Edwardses were the Wileys' near neighbors, and their son Jim was my classmate.

"Val, this is Spen. I'm sorry to bother you," Dad said, "but we may have a little problem here. How's my liability coverage?"

Mr. Edwards said, "It's fine. You have an umbrella policy that covers everything. Don't worry. What's the problem, Spen?"

I knew it killed Dad to have to come out with the whole thing. He told the tale, then finished, "It looks like this could be considered fraud, and Lynn Minter says I may be at risk for a big lawsuit."

"Well, now," Mr. Edwards said, "that does put things in a different light. I'll have to check with the company that issued the primary policy and get back to you."

Poor Dad. Mr. Edwards called back to tell him he was insured against just about everything except "financial damages brought about as the result of criminal activity"—the last thing Dad wanted to hear.

That afternoon I discovered, to my amazement, that Frog had escaped the force of Mr. Kinnick's wrath, viewed only as an innocent bystander to my "vicious" prank. That night I went to bed without supper and stayed in the family doghouse for weeks.

There was one piece of good news, though. Mr. Minter solicited and received a gracious letter from Art Linkletter, saying he would take no legal action against me for impersonating him on the telephone. He even wished me luck in my budding broadcasting career, which at that point was definitely on hold. I wish I still had that letter.

Over time, things simmered down. The FBI never called, the threatened lawsuit faded away, the newspaper dropped the story, and before long the incident was all but forgotten, as often happens in a small town as soon as the next excitement comes along. To my relief, my family rarely spoke of the incident again after I promised to focus my broadcasting activities in a more constructive way.

As for Frog, who followed in his dad's footsteps to become a doctor, I felt terribly sad to learn recently that he'd passed away after a lengthy illness. Frog, old buddy, wherever you are, I hope you won't mind the story being told. Maybe it will even give you another laugh.

*

In fact, my brief notoriety from the telephone prank may have played a role in my first job offer. A family friend, Mr. Jerry Stone, probably thinking my ambitions needed more positive channels, spoke to WKPT's program director, Martin Karant, about my interest in broadcasting. A few days later Mr. Karant called to invite me to audition as a part-time announcer. I got the job but was fired two weeks later when a couple of the sponsors refused to have their commercials read in my cracking, adolescent voice. Obviously I was too young to know what I was talking about.

The following year, blessed with a deeper, steadier voice, I made a fresh start at WKPT and earned the princely minimum wage of $1 per hour for playing records, covering local events and reading news and commercials after school and on weekends, all under the close supervision of Karant. Marty, as we called him, was a first-rate broadcaster whose daily music program, *The Five O'Clock Shadow*, was mandatory listening for local high-school kids. Teen-age hearts throbbed when he introduced music requests: "This next one, 'Fly Me to the Moon' by Frank Sinatra, goes out this afternoon for Judy F. from Tommy M."

Marty would chat about the songs and local happenings, and he was an institution in our town. From the start I knew how lucky I was to have him as my mentor. Others at the station who encouraged me included Paul Overbay, the station's general manager and father of my schoolmate Zelma, and Charles Deming, who presided over the morning *Gloomchaser* program.

My biggest thrill came when Marty asked me to fill in for him while he went on vacation. I was sure I had moved up to the big leagues. Later, after I was given my own 15-minute record program, I introduced a song with: "This next number is by the well-known singer Nat King Cole, who came up the hard way, born in a slum on Chicago's East Side."

Marty, who'd once lived in Chicago, stuck his head into my broadcasting booth while the record played. "John," he said with a straight face, "Lake Michigan is Chicago's East Side. So unless Nat King Cole was born with fins, he must have grown up somewhere else—like maybe the South Side." Embarrassed, I vowed to be more diligent in checking my facts.

One memorable Thanksgiving afternoon at the station when I was a holiday replacement disc jockey, Charlie Deming poked his head into the control room.

"John, it's time you flew on your own. You have about fifteen minutes left in this music program, so sign it off then and join the NBC network at 3 p.m. as scheduled."

Gulp. With that, Charlie turned, walked out of the control room, down the stairs and out of the building. Alone and scared, I quickly discovered that while I knew how to play records and do a music program, I had no idea how to end one. As 3 o'clock neared I began to panic. It was time to sign off the music program, but I had just introduced a long recording by Frank Sinatra that would run well past that time.

Without my knowing it, Charlie had left the coffee shop across the street and slipped back into the station to appear at the control-room door at the last second, to my immense relief. Sensing my panic, he said in a calm voice, "Turn down the Sinatra song, talk over it and end the music program, then give the station identification, read the thirty-second commercial in front of you, give the time, and throw the switch to join the network at 3 o'clock straight up. Do that now."

After I somehow managed to join the network on time, Charlie patiently explained back-timing, a routine that is second nature to every D.J. or radio and television producer.

"You trapped yourself," Charlie said, "putting on a three-and-a-half-minute song that left you no time to do what you had to do before joining the network. You need to back-time every broadcast you do."

I swallowed hard. "How do I do that?"

"Start with the time you have to join the network, then subtract the time of your final recording, the time to sign off the music program, time to read the commercial, and so on. That will give you the time to begin ending the program."

God bless Charlie. A simple but vital lesson in basic broadcasting.

George Collins, one of our best announcers, called me into the control room with great excitement one day. "John, you've got to hear this song by an incredible new singer from Memphis, named Elvis Presley! It's called 'Heartbreak Hotel.'"

I listened, then told George in no uncertain terms that I didn't think it was anything special. Nor did I get excited about this young hopeful later on when my classmate Billie Mae Smith gushed about her date with Elvis after he gave a show in town. So much for my ability to judge musical talent.

Although Marty Karant has passed away, I can never forget the many ways in which he helped me. Once I was doing a live remote broadcast at the dedication of a new suburban post office when Marty suddenly appeared.

"John, your power cord got disconnected. You've been talking into a dead microphone for half an hour."

Did I ever feel sheepish. That was typical of Marty, to take the time to drive all the way out from town to tell me and offer an important lesson: "For pity's sake, John, whenever you're on the radio, always wear headphones, so you'll know whether you're really on the air."

I owe Marty a lot, for he taught me how to organize a newscast, how important it is to prepare well before going on the air, and so many other things. Even in those early days I dreamed of becoming a network news correspondent, working as a reporter at the White House, and perhaps someday anchoring the news, although the term "anchor" was not yet in vogue.

While many of my high school friends seemed to have given little thought to what they might do when they grew up and left school, I knew I was going to be a radio and television reporter. There was no doubt in my mind. I even wrote an eighth-grade theme about the future of television, misspelling the word "television" throughout. (Aptitude for spelling did not, unfortunately, arrive with my new broadcasting voice.) My parents and school friends were curious about my often-stated ambition to be a news reporter and seemed to wonder where in the world I got such an idea, but they were always supportive.

⁂

During those high school years, autumn always arrived like the pilot for *Happy Days.* Our after-school gang crowded into Armour's Drug to drink Cokes and hang out for a couple of hours. I'm amazed now at how tolerant the store's owner, pharmacist George Armour, was. The most any of us ever spent at his soda fountain was probably a half-dollar, yet he always had a smiling welcome for us even though he knew that for those two joyous hours our excited commotion would discourage any grown-up customer from coming in to the drugstore at that time of day. But on Friday afternoons if our state championship football team had a home game, we didn't go to Armour's, but trooped downtown to wait in front of Freels' Drug for the thrill of seeing our high school band march down Broad Street, always with a costumed "Indian" brave and squaw right behind the drum major. All Dobyns-Bennett teams were called "the D-B Indians," and neither we nor anyone else had heard of politically correct. My girlfriend, Betsy Latimer, played snare drum in the band, and over the course of two years I toted that drum many long miles.

On those home game fall Friday nights it seemed as though the whole town turned out for high school football under the lights. Many star Dobyns-Bennett athletes went on to excel at such schools as Princeton, Davidson, Vanderbilt, the University of Tennessee and Georgia Tech, coached at the latter by Kingsport native Bobby Dodd. After the game came the Football Frolics—casual teenage dances at the Civic Auditorium where I enjoyed dancing with Betsy to "Blue Moon" and "The Tennessee Waltz." When basketball season came in, it was sock hops in the school gym after the games. Saturday nights were often spent in Dad's car endlessly circling local drive-in restaurants, either the Dutch Boy Grill or the Texas Steer. Both served as rendezvous points for high school kids in search of action that never seemed to materialize. At least we knew where everybody else was.

It was such an innocent time, when being caught with a weapon in school meant you had a slingshot in your pocket—a time when a bottle of aspirin came without safety seals, because no one had yet tried to poison a perfect stranger.

During the years when I was growing up, Kingsport and surrounding Sullivan County were ostensibly "dry," the sale or possession of liquor, wine or beer being strictly forbidden. Dad complained that the law arose from an unholy alliance between the preachers and the bootleggers. I knew we had plenty of both, but my parents and their friends weren't keen on dealing with the latter. With Virginia's state-run liquor stores only a short distance away, embarrassing situations did arise, as when a few prominent Kingsport matrons planning a large cocktail party drove to the picturesque town of Abingdon to lay in supplies. Crossing the Tennessee line on their way home, they promptly had their car stopped and their trunk load of liquor confiscated.

Sometimes Dad took me with him on the 8-mile drive to Gate City, Virginia, which had another state-run liquor store. On the way to the state line we'd stop at a roadside stand where he'd buy a bushel of apples and two large baskets. In Gate City, after he bought the liquor, he put the bottles in the bottom of the baskets and covered them with apples in case we got stopped on the way home. It never happened, but the apple-basket caper wouldn't have fooled anyone, as it was a widely known and used practice. In those days the Palmer family ate a lot of apple pies.

As a top sales executive with Tennessee Eastman Company, Dad did a great deal of entertaining after work. His business associates and customers from around the world were often invited to dinner at our house, and I looked forward to hearing what life was like in such places as Australia, England and Mexico. At these dinners the wine and liquor always flowed freely, and after one of them Dad was taking customers to a nearby town to catch the train when he was arrested for DWI—driving while intoxicated. His driver's license was revoked for 60 days, and that incident set the stage for one of the biggest battles my father and I ever had. The local newspaper, as a matter of policy, always printed the names of anyone convicted of DWI in our county. In view of Dad's executive position with the town's biggest industry, he and his friends tried hard to get the editor to make an exception for him, but the newspaper wouldn't budge. Their only concession was an agreement to put the DWI notices on the paper's back page. When I told Dad I agreed with the editor's policy he was furious again. Where was my family loyalty? Where was my loyalty to him? It didn't happen then, but later on, after Dad joined Alcoholics Anonymous and remained sober for the rest of his life, I was prouder of him than ever before.

Another clash with my father occurred over a county election for sheriff. As far as I could tell, the Republican candidate seemed to have only one outstanding qualification: a promise not to raid the slot machines at Ridgefields Country Club, of which my dad was then president. The Democratic candidate, on the other hand, had experience in law enforcement and a degree in criminal law.

I challenged Dad: "Which man would you rather see as sheriff? What if one of your daughters was kidnapped? Who would you want as sheriff, the man with the degree in criminal law, or the guy who promised not to raid the slot machines?"

The argument lasted for weeks until Election Day, when Dad walked into the house from voting at Washington School, slammed the door, and said, "You win, son. I voted for your damn Democrat." We never spoke of the sheriff again.

In high school my friends and I did a little drinking, but not much. It was usually just beer, but if we felt really daring we'd head out past the Eastman plant to Long Island and Dolan's Coal Yard for some moonshine. Some older kid had told us the drill: park the car next to a large pile of coal, honk twice, turn off the headlights, and wait until a good ol' boy in bib "overhauls" sidled up to the driver's side to ask what you wanted. It was always the same—white lightning,

$2 a quart and ice cold from being underwater in the river sluice where the sheriff's hound dogs couldn't catch the scent. We joked that the stuff was so potent it burned its own intestinal tract, and fortunately none of us went blind from drinking it.

*

From the time I could first hold a rod until the day I left for college, Dad and I spent thousands of hours fishing at nearby Cherokee Lake. More times than I can count, during our many trips to the lake Dad recited his favorite fisherman's prayer: "Lord, suffer me to catch a fish so large that even I in talking of it afterward shall have no need to lie." He taught me the joys of fishing: how to cast a surface lure for bass, then the art of throwing a tiny handmade fly into a roaring stream in hopes of fooling a trout, and later how to listen over the roar of a charter boat engine for the subtle zinging sound of the outrigger signaling "fish on."

One of the best things about a fishing trip is the anticipation; another is talking about it after you get home. The lessons I learned on the water made good guidelines for life: commitment, diligence, perseverance, optimism and most of all, patience.

When I was 15 Dad taught me to drive on those trips home from the lake, and the car radio provided my introduction to country music with such songs as Roy Acuff's "Great Speckled Bird" and Little Jimmy Dickens's "Take an Old Cold Tater and Wait." During those trips to and from the lake we had talks ranging from school problems to ethics, sex and marriage. I've never forgotten Dad's thoughtful answer when I asked how I would know I ought to get married.

"You'll know. It's not a question of whether you can live with a woman for the rest of your life—it's when you know you can't live without her."

Thirty years would pass before I found the right woman, but when I found her she passed Dad's test in a flash.

As sales manager for Eastman's Plastics Division, Dad had a passion for his product. He loved plastic. He believed in plastic and was constantly on the lookout for new uses. Our family was the only one on our block, or any block anywhere in 1950s America, that had all-plastic doorknobs, plastic telephone covers, plastic Venetian blinds, plastic toilet seats, plastic hubcaps, even plastic duck decoys. Anything and everything that could possibly be made of plastic was found around our house, except that Mom drew the line at plastic plates.

One winter Dad brought home a couple of 12-gauge shotguns and a dozen of those plastic decoys so he and I could try duck hunting on the lake. Despite our best efforts neither of us ever killed a single duck, but we managed to sink most of the plastic decoys.

Always encouraged to take part in outdoor sports, I was also fifteen when I decided to try my hand at rabbit hunting. While Dad was out playing golf I took out my shotgun and a box of shells, lent Dad's gun to a buddy, and went off with him into the woods in search of rabbits or whatever wild game we could find. When Dad came home to discover that I was out with the guns he got on the horn to his beleaguered insurance agent again.

"Val, Spen Palmer. I want to extend that umbrella policy we carry."

"It's already broad," Mr. Edwards said.

"I don't care. I want you to make sure it covers hunting accidents including"—or so the family story goes—"all acts ranging from manslaughter to mayhem that might be perpetrated by my son John." Dad loved insurance, and Val Edwards loved selling it to him.

⁂

Best-selling author Lisa Alther, also from Kingsport, wrote in her novel *Kinflicks* that girls in her fictional town grew up fearing two things: sperm and Communism. That's a very funny line, but I would add a third fear for both boys and girls: the terror of poliomyelitis.

That crippling disease haunted our youth. Without warning, it could and did strike children, paralyzing many for life, leaving some unable to breathe on their own and doomed to life in an iron lung. A couple of our schoolmates wore steel braces on their legs because of it, lucky to have survived. We'd all heard of Sister Kenny and her healing work, and we filled the slots in March of Dimes booklets with silvery 10-cent coins. We saw newsreels of President Franklin Roosevelt, crippled in adulthood by polio, as he enjoyed the therapeutic pools at Warm Springs, Georgia. One summer our town's public swimming pool and local movie theaters closed for fear of polio, although the nearest outbreak at the time was in Charlottesville, Virginia, 270 miles away. Such was the pall of fear cast by that terrible virus.

Years later as a national news reporter I would be privileged to meet and interview Dr. Jonas Salk, the scientist-developer of the vaccine that immunizes against polio and has saved future generations from the ravages of the disease. I'll write more in a later chapter about this dedicated and admirable man, saying here only that my childhood awareness of the scourge gave me a special admiration for him and his work.

*

In the years immediately after World War II, race relations in Kingsport, at least on the surface, continued to be good despite the early stirrings of unrest in other Southern cities and towns as impatient black veterans returned home. Although our town's bus station and dime store had separate drinking fountains marked FOR WHITES ONLY and FOR COLORED ONLY and the bus station waiting rooms were labeled the same way, I don't recall anybody making a big deal about it. It wasn't right, but it was just how things were.

Kingsport had separate and supposedly equal school systems for the two races, but that would eventually change after the Supreme

Court decision of 1954, a few weeks before I graduated from high school. Brown v. Board of Education forever altered the political and social landscape of an insufficiently conscience-stricken nation and hastened the process that would lead, 10 years later, to the passage of the Civil Rights Act outlawing segregation in restaurants, hotels and other public places.

Although Kingsport is a religious community, as evidenced by the circle of churches that serves as the town's geographic and architectural hub, in my young years local preachers rarely discussed racial injustice. As president of the Christian Youth Association during my senior high school year I didn't have righting racial injustice on my agenda either. While I regret now that as a teenager I didn't speak out against the racial injustices, my generation was subject to strong societal pressures to conform as well as to succeed. Going against the grain or making a spectacle of oneself was not encouraged. I hope I redeemed myself later as a reporter, when I took full advantage of my opportunity to give the civil rights struggle the coverage it deserved.

Our family belonged to First Presbyterian Church but rarely attended services other than at Christmas and Easter. All the same, my father insisted that I attend Sunday School every week and drove me there on his way to play golf at the country club. An agnostic himself, Dad told one of my friends he didn't mind being seen as a hypocrite for insisting that I attend Sunday School when he didn't go himself. In that as in so many other matters, he had his reasons.

"I want John to have the knowledge to make his own decision about religion. I'm willing to be hypocritical where John's concerned, but not where I'm concerned."

In later years he explained to me that he was agnostic because he was still searching for spiritual truth. On the other hand he was contemptuous of atheists: "How can they be so sure there is no God? How can anyone know?" In their final years Mom and Dad found a spiritual home in the Unitarian Church.

*

Although my grades were less than stellar, my high school years were generally happy ones. As for sports, I enjoyed golf and fishing then and still do today. One fall I gave Golden Gloves boxing a try but quit after my second bout, when I realized that getting hit repeatedly in the face was not my idea of fun.

During my last few months of high school I became fascinated with the Army-McCarthy hearings, carried live on television every day from April to June. Sen. Joseph McCarthy used the hearings to conduct his witch-hunt for the Communists he believed had infiltrated the federal government. Those hearings were the first nationally televised congressional inquiry, a landmark in the emergent nexus between television and American politics.

My mom, knowing of my interest in journalism and politics, allowed me to spend many hours at home watching the hearings during afternoons when I should have been in school. To this day I can still hear the words of the Army's special counsel, Joseph Welch, admonishing Sen. McCarthy: "Until this moment, Senator, I think I never gauged your cruelty or recklessness. You have done enough. Have you no sense of decency, sir, at long last? Have you left no sense of decency?"

On Sunday nights during this same period, Mom, Dad and I usually watched the 11 o'clock news on CBS with newscaster Don Hollenbeck until the evening when a different newscaster appeared to report that Hollenbeck had died that day. We later learned from the newspaper that he had taken his own life, after relentless accusations by New York newspaper columnist Jack O'Brien that he was a "pinko" or Communist. Hollenbeck was one of Edward R. Murrow's "boys," and his tragic story is part of *Good Night and Good Luck*, the movie about Murrow's heroic exposure of McCarthy.

In high school what I really loved was debate, extemporaneous speaking, appearing in school plays, and serving as announcer for the weekly 15-minute radio broadcast every Friday afternoon from our high school auditorium. I'm sure I loved those activities because they were areas in which I could excel. With the help of my debate coach, Nancy Necessary (later Mrs. Pridemore) and my brilliant debate partner Shelby Outlaw, we made it to the state forensic league finals two years in a row.

Miss Necessary was an unforgettable personality, one of those special high school teachers students remember all their lives. Decisive and enthusiastic, she was always ready with helpful suggestions and encouragement. Laughter often echoed down the hall from her classroom, yet she quickly quelled misbehavior with a wilting glare from her big blue eyes. An energetic, petite person whose bright red lipstick made a striking contrast to her jet-black hair, she had a huge supply of engaging smiles and often sat atop her desk with one shapely leg crossed over the other so she could see the pupils in the back of the room—the ones most likely to stir up trouble.

From her desktop perch she would read to us, her black horn-rimmed glasses sliding down her nose as she held the book in one hand and gestured high in the air with her other double-jointed arm. We would watch in studied amazement to see how far backward she could bend that arm—a great trick for holding an audience's attention.

During the years when Miss Necessary taught high school English, debate and drama in Kingsport, she also served as mayor of her Southwest Virginia hometown. Clinchport had a reputation as something of a rough river town, and she armed herself with a derringer and kept it in her purse. I doubted it offered much protection after she assured me it couldn't be fired. All the same, that was one more reason not to rile Miss Necessary.

The summer after my sophomore year in high school, with her encouragement, I took an even more ambitious fling at acting at age 17, joining the 80-member cast of *The Tide of Freedom* in Bristol, Virginia, a historical drama produced in a natural-bowl amphitheater at Virginia Intermont College 30 miles or so from home. I played three roles: James Robertson, an Indian fighter and founder of the state of Tennessee; and two Indians, Hanging Maw and Dragging Canoe. For the Indian roles I had to cover my body in brownish-red paint each night before the show, and when it was time to shift to Robertson I donned a heavy buckskin suit over the paint. I came to dread those hot summer nights during July and August, every pore covered with body paint as I sweated through seven performances each week, for which I was paid the magnificent weekly wage of $55.00.

I was the youngest member of the cast in a fast crowd of actors, many of them New York professionals who liked to party until dawn every night. On one of those hot and now unforgettable evenings, the cast rented a farmhouse just outside of town, filled the bathtub with gin and, as I can best recall, floated some sort of blue flowers atop the aromatic sea.

Shortly after midnight, I found an available bunk and crashed after consuming what must have been a colossal amount of gin, because the next morning, despite being shaken and doused with cold water, they couldn't wake me up. It had rained heavily overnight, washing out the road, and although my colleagues called an ambulance, the driver couldn't make it all the way to the farmhouse. In my alcoholic coma I didn't remember a minute of it, but I'm told that my fellow actors, most of them shaky at best, wrapped me in a blanket and carried me about a mile to the paved road, undoubtedly fearful of being hauled up in court for contributing to the delinquency of a minor.

Several hours later I awoke in the emergency room of the Bristol hospital attached to a stomach pump with tubes down my throat and a blistering headache. I've never tasted gin again, and to this day even a sniff of that hazardous substance sends me out of the room. It was probably a good thing I learned at that early moment in my career to beware the pitfalls of Mother's Ruin. Fortunately Miss Necessary never knew of her protégé's fall from grace.

Back in school that autumn, another life-changing day arrived when the same lady asked me to stop by her desk after class. She led me to her bulletin board and pointed to a poster from Northwestern University that offered high school students a summer opportunity to sample college life studying radio and television between their junior and senior years.

"Apply for that, John!" she commanded. "You're qualified, and they're probably looking for diversity, so being a hillbilly from Tennessee should give you an advantage." She'd spent summers studying at Northwestern herself, so she knew what she was talking about. We were both well aware I was no more a hillbilly than she, but on paper up North it might look that way.

I applied, was accepted, and spent a rewarding and wonderful six weeks on the shores of Lake Michigan at Northwestern, after which I won a fellowship to attend the university. That fortuitous trip to the bulletin board and Miss Necessary's insight and insistence put me on course for my career in broadcasting and journalism. Every young person should be so lucky. Not only did I receive a fellowship to Northwestern, automatic acceptance to the university was part of the deal, so I didn't have to suffer through SATs as many of my classmates did.

Over the years I've returned home to Kingsport often to see old friends and speak at various events. One of my greatest joys was hosting the dedication of the new high school theater in honor of the teacher who gave me so much inspiration and support. To know Nancy Necessary Pridemore was to love and admire her, and I did both.

3

OUT IN THE WIDE WORLD

MY FOUR YEARS at Northwestern University were among the best of my life. I majored in political science, history and communications, while keeping my focus on the unwavering goal of becoming a journalist. Northwestern had high academic standards, but it was also something of a party school. One surprising acquaintance I made at Northwestern, less than ten years after the war, was a German exchange student named Helmut. Helmut was quite a beer drinker, and after a few cold ones we could sometimes persuade him to demonstrate the Nazi goose-step for us. During my years there we had lots of parties on and off campus and in the watering holes of nearby Chicago. Summers were spent back home in Kingsport working at WKPT, where my salary soared to a whopping $3 per hour. That NBC-affiliate connection would prove to be the foundation for everything that came afterward. At the time I had no idea how far-reaching its influence would be.

Before I received my diploma in June of 1958, I applied to Northwestern for graduate work in journalism, hoping to come back to complete a two-year degree. At the same time I submitted an application to NBC for the first annual Earl Godwin Fellowship for study at the Columbia University School of Journalism, to be awarded jointly by the network and RCA in honor of a Washington correspondent. I might not be accepted at either place, but with my life direction clearly in mind, before I launched myself on a serious journalism career I thought it was time to have a little unencumbered fun.

*

And so that summer my classmate and SAΣ fraternity brother John Gillin, who later rose to be a very senior vice-president of Coca-Cola Company, and I set off on a two-month grand adventure traveling to Russia and central Europe. With my long-range goal of becoming a foreign correspondent, I thought seeing some of the rest of the world would be good for me.

The Cold War was at its height, with Khrushchev in power in the Soviet Union and General LeMay heading the Strategic Air Command—momentous times.

We applied to Intourist for student visas, and to our astonishment were both given visas for Moscow and Leningrad. Neither of us had ever been to Europe, which meant we'd be seeing Russia when we didn't even know what the rest of Europe was like. And after we got there we couldn't tell what was European and what was purely Russian.

We flew first to Helsinki on the longest day of the year, and after we landed went to a park where hordes of Finns were out for a Midsummer Night's festival. To our amazement, the entertainment was a troupe of Africans in grass skirts, performing native dances and brandishing spears. The pale-faced Finns were fascinated with these African dancers—absolutely the last thing we'd expected to see at the top corner of Europe.

The next day we flew on to Leningrad on Aeroflot's equivalent of a DC-3, where we chatted with a fellow passenger who was a writer. "I don't know whether they'll let me back in," he said, apparently because the powers-that-be didn't approve of his writings. After a plump stewardess came back with a basketful of oranges and handed one to each of us, he told us, "Citrus fruit is hard to come by in the Soviet Union, so giving us an orange means they're being very nice. A good sign."

In Leningrad the first thing that struck me was the paucity of cars on the street. When one of the few we saw ran a stop sign and nearly hit somebody, a policeman whistled the driver down, dragged him out of the car, beat him thoroughly, threw him back into the driver's seat, and let him drive away. We figured it was the spontaneous Russian version of a ticket.

During our sojourn in the Soviet Union, Intourist saddled us with an officious minder named Vera. She was showing us the gardens of Peter the Great's Summer Palace when a MIG fighter plane roared through the sky about 50 feet over our heads. "I saw a man in that plane with a cigar in his mouth," Vera said, giving me a sly look. "I do hope it wasn't General LeMay." A little Russian joke?

From Leningrad we took the train to Moscow and arrived coated with soot, so the first thing we wanted to do in the Peking Hotel was to take a shower. Every floor in Russian hotels had a female employee who sat at a desk to keep tabs on the guests' comings and goings. Our floor lady—the *dezhurnaya*—handed us our key, which weighed at least half a pound. We couldn't put it in our pocket and carry it off, so we had to turn it in whenever we went out. No doubt that was the whole idea.

Once settled into our room, I got first dibs on the adjoining bath, which had a hand-held showerhead. I was standing in the tub spraying myself with abandon when every inch of the surrounding tile and plaster fell off the walls into the tub with a colossal crash. So there I stood, buck naked, debris nearly up to my knees and water flowing everywhere.

John heard the crash and threw open the door. "Good God, Palmer, what happened?"

"Look at this! I'm buried in this tile! Turn this thing off!" We'd never heard the word *gulag*, but I said, "I don't know where you're going from here, but I think I'm going to Siberia!"

Worried sick, we were very aware of the Cold War atmosphere, certain the room was bugged and that Big Brother was listening. John tossed me a towel and went for the floor lady, who, when she saw the mess we'd made, shouted the Russian equivalent of "Oh my God!" I needn't have worried. She was the mortified one, distressed that such a thing had happened because it made the Russians look bad. Immediately she moved us to a much bigger and nicer room and issued another half-pound key, but this time there was no adjoining bath. We had to send for her again to ask where it was, so I found the word for "bath" in my phrasebook and tried it out, miming soaping myself all over, but she seemed to have no idea what I meant. John and I just kept repeating the same word. When she finally caught on, she exclaimed the very same word we'd been saying all the time, in a why-didn't-you-say-so tone. She took us down the hall, drew the bath, and provided everything else we wanted.

In Moscow we somehow escaped Vera's clutches long enough to go to a nightclub. We'd met up with a couple of girls and invited them along. When we found the place, prospects of getting in at first looked slim, because there was a long line of young people waiting outside. We were about to turn away when the young

Russians realized we were Americans and insisted that we go to the head of the line. We objected, saying we didn't do that in America, everyone had to wait his turn, but they wouldn't take no for an answer. They pushed us up to the door, and one of them held my passport up to the glass to convince the doorkeeper to let us in. Once we got inside the place was jam packed, and a woman attendant tried to give us a front-row table occupied by six Russian officers and their women. We flatly refused, preferring to stand in the back, but she made them vacate the table anyway, and it stayed empty the whole time we were there.

Back on the job the next day, Vera took us to see those beautiful spotless subways an immense distance underground, one of the country's engineering marvels. As we were being carried down long, long, long escalators to the trains, I commented to Gillin, "Wow, I bet these made terrific bomb shelters during the war!"

At that Vera chimed in. "Tell me, John. Why do you Americans always speak of war and killing? Why is this so much a part of your life?"

I had a ready answer. "As a kid growing up, World War II *was* a big part of my life. We plan to visit a lot of battlefields around Europe. I want to see the Maginot Line from World War I, and the battlefields where Americans fought in World War II. Knowing what your people went through from the Germans, I merely thought how good it must have been to have such a place to go during the bombing. Nobody else in Europe had places so deep, so far down underground." I suppose I hit pretty near the truth, because for once Vera had no comeback.

Up on the streets we were fascinated to see many older women all in black, with black kerchiefs on their heads, sweeping the pavements with twig brooms. Not yet having been anywhere else in Europe, we hadn't seen the blue-uniformed Frenchmen washing out their gutters, and I was berated several times for trying to photograph the Russian women street-sweepers. Many of them must have been war widows, for the Soviet Union lost the best part of an entire generation of its men in World War II, ended just 13 years before.

My greatest frustration in Moscow had to do with a specific place I was determined to see. Over and over I'd asked Vera to arrange a visit for me to Radio Television Moscow. Already planning to go into radio and television, I wanted to see how the Russians did it. Furthermore, I was doing little radio pieces for WKPT, the hometown station that had given me my start. I had a little tape recorder and letters of introduction so I could meet the various correspondents, but every time I asked Vera to arrange it she'd say: "Today we are going to agricultural farm. We are going to see turnips grow and potatoes, and in afternoon after nice lunch in country villa, we go to manufacturing plant where they make tires." In short, everything but Radio Moscow. We went to the Bolshoi at night, all the usual tourist sites, but no appointment for me at the radio and television center.

Finally I took matters into my own hands. "Today, Gillin," I told him with a wink, "you go to the factory. I've got a very bad stomachache. I may even be getting the flu. You go, I'll stay in."

We went down to breakfast, but I ate very little and then went back upstairs to watch from the hotel window as my buddy got on the bus, the door closed, and the bus pulled out. Fifteen minutes later I walked quietly down the stairs and out to the street. Even though nobody was around, I walked a few blocks before hailing a taxi. "Radio Moscow," I told the driver, who took me straight to the gate and let me out. There was a big fence all around the large, imposing building and a guardhouse, so I just walked up and announced who I was and what I wanted to see. And then I waited.

A short time later came a group of musicians, and one carrying a violin case must have figured me for an American, because he spoke to me in pretty decent British English.

"I toured the United States with an orchestra in 1934. What is it you want to do?"

I explained that I hoped to meet the program director, that I had letters of introduction and had been asking Intourist to arrange it, but for some reason they wouldn't make the appointment.

"You stay here," he said. "I'll go inside and see what I can do."

He spoke to the guard in Russian and went in, and five minutes later someone came out for me. At that time Radio Moscow was the umbrella organization for radio, television and all broadcasting, and I was taken to be introduced to its director-general. Cordially received, I was also given lunch and a tour of the facility—all very informational.

As the director-general and I sat down afterward for a chat, I said to this important man, "Now let's look at your programming." Talk about nerve; I had it in spades. "Where's your *Meet the Press*? Where's your *Face the Nation*? Where's your *Youth Wants to Know*?" The last was then a popular U.S. program.

He folded his hands across his middle. "Oh, I see." His tone was sarcastic. "You're talking about your Sunday afternoon broadcast ghetto—the question-and-answer sessions where you drag public officials before journalists and question them as though they were not doing a good job. Oh, yes, I am very familiar with that. No, no. We have no such programs as that here."

"Well, in a democracy," I said, "it's a good thing to have such programs, because if someone's not doing a good job they can be exposed."

He glared. "If they're not doing a good job, it's up to their superior to handle it. It's not journalists who should question them. How would journalists know what problems these people confront?"

All of 23 years old, I was unstoppable. "Let's use an example. What if City Hall here in Moscow catches fire today? Maybe the fire department is a bit slow in responding. Maybe they should have had higher ladders to get people off the upper floors. Maybe they didn't have enough water for their hoses." To which he replied, "In case of a fire, the only ones who need to be concerned are the firemen, and they were called right away."

That evening after my friend John got back from his outing

we both went down to dinner, which always began with *borscht* I loved. At the head of the table sat Vera, who suddenly turned brightly to me.

"Well, John, I was so happy to learn that your stomach problem cleared up so quickly! The bus had hardly pulled away from the hotel before you got feeling better. We're very happy for you. I'm just sorry that you had so much difficulty at the gate of Radio Moscow, because I would have been *happy* to arrange for you a car so you could just go right in with an appointment. We do things with appointments here."

Stunned by how much she knew, I tried not to let on. "Vera, how many days have I asked to go there? Always you'd say tomorrow, today we have to do this and that—"

"Here things take time," she said.

"I know, but after so much time went by and nothing happened, I decided that if it was going to happen, I'd have to see about it myself."

She knew I had gone there. She even knew up until the point that I got out of the taxi three blocks from the hotel to walk back, and she wasn't even back from the factory visit at that time. Someone else knew. Someone else was watching. That was an eye-opener.

*

After leaving Russia, Gillin and I continued our travels in Europe. It was during a stop in Germany that I went by the American Express office in Frankfurt to check for mail. There I was handed an envelope from NBC marked URGENT, containing two pieces of incredibly good news: an offer of admission from the Columbia Graduate School of Journalism in New York, plus a letter awarding me the Godwin Fellowship to cover all expenses for the fall term. I was ecstatic. Rather than two more years at Northwestern, I could complete the work in one year in New York. That was one of the happiest days of my life, and John and I celebrated into the early morning hours at a nearby beer garden.

The Columbia Journalism School, founded by Joseph Pulitzer in the early 1900s, is one of the top-rated journalism schools in the country, touting New York City as its laboratory for aspiring young writers for print and broadcast. One more of the lucky breaks that seemed to fall my way. So in the fall of 1958 I went on to Columbia, having studied mainly political science and history as an undergraduate, but never journalism. At Columbia there were only about 80 of us in the class, and the professors told us, “New York is your laboratory.” We covered all kinds of stories, and I learned a great deal. We studied all aspects of journalism, including ethics and the laws of libel and slander. Columbia was also the venue for one of my great mistakes in journalism, but better there than out in the real world.

Every week our journalism class put out a newspaper. For that paper, one memorable day I was assigned to cover a Kiwanis Club luncheon on Wall Street where the speaker would be one of three federal appointees monitoring the corrupt affairs of the Teamsters Union. I took the subway downtown and arrived at a small private dining room upstairs over a bar just as the monitor began to speak. He went on and on about what a bad corrupt guy Jimmy Hoffa was, saying he was a scoundrel, could not be trusted, and the like. What’s news about that? I thought. Everybody knows it. I wrote my story in longhand during the subway ride back to Columbia and once back in the classroom told my professor Larry Pinkham that as soon as I could type my piece I’d be ready to hand it in.

“That won’t be necessary.” Pinkham took the paper from my hand and tore it to pieces in front of the class.

I was floored. “Why did you do that?”

“Because the Teamsters monitor story is the paper’s lead, and since you didn’t phone in any bulletins on your story immediately after the speech, the paper has to go with the wire-service version.”

I was crushed. I hadn’t done my homework. Of the three Teamsters monitors, one had been pro-Hoffa, one anti-Hoffa, and the third neutral until the third man seized the occasion of the Kiwanis

Club luncheon to come out against Hoffa. The speech I had just heard made it clear that two out of the three monitors—a majority—now opposed Hoffa, and he was finished. Disgusted with my performance, Pinkham suggested that I leave the building. My classmates watched in silence as I turned and did just that. It was a humiliating but vital lesson about the need for preparation before any interview.

One friend in grad school with whom I shared more than a few beers was a Russian by the name of Oleg Kalugin, a Fulbright exchange student who told me he'd come to the United States to study American journalism. Oleg was also working part-time as a guide at the United Nations, and I thought he was just an interesting guy. But another of my professors, John Hohenberg, took me aside one day and warned me that my friend was probably a colonel in the KGB and thus here on a spy mission.

In my youthful naïveté, I stuck up for my drinking buddy. "Just because he's a Russian doesn't make him a spy," I said, dismissing what I considered Hohenberg's alarmist view. I thought no more of it until three years later, when I was handed an AP bulletin while anchoring a newscast at WSB-TV in Atlanta. Shocked and amazed, I had to read it on the air:

"U.S. military authorities today charged a Russian by the name of Oleg Kalugin with spying after he was arrested on a Baltimore street last night, while accepting top-secret microfilm from an American military official." As soon as I got off the air I went straight to the phone and called my mentor to apologize. Oleg, then serving as a press officer at the Soviet Embassy in Washington, was also the KGB's Washington station chief at the time of his exposure as a spy. Declared *persona non grata* by the State Department, he was ordered to leave the country. Back in Moscow, he rose to the rank of major general and eventually headed KGB spy operations aimed at the United States. *Touché*, Professor Hohenberg! Kalugin later became a critic of the agency and was given asylum in this country and U.S. citizenship. He claims today that he did not spy while a journalism student at Columbia.

"I was not supposed to spy," he said. "It was a reconnaissance trip.

I was supposed to make as many friends as possible to prepare fertile grounds for my future work, to familiarize myself with the United States and its ways of life."

I guess I was one of those friends.

*

Speaking of Communists, one of the most interesting speakers who came to Columbia while I was there was Fidel Castro, in the States to address the United Nations. He and his fellow revolutionaries stayed in a Harlem hotel, and all sorts of stories circulated about their bringing live chickens and cooking them in the room. I was in a foreign-policy seminar at Columbia, and we, along with everybody else in New York, invited Castro to come and speak to us. To our surprise, he accepted our invitation. When the day arrived no more than 17 of us were in the seminar, maybe even fewer, and the talk was scheduled for the Latin-American Room, one of those rooms that looks as though nobody had ever entered it, with beautiful polished furniture and carpet about two inches thick. Just a room to look at, you'd have thought.

We students were jammed into the room, then here came this rangy, bearded Cuban revolutionary who'd overthrown the despotic Batista, got rid of the prostitutes and gamblers, who believed in agrarian reform—a man I considered quite a hero at the time. Along with him came his fellow revolutionary and right-hand man Che Guevara, all of them in military uniforms with cartridge belts across their chests. The New York press was there, but they weren't allowed to ask questions. We graduate students were the only ones allowed to do that.

When Castro addressed us in his broken English I was quite taken with the man. He would occasionally ask an aide a question in Spanish while standing right behind him, arms folded over his chest, was his trusted lieutenant Guevara. And Che Guevara was smoking a cigar—Cuban, no doubt. People could smoke anywhere then, but it made me uneasy to see him smoking a cigar in this fine room with a carpet so thick you could bounce on it, and no ashtrays in sight. He took a couple of puffs on his cigar, dropped it on the carpet, and ground it into the carpet under his boot heel to put it out. The look on the face of the dean of the Journalism School was a sight to behold—the horror of seeing this revolutionary grind his cigar into that wonderful carpet. Nobody said a word. These guys had been in the mountains, fighting a guerilla war for years, and maybe that's just the way they lived, but I did suspect that the cigar bit might have been an in-your-face gesture on Guevara's part.

Years later when I was working in the Middle East I was sent to a non-aligned summit conference in Tripoli, and there was Castro again. I figured he wouldn't remember me, and he probably didn't, but at the first photo op when no correspondents were allowed in I told the sound man, "Give me your microphone, I'll take your place." While the photographers took their pictures I moved slowly around the room until I could walk over to where Castro sat and speak to him.

"Chairman Castro, I'm John Palmer. During your visit to Harlem when you addressed the United Nations, you also spoke to my group at Columbia Journalism School."

"Jes, jes," he said.

"May I ask you a few questions?"

He thought for a moment. "Not suppose to have questions, but jou can ask me one or two."

At that I asked some question or other and edged up closer to his chair. When he broke into Spanish to answer, I interrupted. "Oh, Mr. Chairman, would you please speak English?"

"My Eenglish, she not so good anymore," he said.

I said, "I remember your English was pretty good when you spoke to us at Columbia."

"Jes, but that was a long time ago, and because of American government not inviting me, not letting me in, my Eenglish, she not so good anymore."

I got in a few more questions, which he answered about half in "Eenglish" and half in Spanish, and we got a little bit of a story out of it for NBC News. By that time I'd become rather disillusioned with Fidel Castro, because while some of that promised agrarian reform did take place, the Cuban people also suffered considerable repression. Any fair-minded jury would probably be hard pressed to say who had the worst effect on the Cuban people, Batista or Castro, for both had excesses in their own way.

*

In the fall of that first year at Columbia, I was assigned as an intern to work with the celebrated veteran New York City journalist Gabe Pressman, one of the pioneers of television news. I was with him on election night when I witnessed just how cruel politics can be. We were ushered into a private hotel suite where New York's Governor Averell Harriman was watching election returns on television, hoping, of course, that voters would return him to the Executive Mansion in Albany. You could tell from the pained expression on his face that things were not going well. His opponent, Nelson Rockefeller, had built up an insurmountable lead. When the television anchor declared Rockefeller the winner, Harriman's wife Marie, watching the election returns in a bedroom, let out a scream.

"Oh, God! This will kill Ave! He gave all he had as governor, and now the people have turned their backs on him! He has nothing left!"

All of us in the suite—Harriman, several campaign aides, Gabe and I—had clearly heard her outburst, which continued with audible sobs and weeping. An aide summoned a doctor to give her a sedative, and eventually she calmed down. An hour later, I stood in the back of the hotel ballroom as the governor, his face drained of color and seemingly frozen in shock, walked on stage accompanied by his wife to concede defeat. As he spoke, Mrs. Harriman's hands trembled, and her red, swollen eyes and heavy make-up failed to conceal her look of total devastation.

On our way out of the hotel that night, I said to Gabe, "I had no idea politics could be this rough."

"Just wait," he said. "You'll see. It can be a lot worse."

*

After grad school I worked for a few weeks in the CBS film library in New York, and then, because my college deferment had ended, flew home to Kingsport and joined the U.S. Army Reserve. Believe me, six weeks of boot camp at Fort Jackson, South Carolina, under a broiling August sun is no walk in the park.

As I lined up in formation on my first day there, my company commander called out, "How many of you men graduated from high school?"

Most hands went up.

"How many of you have a college degree?"

Three hands went up, including mine.

"Anyone have an advanced graduate degree?"

Fearing the worst, I held up my hand.

"Great," said the lieutenant, then addressed the massed greenhorns. "Private Palmer will now show us how an educated man picks up cigarette butts around the compound. Everyone else, dismissed."

After boot camp I was sent to Third Army Headquarters at Fort McPherson, Georgia, where I was supposed to work as a broadcast specialist. But the Army had mistakenly tagged me as a computer specialist, and when my new commanding officer realized I had no special computer skills, he assigned me to several weeks on a leaf-raking detail. Obviously the U.S. Army didn't see me as any journalistic hotshot.

Finally somebody must have realized I was overqualified for the jobs being assigned to me and sent me off to produce radio programs urging young men to join the army and see the world. What I really wanted to tell them was that enlistment would guarantee a course in the fine arts of picking up cigarette butts and raking leaves. Six months later I was discharged and ready to pursue my dream of reporting where it might matter.

4

CLIMBING THE LADDER— ATLANTA

THE INVITATION CAME in a phone call from the governor's office. "Mr. Palmer," the caller said, "the Governor and Mrs. Vandiver would like you to join them for dinner tomorrow night at the mansion."

Wow! It was March of 1960, and I'd held down my first job in television news, at WSB-TV in Atlanta, for all of six weeks. A dinner invitation from the governor of Georgia—that was heady stuff.

I'd applied for the job as a reporter for the station when an army buddy told me of an opening. After a lengthy interview process and a strenuous studio audition, the station's program manager, Mark Tolson, offered to hire me at the princely salary of $95 a week. Thrilled though I was, I had the nerve to respond that I couldn't consider accepting for less than $100 a week. After all, I had a master's degree in journalism from Columbia University.

Tolson then kept me hanging for three days while I worried that I had blown my career over a measly five bucks. Finally he called.

"The job's yours, Palmer, and we'll pay you a hundred bucks a week on one condition—that you swear not to tell our other reporters what you make."

I began as a street reporter covering politics, crime and whatever else was happening, as well as doing the local news cut-ins during NBC's *Today* at 7:25 and 8:25 each weekday morning. As it happened, Governor Vandiver was a fan of *Today* and saw my local news reports, hence the dinner invitation.

Ray Moore, my news director and mentor at WSB-TV, must have witnessed my unbridled excitement in the newsroom at being invited to dine with the governor, because he called me into his office for a chat.

"John, why do you think the governor of Georgia, whom you've never met, has invited you to dinner?"

"I don't know, but I'm going."

"Sure, you should go. But don't you imagine your invitation might have something to do with the fact that you report daily to the public about the governor's activities, so that it's very much in his interest to develop a personal relationship with you?"

Ray was right, of course, giving me my first lesson as a working reporter about vigilance regarding possible conflicts of interest.

Hal Suit, Ray's second in command, was less restrained in his advice. "You may be only twenty-five years old, but you are a reporter, so remember that when you go there. And another thing. Keep in mind that the governor puts his pants on every morning just like you do, one leg at a time."

Off I went to what was then Rich's Department Store, bought

a new suit, and showed up at the front door of the Governor's Mansion promptly at 8 p.m. after nervously circling the block for half an hour.

It was a fine dinner, except that the main course was quail the governor himself had shot on a South Georgia hunting trip. I did my best to respond intelligently to our discussion of politics, race relations and other issues of the day, struggling all the while to separate birdshot from every mouthful and deposit the pellets as discreetly as possible in my napkin. In the months to come that conversation would give me insights into Vandiver's thinking about race relations in particular as he confronted the volatile issue of desegregation at the University of Georgia and in Atlanta's public schools.

It was a very fortunate break for me that I began my career at WSB-TV, one of the premier television stations in the country, and the first television operation in the South with an outstanding news department. Housed in an impressive building known as White Columns on Peachtree, the station evoked the grandeur and tradition of the South, warmly welcoming visitors through its dignified front entrance into a state-of-the-art facility. Even more fortunate for me, my first boss was Ray Moore, a man of great integrity who guided us through our coverage of the civil rights struggle with innumerable personal examples of fairness and courage.

In those early days of television we shot black-and-white film that had to be processed and then edited by hand—a tedious operation—so that once we'd shot the film, several hours had to elapse before it went on the air. No video from helicopters, no satellites, no computers, no cell phones, just old-fashioned feet-in-the-street reporting.

During the time I was covering news in the early 1960s, television stations didn't have the equipment to go "live" without bringing in a huge van with big cameras and tons of heavy equipment. And that took time—but it allowed reporters time to gather the facts before going on the air. Nowadays, with satellite dishes and portable cameras which can be set up in minutes, reporters often don't have time to do the reporting they need to do before they have to go on the air "live." All too often the emphasis now is on being first on the air at the expense of accuracy. On the other hand, today's viewers see the story unfold as it happens and follow along as the story develops. One such example was the day-trader shootings in Atlanta a few years ago, where viewers saw terrified people running away from a building, the police going in, the discovery of the perpetrator in his car miles away from the shooting scene—saw everything just as it happened. So that kind of reporting, although it may be short on facts, does bring the viewer a sense of immediacy.

At every step of the way in my career I've had to jump through various hoops, and every one of them brought its own lessons, some painful, some fortuitous. And today everybody else coming into the business is also jumping through his or her own hoops. I can honestly say that I've learned something from every situation and every person I've had dealings with in the business, either as a mentor or someone to try not to be like.

As great a start as WSB-TV was for me, at first the job had one downside. Since the station's news department was not then separate from the program department, we reporters had to read commercials along with the news. We didn't do them on our own newscasts, but we did them on other newscasts, which were always live. Out of all the commercials we had to do, I favored one for Rich's, because it was very institutional, quality, about the store's great Southern heritage, no hard selling. I'd sit in a nice wingback chair beside a fake gas fireplace reading the commercial off the teleprompter which always ended with me saying, in as deep a voice as possible, "Rich's, a Southern institution since 1866."

Another commercial I had to do, early in the morning during the local cut-ins on the *Today* show, called for much greater agility. Every morning I lined up 24 coffee cups on a tray and put a spoonful of instant Luzianne Coffee into each one, then at the appropriate time poured boiling water into all 24. The sponsor wanted to demonstrate how one little jar of instant could make so many cups of coffee. I did it so many times I remember it verbatim. The camera would open with a close-up on a small paper cone labeled "Money Saver." Then I'd say, "Hmm! Wonder what it is! Says Money Saver! Let's see!" At that, I'd lift the cone. "Ah! A jar of instant Luzianne Coffee and Chicory, the coffee so rich you use just half as much!"

With about 30 seconds left, I'd pick up a kettle of boiling water and fill all twenty-four of those cups, trying to spill as little as possible, and at the same time read the teleprompter. I used to compare that exercise to being a one-armed paper hanger.

Guy Walters was a director at WSB before he went to California and made a fortune with a program called *The Dukes of Hazzard*, and we once played a terrible trick on him. Any time a commercial got messed up or the announcer didn't do it correctly, we'd have to do a "make-good" for the sponsor—in other words, do it over. So on the schedule where it said "Make-good for Luzianne Coffee" we set up our joke. All of us were in on it except Guy. The control-room team planned to run a commercial on air that was already on film, standing ready at the exact moment to switch everything. The viewer would see a commercial on film fed smoothly from the transmitter, but in the control room all the monitors were rigged to make it seem that the live action in the studio was what went out. Everybody had to have tremendous coordination to throw the right switch at the right time, because one slip would be disaster.

To lay the groundwork for the joke I went into the studio and let Walters rehearse me over and over: "Wonder what it is! Says Money Saver! Let's see!" The same damn thing, time after time. Finally Guy said, "Okay, we're fine, we've got it down. In three minutes we'll come out of the *Armchair Playhouse* and go to your commercial. Stand by."

At that point, while Guy was concentrating on something else, the floor manager helped me to stash under the counter where the Luzianne coffee always sat every major competitor's brand of instant coffee: Chase and Sanborn, Maxwell House, half a dozen others. I then removed the Luzianne jar from beneath the wonder-what-it-is-Money-Saver cone and substituted Chase and Sanborn. When the countdown came, *5, 4, 3, 2, 1, CUE*, I said, "Hmm! Wonder what it is! Says Money Saver! Let's see!" I lifted the cone. "Ah! A jar of—oh my God, it's Chase and Sanborn!" I grabbed the jar out and tossed it onto the floor, grabbed another jar from underneath and slammed it onto the counter. Walters couldn't believe what he was seeing.

"Oh my God!" I yelled again. "It's Maxwell House!" I snatched that one out and away and kept sliding one jar after another onto the counter, all the wrong brands.

Walters went wild, hollering, "CUT! CUT! GO TO BLACK!" When the guy operating the control board couldn't find the right switch to throw, Walters turned around and started pounding on the shoulder of the technical director, shouting, "KILL AUDIO!"

I was still bringing up jar after jar of competitive coffee brands, with Walters screaming at everybody, until finally the tech director managed to take him by the arm and say, "Guy . . . Guy . . . it was a joke. Just a joke."

At that Walters turned and walked out of the control room, walked down the hall and out of the station, and got in his car. As far as I know, there were no repercussions from it, but later we felt really bad about putting such a terrible strain on the man. He could have had a heart attack.

Another commercial gone wrong, this time by accident, was for Armour Franks. When I did it correctly, I'd take a knife and slice down the middle of the wiener to split it open and show in close-up how nice and pink the meat was inside. On the air live, anything could happen, and sure enough, on one try with that knife I didn't stop slicing with the wiener itself but ran the blade straight into my own finger. There I was on the air live, blood just spurting from my finger onto the sponsor's precious hot dog. That was one commercial I never had to do again, and it came as a tremendous relief to me and the other reporters when the news department decreed that reporters no longer had to read commercials on the air.

Once I was anchoring the 6 o'clock news when cameraman Dick Goss got stuck in rush-hour traffic on the southwest highway while heading back to the station with film of an event he'd just covered. I wanted to lead my broadcast with that story and shouted at him over the two-way radio in the newsroom:

"Listen, Dick, get out of the station wagon and leave it, run to the nearest side street, hail a taxi or commandeer a private car, and get that film to the station pronto!"

Ray Moore, overhearing my rant, called me into his office to favor me with more of his good advice. "John, while I admire your efforts to get the story in-house and on the air, we'll need that station wagon to cover stories tomorrow, and the next day, and the next. Think about it. You've just ordered Dick to abandon it in the middle of a busy expressway during rush hour. Would you like to rethink that decision?"

Again a wiser, cooler head prevailed, and I gained another lesson in journalism and life.

Ray taught us well. I remember when my friend and colleague George Page led the 11 o'clock news with a report that an 8-year-old black child known as Little Harvey had been hit by a car and killed that night on the Marietta highway. It happened that Little Harvey was known to untold numbers of Atlantans who'd dined at Aunt Fanny's Cabin, a popular restaurant on the outskirts of the city. Named after the restaurant's owner, who'd virtually adopted him, the young boy would come to your table holding a blackboard listing the menu specials—country ham, southern fried chicken, grits, okra, black-eyed peas, corn muffins and the like. The youngster charmed everyone who met him.

The next morning Ray asked Page why he had led with Little Harvey's death when there was so much other important international and national news.

George replied, "Because his death directly affected tens of thousands of Atlantans."

Ray smiled. "You did exactly right."

With Ray to teach us, we were all learning.

*

When I moved to Atlanta in 1960, the city had a population of fewer than a million and had just recently outstripped Birmingham, Alabama, as the unquestioned economic and industrial headquarters of the South. Although Atlanta was the leader of the so-called New South, like other cities and towns in the region it was racially segregated. If a black family moved into a white neighborhood, a cross might be burned on their front lawn. Jim Crow was still very much in evidence. Blacks were required to sit in the back of the bus. Black children did not attend school with whites. Drinking fountains, waiting rooms for buses and trains, and toilets were still labeled COLORED or WHITE. Blacks had their own movie theaters, restaurants, and hotels, and as Ray Moore recalls, "When heavyweight champion Cassius Clay came to Atlanta, there was only one black-owned motel where he could find a room."

Fortunately times changed. In 1996 Muhammad Ali—no longer Cassius Clay—was Atlanta's honored guest, invited to light the Olympic Torch and occupy the presidential suite at a five-star hotel.

For a time during that period a man by the name of Lester Maddox, who was later elected governor of Georgia, got considerable national news coverage for his racist rantings and actions. While I was at WSB he was running the Pickrick Cafeteria not far from Georgia Tech, a popular eating place. The food was a real bargain: home-style cooking that featured green beans cooked with fatback for 17 cents a bowl, creamed potatoes, delicious fried chicken and roast beef, cornbread, all quite good and moderately priced. A couple of the station engineers were going there to eat one night and invited me along. I'd heard about Pickrick but never eaten there. When we walked in, I noticed stacks of racist literature on display up front, along with a parrot in a cage squawking out "Hello, nigger! No niggers here!"

We collected our food and had sat down to eat when Lester got a microphone and made this blatant announcement: "We'd like to welcome to the Pickrick John Parmer of WSB! He's here eatin' some of our delicious Pickrick food, and I just want to welcome him tonight!"

Fortunately there weren't many people in the place that night, because I was mortified to have my presence in such a racist atmosphere trumpeted for all to hear. Very embarrassing. The other guys started snickering, because they saw me turn red in the face. I never went back. Holding an axe handle, Maddox once chased out some people who were trying to integrate the restaurant. When that got him notoriety he adopted the axe handle as his trademark. Later he even had a shop in Underground Atlanta that sold axe handles, and it probably helped him get elected governor.

It was on a later visit back to WSB that I heard a funny story about Maddox after he became governor. Upon election, he promptly announced that he was opening the governor's office once a week for anybody who had a problem and wanted to talk to him about it. So WSB sent a reporter out to wait on the steps and stop people in line to ask, "What are you going to talk to Governor Maddox about today?" They'd get such answers as, "Well, my corn crop failed, and I want some gov'mint aid." One woman came up with her hair in curlers tied up with a kerchief, and when the reporter asked why she was there, she said, "I'm Miz Maddox, the governor's wife. I've come to get Lester's paycheck." It wasn't my story to cover, but it was good for a laugh.

Atlanta gave me opportunities to cover stories I never imagined I'd be covering. One was a Ku Klux Klan rally at Stone Mountain, Georgia, beneath the colossal sculpture of Confederate generals that covers one whole side of the mountain. David Brinkley then had a national program called *David Brinkley's Journal*, and on one or two occasions we were sent out to do a piece on the Klan for it.

Our cameraman and I went out to Stone Mountain on a hot summer night for what turned out, for me, to be a frightening experience. The rally took place after dark on private property, a field owned by powerful segregationist J.B. Stoner at the foot of that great granite monolith. To get there, we drove along a winding road lined by shanty homes, and as our headlights turned this way and that we could see the faces of black families with small children sitting on their porches watching the cars come, probably terrified as they stared at the spectacle of so many cars shining their lights and honking their horns.

When we reached the field we saw that the white-robed Klansmen had pulled up a big flatbed truck with a microphone on the back, with two or three hundred people gathered around. It was sobering to see just how many people had come and parked all around that field, to sit on or stand around the hoods of their cars and trucks. As they often did, the Klan had brought in a preacher to provide scriptural justification for their segregationist aims. The preaching and ranting went on for some time, always including vituperation against the "lying Atlanta newspapers." By no means were we reporters regarded favorably, because I was working for WSB, which was owned by Cox Communications, as was *The Atlanta Journal-Constitution*. Nevertheless, we were there.

In a way the KKK was using a very up-to-date dramatic technique, for at a given point some signal triggered the culmination of the event: a cross set afire high atop the mountain, so far away that we couldn't get a clear picture of it, with a second cross burning close by. The whole thing gave me the chills. That was one of the last KKK rallies in Stone Mountain, and things have changed, because today the city of Stone Mountain has a black mayor and a large, middle-class black population.

On Sundays at WSB-TV, I was the news reporter on a television program hosted by my friend and fellow reporter George Page. On one Sunday during the height of the civil rights struggle and the lunch-counter sit-ins, George decided to have Dr. Martin Luther King, Jr. on the program. When the program's sponsor, the George Power Company, saw an ad in the morning paper listing King's appearance, company executives were irate. At the time, Dr. King was viewed by many as a "troublemaker" and an "agitator." I was in early that Sunday morning and took the calls from the company. While listening to their protests, I insisted that Dr. King was a newsworthy person and would be on the program despite their objections. George, the program host, and station manager Mark Bartlett agreed, telling Power Company executives that program sponsors could not dictate content on a news program. The solution: sponsorship of the program was withdrawn and Dr. King appeared as scheduled.

At the end of the program, George announced, "Our guest next week is Calvin Craig, a paint sprayer from the Ford Motor Company and Grand Dragon of the Knights of the Ku Klux Klan." With that, the power company was again up in arms. As journalists we viewed that kind of coverage as essential, because civil rights was the central issues of the day. And, after all, there was only one power company in the state so people had to buy their electricity from Georgia Power or else live in the dark. So what were they afraid of? Power company officials said they sponsored the program to create goodwill and soon moved their sponsorship to the less controversial daily weather report.

The station provided news on both radio and television, and WSB's coverage could range from the big picture to the extremely local scene. A reporter named Aubrey Morris used to cruise Atlanta's roads in what was called Radio Car 750 looking for news. If he thought something was newsworthy, he would break in on regular programs.

Atlanta still had trolley cars at the time, and after an overnight ice storm, at 7 o'clock that morning Aubrey was out touring around. He broke in on the regular program: "This is Aubrey Morris! The city of Atlanta, for all practical purposes, is closed! The trolley wires are frozen, the maids can't get to work, nobody can move, you'll never get your children to school or get to work yourself."

A few minutes later Atlanta Mayor William B. Hartsfield joined Aubrey on the radio: "Aubrey, you have just shut down my town, and I wonder under what auspices you have closed the city of Atlanta this morning. You have closed our schools and you have shut down our transportation system." Aubrey said, "Well, Mr. Mayor, I've been out in it, and it's just dreadful out here."

The mayor came back on in that calm voice. "Let me say right now to everyone in Atlanta, the trolleys will run later on in the morning, we will have school today, and the city will not shut down." The prestigious mayor of Atlanta had spoken.

*

While reporters at WSB-TV would often cover events for NBC News programs, from time to time network correspondents would also be sent to Atlanta to work out of our newsroom. Once I told visiting NBC News correspondent Herb Kaplow that someday I'd like to do the job he did. Herb had then been on the road for almost two weeks and was looking forward to going home to Washington that night when the phone rang. It was the NBC News assignment desk in New York, asking him to grab the next plane for Miami. A boatload of Cuban refugees had washed up on the Florida coast, and the network wanted Herb to cover the story.

I saw the pained expression on his face as he phoned his wife. "Don't bother to hold dinner," he said. "I won't be home tonight. They want me to go to Miami."

As he walked out of the newsroom Herb turned to me and shook his head. "So, kid, you want to be a network correspondent, do you?"

I shouted after him, "Yes! I do!"

On another occasion David Brinkley came to our station to do some reporting for The Huntley-Brinkley Report. By then Brinkley was a household name in America and one of the most celebrated television news anchors of our time, so I was thrilled to be assigned to interview him in his Biltmore Hotel room about NBC's coverage of the upcoming national election. The interview seemed to be going just fine when our cameraman, an inexperienced freelancer, suddenly switched off his camera and appealed to me.

"John, I'm afraid my focus may not be right. How far do you think it is from my lens to Mr. Brinkley's nose?"

Numb with embarrassment, I hadn't come up with an answer when Brinkley spoke up.

"I have a suggestion. Go out and buy a box of cigars. Then throw away the cigars and put the empty box in your newsroom with a sign saying, 'Deposit twenty-five cents for each word mispronounced on the air.' As soon as you have a couple of dollars in the box, go out and *buy a measuring tape, for God's sake*."

After we aired the somewhat out-of-focus interview Brinkley stopped by the station to say goodbye and asked a secretary to order him a taxi for the airport. I quickly volunteered to drive him, and in another lucky break for me if not for him, his flight was delayed two hours, so we had time for dinner together at the airport. For me it was great, but it had to be frustrating and far less pleasant for Brinkley as dozens of people came over to our table asking for his autograph. He told me between sieges that he found it well-nigh impossible to venture outside the studio anymore to cover news events because the unwelcome attention so often overshadowed the story he was there to cover.

*

The early 1960s were years of great change in the South and especially in Atlanta, which became a major organizing center of the civil-rights movement, with the Reverend Martin Luther King, Jr., and students from Atlanta's historically black colleges and universities playing major roles in the movement's leadership.

On Oct. 19, 1960, a sit-in at the lunch counters of several Atlanta department stores drew national media attention when it led to the arrest of Dr. King and several dozen black students. Despite this, Atlanta's political and business leaders fostered the city's image, in Mayor Hartsfield's words, as "a city too busy to hate." And for the most part the slogan was true.

I first met Dr. King at a demonstration outside Lebs Delicatessen near Five Points in downtown Atlanta. Lebs was an Atlanta institution, offering oversized stuffed corned-beef sandwiches and mouth-watering kosher dills stacked in metal bowls on every table. Like other restaurants in Atlanta at the time, Lebs refused to serve blacks, so civil rights demonstrators made it a special target, figuring that a Jewish owner should know better than to discriminate.

On one occasion when Dr. King took part in a demonstration at Lebs, I managed a brief interview with him for television as he was led away to a police car in handcuffs. Amid all the shouting and confusion, I shall never forget the absolute serenity I saw in the man's face. In the weeks and months that followed, I interviewed Dr. King several more times while covering civil rights demonstrations in other Southern cities and later when he took his crusade north to Chicago.

Even at the time I knew that Dr. King was no ordinary civil rights leader. By the time I encountered him in 1960 he was already a national figure, having led the Montgomery bus boycott that began when seamstress Rosa Parks refused to comply with the Jim Crow law that required her to move to the back of the bus. King had already helped to found the Southern Christian Leadership Conference, a group created to harness the moral authority and organizing power of black churches for nonviolent protests in the service of civil rights reform. Always I was impressed with his quiet dignity in the face of threats and verbal abuse. He was without a doubt the most inspiring person I ever met. Even in later years when I became an NBC News correspondent, interviewing presidents, senators, astronauts, other Nobel Prize winners and world statesmen, none measured up to the inspirational qualities of this visionary man, who exuded faith and love for his fellow human beings. Of course he had flaws, like the rest of us, but I found him to be truly a man of grace.

He loved to laugh and had a surprising sense of humor. A lawyer friend of mine, who more than once was called on to bail Dr. King out of some Southern jail, remembered traveling by car with King through Mississippi during the dark days of the civil rights struggle. King, who was behind the wheel, said, "You know, I could use some exercise. I know a bowling alley up ahead where we could stop."

"No!" my lawyer friend exclaimed. "That bowling alley is run by the most hateful, out-of-control racist in Neshoba County. He'd just as soon shoot you as look at you!"

"Oh, come on," King said as he pulled into the bowling alley's parking lot. But then with a hearty laugh he gunned the car, scattering gravel, and drove off, much to my friend's relief. Humor was one way Dr. King dealt with the tension and fear that were his daily companions.

In January of 1961 the emerging civil rights struggle burst into the forefront when a federal judge handed down a decision ordering the University of Georgia to accept two superbly qualified black students who had been denied admission. Both Charlayne Hunter and Hamilton Holmes had attended Atlanta's all-black Turner High School, where Holmes was valedictorian, senior class president and co-captain of the football team. Hunter had finished third in her graduating class and had edited the school newspaper.

The presence of Holmes and Hunter on the campus was a decisive test of segregation, as well as being one of the defining moments of the national civil rights struggle. As they arrived on the North Campus to register for classes, the two courageous young people were met by a crowd of reporters and students, the latter chanting, "Two-four-six-eight! We don't want to integrate!" All was relatively quiet, however, until the third evening after their arrival, when a mob of students hurling bricks and bottles descended on Hunter's dormitory. Police finally had to use tear gas to disperse them.

I was there that night covering for WSB-TV, along with Ray Moore, who did double duty as a cameraman, and NBC News correspondent Frank Bourgholtzer. As we crouched behind a tree, handkerchiefs over our noses to mitigate the tear gas, we watched Georgia state troopers escort the two students out of their dormitories amid the cheers and jeers of the crowd. The dean of students had withdrawn them from the university, saying it was "in the interest of your personal safety and for the safety and welfare of more than 7,000 other students at the University of Georgia."

Within days, a new court order sent Hunter and Holmes back to the university, which posed a new dilemma and put Governor Vandiver in a bind. Some months earlier, the Georgia legislature had passed a law ordering the university to shut down if blacks were admitted. And Vandiver had won election on an unequivocal campaign promise: "No, not one, not one Negro will go to school with a white child while I am governor."

On the evening of Jan. 18, 1961, in an address carried by WSB-TV and fed to every other television station in Georgia, Governor Vandiver stood before a special session of the all-white Georgia Assembly and ate his words, asking the legislature to change the law to allow the university to remain open. In spite of bitter attacks against him by rabid segregationists, the lawmakers acquiesced.

I stood in the balcony of the Georgia legislature on that historic night realizing that I had just witnessed a great turning point in the history of the South. Later, I drove by the Governor's Mansion a few blocks from our TV station to find it ringed by scores of armed state troopers, ready to hold back the expected racist mobs who felt the governor had betrayed them. Those mobs never materialized. The people of Georgia did not want their great university closed, even if it meant admitting black students.

Charlayne Hunter went on to become a writer and reporter for both the Public Broadcasting System and *New York* magazine before taking a position as CNN bureau chief in South Africa. Hamilton Holmes became a physician and trustee of the University of Georgia, and when he died in 1995 the Georgia legislature named a highway after him.

While desegregation of the university was a big step for the state and the South, Georgia had another hurdle to clear late that summer. The deadline for compliance with a federal court order mandating desegregation of Atlanta's public schools was at hand. Civic, business and church leaders joined Atlanta's Mayor Hartsfield in a powerful initiative to avoid the mistakes made in New Orleans and Charlotte during desegregation of those cities' schools. A flurry of meetings, conferences and public forums took place, all aimed at preparing city residents for the entrance of nine black students to previously all-white schools on Aug. 31, 1961.

The *Atlanta Journal-Constitution*, vilified by rabid segregationists as "those race-mixing, lying Atlanta newspapers," carried numerous editorials advocating a peaceful transition. At WSB-TV, Ray Moore produced documentaries on desegregation in New Orleans showing that unfortunate city's reaction of widespread violence, along with a portrayal of the troubles in Charlotte. The programs' overriding message was, "Don't let it happen here."

Ray carefully planned our television coverage plan for "D-Day"—public school desegregation day in Atlanta. In the weeks leading up to that day everyone in the newsroom, including reporters, film editors and secretaries, was required to learn to shoot news film, as we planned to cover every entrance at the four desegregating schools at the same hour on the same day. All of us novice cameramen were told to shoot sparingly, so as not to overload the film-processing machine. Police set up a "no man's land" around those schools. Photographers, kept well back from the school entrances, could only snap pictures from a distance.

One of our reporters, Don McClellan, went to Murphy High School and befriended a lady who lived across the street from the school and whose porch provided an excellent vantage point. She was happy to cooperate and even let him use her phone to call back to the station. From my own position across the street from another school, I saw two black children enter without incident. It was the same at the other three schools. The city had faced a big challenge and met it with aplomb, decency and good sense. Atlanta had turned a corner toward becoming the great city it is today.

The final legal barrier to racial equality in Georgia fell the following year, when Federal Judge Griffin Bell ruled that the state's county unit system of voting violated the principle of "one man, one vote." That antiquated system, in place since 1917, gave disproportionate voting power to Georgia's rural counties, then bastions of racial segregation. Aubrey Morris, by then WSB Radio's news director, and I happened to be visiting Georgia's Sen. Herman Talmadge in his Washington office when the senator interrupted our interview to take an important phone call. An aide was calling to tell him that the U.S. Supreme Court had just upheld Judge Bell's decision, striking down Georgia's county unit system as unconstitutional. Sen. Talmadge, who owed his political career to championing the cause of segregation, was also a very smart politician who immediately recognized the decision's impact on his political future in Georgia.

"Things will never be the same down home," he told us. "No longer will candidates in statewide races win by campaigning against Negroes, because they just got empowered by the Supreme Court, and their vote will have to be courted."

Talmadge took his own advice, transforming himself from a staunch segregationist to a moderate who would eventually draw strong support from Georgia's poor black population.

In just two years, but after far more years of struggle, Georgia had led the South in its crucial advance toward racial equality. Has the forward-looking spirit of that time endured? Not everyone thinks so. Ray Moore, my early mentor and friend, recalling the momentous times he and I were both on hand to record, recently stated his own sobering assessment of present-day black/white relations in America.

"Today, we have drifted apart," Ray wrote. "The LAWS are stronger, but the SPIRIT of brotherhood is weaker."

Many journalists whose writings and broadcasts supported the civil-rights movement had to endure serious threats. Perhaps the most influential of these journalists was Gene Patterson, then editor of the *Atlanta Constitution*, who followed in the footsteps of its legendary editor Ralph McGill. Every day, Patterson wrote directly to his fellow white Southerners urging them to change their ways. His words were so inspirational that Walter Cronkite asked him to read, live on the *CBS Evening News*, his most famous column, "A Flower for the Graves," reflecting on the Birmingham church bombing that murdered four black children. Here is an excerpt from that column, dated Sept. 16, 1963:

> A Negro mother wept in the street Sunday morning in front of a Baptist church in Birmingham. In her hand she held a shoe, one shoe, from the foot of her dead child. We hold that shoe with her. Every one of us in the white South holds that small shoe in his hand. It is too late to blame the sick criminals who handled the dynamite. . . . The charge against them is simple. They killed four children. Only we can trace the truth, Southerner—you and I. We broke those children's bodies. . . . We know better. We created the day. We bear the judgment. May God have mercy on the poor South that has been so led. May what has happened hasten the day when the good South, which does live and has great being, will rise to this challenge of racial understanding and common humanity and in the full power of its unasserted courage, assert itself.

Race relations and the civil-rights struggle in the South dominated our coverage during my two and a half years as a reporter and news anchor at WSB-TV, but there were other stories, some memorable and some not so memorable. One I would like to forget occurred during my first six months at the station. I was a substitute anchor for the noon news at the time, and we had what was called a "running story" with a new development almost every day. This story concerned a purse-snatcher—no big deal on the cosmic scale, but it got the attention of nearly everybody in the city. The purse-snatcher was a bold fellow who would run into a department store or dress shop, grab a woman's purse, and flee before anyone could react. This happened day after day, so often that the *Atlanta Constitution* began running a little front-page box listing the elusive purse-snatcher's strikes of the previous day.

Finally just before Christmas I heard on the police radio in our newsroom that a man accused of being the purse-snatcher had been arrested and was being brought to police headquarters for booking. Cameraman Dick Goss and I arrived just in time to get pictures of the suspect, in handcuffs, being led into the clink. We rushed back to WSB-TV where the film was quickly processed and handed to a technician in the projection room to be included with other news film on the noon news. I dashed to the studio, straightened my tie, and said, "Good afternoon. A man accused of being the long-sought purse-snatcher has been apprehended, and we have exclusive film of the suspect taken within the hour."

At this point I saw film pop up on the TV monitor in front of my desk and, also to my horror, shock on the studio crew's faces. The wrong film had been loaded into the projector, and the man we were showing on television and identifying as the purse snatcher was Dr. Claude Purcell, well known to most Atlanta residents as the state superintendent of schools. I immediately apologized on the air, and Dr. Purcell was gracious enough not to sue. It was the first of several painful experiences with the old axiom in television news, otherwise known as Murphy's Law: "If anything can go wrong, it will."

Another of my early assignments at WSB-TV was coverage of the opening of the Southeastern Fair to come up with a feature story. My cameraman and I scanned the midway and found one attraction impossible to miss. The banner above the booth urged us to

SEE SAILOR KATZIE AND HIS
20-FOOT BOA CONSTRICTOR!

Eager to make my mark, I set off to do an interview with Katzie, who sported the appropriate sailor suit while wrestling his pet boa. I thought it would make for an interesting, if unremarkable, feature.

Sent to cover the fair again the following year, I found that the same attraction was back, but minus one essential element. The new banner screamed

SEE THE BOA CONSTRICTOR
THAT KILLED SAILOR KATZIE!

Keeping company with the snake this time was the late Sailor's wife, who passed on the sad news. "When I come looking for him one morning, there he laid in the bottom of the cage, dead as a doornail, and that big old snake just laying there looking at me."

No one will ever know why the pet boa turned on its master. A tragedy, yes, but stoic Mrs. Katzie saw no reason to fold the act and thereby sacrifice her livelihood.

Another morning, in May of 1961, while I was co-hosting *Today in Georgia*, a one-hour local program that followed NBC's *Today*, a group of grade-school children accompanied by their teacher arrived at the studio as part of a field trip to learn about television. Our program had just begun when I received a signal to join the NBC network for a news special: astronaut Alan Shepard was about to become the first American to journey into space. With just seconds to go before the lift-off, the teacher, obviously disappointed that our television program had been preempted, corralled her charges. "Okay, boys and girls, back to the buses."

Astounded, I rushed over to suggest that she let her students stay to watch this historic event, one they would remember all their lives.

"No thanks," she said, "we're on a tight schedule, and we're due at the zoo in half an hour." Some things you never forget.

June 3, 1962, was a day that no one alive in Atlanta at the time will ever forget. I was driving with my friend and fellow reporter George Page to Florida for a few days of vacation when we heard the horrific news on the car radio: "A jetliner carrying one hundred and twenty-two members of the Atlanta Art Association, on a tour of art museums in Europe, has crashed on takeoff from Orly Airport in Paris. It is reported that only two stewardesses survived the crash."

We stopped at a little radio station along the highway and asked the person on duty to let us read the AP wire service reports. The news was every bit as horrible as we feared. There were the names of the cream of Atlanta society, all dead. I knew many of them personally. We immediately turned around to drive back to Atlanta and go back to work, as the city struggled to deal with its loss. In the months that followed, the people of Atlanta, along with the French government, settled on a means of honoring those prominent citizens who lost their lives by creating a magnificent Arts Center.

That same year, Atlanta and the rest of the country held its collective breath during a terrifying autumn week while the Cuban missile crisis unfolded. On October 22, President John F. Kennedy informed the world that the Soviet Union was building secret missile bases in Cuba, a mere 90 miles off the Florida shore.

Early in the crisis the entire radio and television staff of WSB was asked to assemble in the big TV studio, to be told that WSB Radio was being taken over by the United States government. All subsequent programming would come from Washington to be broadcast in Spanish to the Cuban people, assuring them that the United States, regardless of what action it might be forced to take, bore the Cuban people no ill will.

Our chief engineer spoke up. "That switch-over will take hours to accomplish."

"No, it won't," a State Department official said. "The work has already been done."

That was a scary time for me and the whole nation, with the two great powers teetering between war and peace. After weighing such options as an armed invasion of Cuba and an air strike against the missiles, President Kennedy settled on another course. In addition to demanding that Soviet Premier Nikita Khrushchev remove all the missile bases along with their deadly contents, Kennedy ordered a naval blockade of Cuba to keep Soviet ships from bringing more missiles to the island.

I stocked up on nonperishable food and cans of water in the basement of my rented house in suburban Sandy Springs, as did many others, to prepare for possible nuclear war. In the end, of course, Premier Khrushchev backed down.

A good many years later I was interviewing Secretary of State Dean Rusk and asked about that period when the United States and the Soviet Union marched up to the brink of war. Rusk, a Georgia native who'd grown up in rural Cherokee County, recounted how he'd informed a greatly relieved President Kennedy that the missile crisis was over.

"When I was a boy in Georgia," he'd told the president, "we were so poor we had to make up our own amusements. One of our games involved two boys staring deadpan into one another's faces until one of us blinked, and the one who didn't blink won. Khrushchev blinked."

*

Atlanta had been a great place to get my feet wet in the news business and I'd had the privilege of working for a first-class station with a gifted news director. Now it was time to move on.

5

MORE RUNGS ON THE LADDER—CHICAGO

CHICAGO HAD BEEN in my sights for more than a year, ever since the news director at the NBC-owned and operated station had asked me to join their news team. I had turned down that invitation after my WSB-TV news director Ray Moore suggested that I needed more seasoning before moving to such a large market. "If they love you in September," Ray said, "they'll love you in May."

But that was not the case. When I called to speak with the

executive who had offered me the job a year before, I was told he had left, replaced by Bill Corley as news director. Bill said the television anchor job was no longer open and mentioned that he had only a radio news position to offer. Then he said: "John, you live in Atlanta where you're a big fish. Why not stay in that wonderful place and have a great life?" A curious argument, I thought. Why would he try to discourage me? Nevertheless, I had made up my mind that it was time to try for another rung up the ladder. From my days at Northwestern University, I knew that Chicago was a great news town and a big step up, so I took the radio job, which, incidentally, paid about double my television salary in Atlanta.

Back beside Lake Michigan again during my first week in Chicago in September of 1963, I opened my hotel room door one morning to find a copy of the *Chicago Tribune* with an eight-column headline: FLYNN AND HILL MOVE TO 7. I had no idea who Flynn and Hill were, or what "7" might be. From the story I learned that Flynn was Fahey Flynn, one of Chicago's leading newscasters, and Hill was Hugh Hill, a well-known local police reporter. Both were moving from WBBM, Chicago's CBS affiliate, to Channel 7, WLS-TV, the ABC affiliate.

That was big news? After I read that, I knew I'd come to the right place. Chicago was, and is, the best news town in America—a reporter's dream. Whether you're interested in politics, business, race relations, labor, transportation, crime, government corruption or the weather, Chicago has it all. On top of that, it has a beautiful lakefront and is a clean, vibrant city that works.

I was hired as a radio reporter and newscaster at WMAQ with the promise that I'd be considered for the first television opening. Less than a year later, that promise came true. I was on my stomach having a massage at a health club near the station when the masseur congratulated me on my new television anchor job. That was news to me. The station manager used the same masseur and the masseur knew what he was talking about. I guess masseurs, like hairdressers, learn everything first. From the beginning, I knew I had made the right decision. I quickly found a one-bedroom apartment on the 45th floor of Marina Towers on the Chicago River, just three blocks from the Merchandise Mart and the NBC station with a great view of the city's magnificent skyline. Marina City is a complex of two 60-story circular towers that encompass apartments, recreation facilities, restaurants, banks and of course a marina on the Chicago River, where I kept a boat. There were some interesting tenants. One was Murray "the camel" Humphreys, a Chicago mobster who once worked for Al Capone and was the chief political and labor racketeer of the Chicago Outfit during prohibition. His nickname, The Camel, was derived from his preference for wearing camel hair coats. He died of a heart attack while vacuuming his apartment. At least, that is what his newspaper obituary said.

Once, my Marina City apartment was the site of a gathering of draft evaders during the Vietnam War. My friend and NBC News producer George Page had asked me to find a subject for his network documentary entitled *We Won't Go*, which would follow a draft evader as he fled to Canada to avoid prosecution, as a number of young men were doing during that time. I invited about a dozen draft evaders to my apartment one evening for pizza, being careful not to disclose my purpose and listening to them until I heard one of them say he was going into exile the next week in Canada. He agreed to have Page and his film crew accompany him to Toronto. As soon as the airliner had crossed the U.S. boarder into Canada, they brought out their camera and interviewed him, then followed him during his first weeks in exile as he tried to find a job and a place to live. It was an important look at what motivated many young men to avoid the controversial war in Vietnam.

The morning after my "pizza party" I was visited at my Chicago NBC News office by two FBI agents who asked me about the nature of the gathering at my apartment the previous evening. It seems that several of my "guests" had been followed to my apartment and even the pizza deliveryman reported that he had been questioned by FBI agents as he waited for the elevator to take him up to my apartment. I was fully prepared to champion the first amendment and be taken off to jail for refusing to reveal my sources. "This was a gathering in my private home, with guests whose identity I will not disclose, nor will I reveal what was discussed," I said. With that, the two agents thanked me for my time and left. I never heard about the incident again.

On Friday, Nov. 22, 1963, less than two months after arriving in Chicago, I was having lunch at a restaurant with a friend on my day off when a waiter who knew me came over to our table.

"Mr. Palmer," he said, "you'd better get back to your office, because the president has been shot."

At the time anti-Kennedy jokes were very much in vogue. If this waiter was making one now it was in very poor taste. But his stricken face reflected true distress.

I headed for the door, pausing to join the silent crowd around a television set at the bar. We watched as Walter Cronkite, in shirt-sleeves with unbuttoned collar and loosened tie, relayed a bulletin from the UPI wire: "Three shots were fired at President Kennedy's motorcade today in downtown Dallas." Almost immediately, he followed with another UPI dispatch, adding that President Kennedy had been "seriously wounded, perhaps fatally," and that his motorcade had been diverted to a hospital.

I jumped into a taxi and headed for the NBC station where, at the entrance to the newsroom on the 19th floor, I found two NBC pages holding back station employees so news reporters and writers could work. NBC News correspondent Frank McGee was on the air, talking with reporters on the scene in Dallas.

Within a few minutes bells on the wire machine clanged to signal a major bulletin: FLASH—DALLAS TEXAS, PRESIDENT KENNEDY DIED AT 1 P.M. CENTRAL STANDARD TIME TODAY.

I was stunned, along with everyone else in America.

As the junior member of the news staff, I had little to do and was further discouraged with an admonition from my new boss, Bill

Corley. "John, the best thing you can do is go home and get some rest. We'll need you fresh for relief tomorrow."

I went home, all right, but not to rest. Hour after hour I stared at my television screen in disbelief, knowing that things would never be quite the same again. They never were. It's a cliché, but it's true—America lost much of its innocence that day.

Early on Saturday Corley called me with further instructions. "They think the rifle used to kill the president was ordered from Klein's Sporting Goods here in Chicago. Get over there and see what's going on."

There, a group of FBI agents were huddled in a back room sorting through thousands of sales slips for hours until they found the one they were looking for: a mail-order coupon signed by one "A. Hidell" of Dallas, Texas. The FBI knew this was an alias frequently used by Lee Harvey Oswald, and the handwriting matched that of the man suspected of killing the president.

The next morning, a Sunday, I was monitoring the wire-service machines in the newsroom and watched on television as Oswald was being transferred to a more secure lock-up from Dallas Police Headquarters. Suddenly I heard the sound of a gunshot. I looked up at the television monitor in time to see Oswald on the concrete floor, mortally wounded. The only network carrying the transfer live was NBC, and Tom Pettit, our correspondent on the scene, did a masterful job.

"A shot has been fired," he said. "Oswald is on the ground." Tom resisted the temptation to state that Oswald had been shot until he knew for certain that it was so, a good lesson for every aspiring television news reporter.

The Kennedy assassination triggered anti-gun campaigns in cities nationwide, prompting Chicago television stations to run daily public-service announcements asking residents to turn in their firearms, "no questions asked." The anti-gun movement, coupled with the announcement that President Johnson would make

Chicago his first trip outside Washington since being sworn in, prompted me to dig out my old, all-but-forgotten .22-caliber rifle from the closet so I could get rid of it. It seemed a wise and timely move for a guy living on the 45th floor overlooking the route of the new president's motorcade into the city.

I called Chicago police headquarters. "My name's John Palmer, and I live in apartment 4505 in Marina Towers. I have a rifle I'd like to turn in."

"We'll take care of it," the switchboard operator said.

I had barely hung up the phone when there was a heavy knock came at the door. I opened it to encounter four policemen in the hallway. "We're here for the rifle," one said.

By this time the building manager plus two security guards had arrived in the hallway and a dozen or so neighbors, alerted by the commotion, were peering out of their own doors. I handed the rifle to a police officer, who took it in his gloved hands, held it high overhead just like in the movies, and marched past my frightened neighbors, down the hall toward the elevators.

The officer in charge then asked me when and where I had bought the rifle, when it was last fired, and other such questions. Politely, I declined to answer them all, citing the "no questions asked" policy. With a final glare at me the officer turned to leave, but not before he issued an ominous warning. "Mr. Palmer, I doubt that you've heard the last of this." But I had heard the last of it—although my neighbors continued to eye me with suspicion.

In Chicago one of my first duties soon became an ongoing assignment over the next six years. I covered Mayor Richard J. Daley's morning news conferences at City Hall, and they were rarely dull. The mayor approached every issue and conflict as an attack on his political power and ability to govern, barely tolerating reporters and taking personally the numerous scandals the press uncovered in his administration. Whenever any of us questioned him about some perceived misdeed we could count on the legendary mayor's face turning red with anger.

One of Daly's more famous outbursts came in response to a reporter's question about one of the mayor's son's employment with a company that insured City Hall and many other public buildings in Chicago. Under questioning from reporters Daley replied, "If a father can't look out for his own son, who will?"

Equally famous were his malapropisms, as after his police force was accused of brutality in the 1966 West Side race riots. "The policeman is not there to create disorder," the mayor declared. "The policeman is there to preserve disorder."

In *American Pharaoh*, the mayor's biography by Taylor and Cohen, the authors depict a man rarely concerned with national politics or political theory, living most of his life in the same small, South Side, Irish-Catholic neighborhood of Bridgeport where he was born. Daley dominated the city's political machine through patronage, ruling Chicago for twenty-one years with an iron hand.

Despite his unbreakable grip on the city, or perhaps because of it, Mayor Daley received more than his share of death threats, and after President Kennedy was assassinated the mayor became almost paranoid about his own security. When I was sent to cover Daley's participation in the opening of the Chicago campus of the University of Illinois, credible warnings had already been received that an attempt would be made on his life. During the mayor's brisk walking tour of the campus I noted dozens of police sharpshooters on rooftops, and afterward as the mayor greeted dignitaries behind the speakers' platform he suddenly realized that his bodyguards lagged at least 10 feet behind. Frightened and enraged, Daley lunged through the crowd, grabbed his chief bodyguard by his lapels, and shouted, "Never, never, EVER leave me alone! Do you hear me? DO YOU UNDERSTAND?"

In view of the tremendous stress he was under I thought the mayor demonstrated great courage by simply showing up.

*

One day I was dispatched to a Chicago restaurant where Richard Nixon was scheduled to speak to a civic group. Nixon had been defeated in the 1960 presidential campaign by John Kennedy and had accepted a job with the Pepsi-Cola Company. I hoped to get a quick interview with the former vice-president and positioned my crew on the sidewalk, where I stopped him as he entered the restaurant.

"Mr. Vice President, I'm John Palmer with WMAQ-TV, the Chicago NBC affiliate, and I'd like to talk to you briefly about Cuba."

He said, "Well, look, I'm a little late. I'll make an appearance and give a short talk, take a couple of sips of the soup, maybe have a cup of coffee and eat a bit of bread, but I won't have the main meal. Then I'll slip out and come right down here. I'll be here in 15 minutes. How's that?"

"That'll be just fine," I said. "Thank you."

True to his word, Nixon returned in 15 minutes on the dot. Most Americans who had watched his debate with Kennedy on television thought Kennedy came out on top, because while Nixon was well prepared on content, he had an obvious five o'clock shadow, perspired heavily, and gave long-winded answers. Kennedy, on the other hand, appeared cool, collected and at the top of his game. After losing the election the ambitious Nixon resolved to improve his television technique. I soon saw an example of how intently he meant to go about it.

I'd already put a tape marker on the sidewalk to show him where to stand, and he walked right over and put his toes exactly on the spot.

"Now," he said. "What length do you want? Would you like 15 seconds, 20 seconds, 35 or maybe 45 seconds? Or would you like me to take a minute?"

Never in my life had an interviewee asked me how many seconds his or her answer should be. Nixon apparently felt he'd been burned so many times by giving long, complicated answers to questions that he was determined to exercise editorial control, rather than leaving that to news editors back at the station.

I shrugged. "Just reply as you see fit."

"Ok," he said, "Let's make it 30-second answers"

I went ahead with my questions, and in his head he timed his answers perfectly to the 30-second mark. That was the new Nixon, a paint-by-numbers guy all the way. Kind of frightening.

In addition to my reporting duties with WMAQ, now and then the network called on me to cover stories in other parts of the country. Nothing quite prepared me for the story I would cover in Nashville, capital of my home state. It was the spring of 1964, and the civil rights struggle had spread to cities and towns, large and small, throughout the South.

In Nashville a young civil rights leader named Lester McKinney had been conducting marches and staged demonstrations in an effort to desegregate two holdout restaurants and a cafeteria that steadfastly refused to serve blacks. Every day saw the numbers of protest marchers grow, with a corresponding increase in arrests and violence, so NBC's Chicago Bureau dispatched a news producer, Bob Mulholland, and me to cover the mounting confrontation.

On the afternoon of April 30, several hundred black people gathered at the First Baptist Church and marched three miles to Morrison's Cafeteria in the heart of the Tennessee capital. When the first marchers tried to enter the cafeteria, the manager promptly locked the doors and posted a CLOSED sign in the window. That action triggered a massive response with demonstrators lying down in the street and vowing to remain there until the cafeteria agreed to open its doors to black customers.

Police moved in swiftly to clear the scene, carrying, and in some cases dragging, the passive marchers to waiting paddy wagons. A few officers treated those taking part in this nonviolent demonstration with respect, but others subjected many protesters to physical and verbal abuse. At one point an obviously pregnant black woman was picked up by her hands and feet and bounced repeatedly on the pavement as the police dragged her away.

Maybe it was because this was happening in my home state, or maybe it was the senseless brutality of it all; maybe both. At any rate, seething with wrath, I sat down in the street among the protestors and handed my notebook to the startled producer.

"Here, Bob, you cover this story. I'm joining this demonstration."

Bob, who would go on to become president of the NBC Television Network, explained patiently that what I was doing was selfish.

"Making a personal commitment and getting yourself arrested may make you feel better inside, but think how much more important it is for you to get up and do your job, so 12 million television viewers will know what happened here today."

Eventually I got up and did just that. A few months later, Congress passed the Public Accommodations Law, ending that phase of the civil rights struggle. Yet to this day many other battles against injustice remain to be won. Lester McKinney had argued that Nashville needed to become an open city with equal rights and opportunities for people of all races. At the time, most white residents of Nashville thought their city was already open. Justice, like beauty, is often in the eye of the beholder.

*

In June of the same year, 1964, an item crossing the AP wire caught my attention. A gang of gunrunners in southern Illinois had been arrested in an FBI sting after trying to purchase a huge weapons cache from an undercover agent—enough ordnance to equip a small army.

Dispatched to Springfield to cover the story, I found the U.S. attorney there reluctant to supply me with operational details. He got off the hook by suggesting that I go to the basement cafeteria in his building and look for a heavy-set man with a gray mustache who would be sitting alone at a back table. "He can tell you what you want to know."

Then, to my surprise, he added that the man was an undercover U.S. Treasury agent, posing as a fictitious "General Camillo," who'd paid the gun-runners $17,000 in marked bills just before the FBI swooped down and arrested two members of the gang. At that point he must have realized he'd said too much, for as I was leaving he added, "By the way, this conversation never took place. This is very sensitive information. I'll deny even telling you this and I'll deny we even spoke. This operation is being run out of Washington, and they don't like people talking to the press."

I headed for the cafeteria and found it practically deserted at mid-morning except for the man I hoped to see. When I bought him a cup of coffee, paying with a $20 bill, he scooped up the change and put it in his own pocket. That worried me, because NBC News had a strict policy of not paying for interviews. I decided to overlook it and just listen as he told his amazing story.

He acknowledged he'd been working undercover with the gun-runners for months to gather evidence, even demonstrating the heavy Spanish accent that went along with a general's uniform provided by the FBI.

"You should have seen me," he said. "My chest was covered with so many medals I could hardly stand up straight. Believe me, the gunrunners were *very* impressed."

The "General" said he'd met with the gunrunners to close the deal in a barn near the town of Wapella, Illinois, paying them $17,000 in marked bills for 100 submachine guns, five .50-caliber machine guns, a flame thrower, a 75-mm cannon and several bombs. The FBI agents, hiding in the hayloft, had grabbed the men as soon as the money changed hands. They arrested two members of the gang, one having been associated with a militant anti-communist group that called itself The Minutemen.

Concerned that CBS and ABC correspondents would soon be

on the trail of this hot story, I suggested that "General Camillo" and I take a drive into some nearby woods where we could film a television interview away from public view. He agreed, reluctantly, after I promised that his face would not appear on TV.

Once we got there and my cameraman set up his equipment, the "General" remarked, "You can forget that general stuff. Just call me Jack." My cameraman put Jack in the shadows to conceal his identity, and our interview began.

"These guys sold weapons to Castro," Jack said, "as well as to anti-Castro groups. They made airdrops of contraband weapons over Bogotá, Colombia, and in this country they sold weapons to the John Birch Society."

His last statement set off an alarm in my head. I broke in right away. "How do you know that?"

"By their own admission," he said.

That section of our interview ran on NBC News's *Huntley-Brinkley Report* that same evening, and the next day the ultraconservative John Birch Society informed the network that it was suing NBC along with Messrs. Huntley, Brinkley and Palmer. The lawsuit made the papers, with this headline in the *Chicago Daily News*:

NBC NEWS AND LOCAL REPORTER SUED
FOR $10 MILLION

All I could think of was how long it would take to pay off my share of that amount—one hell of a chunk out of my paycheck for the rest of my career and then some. But NBC's lawyers put me at ease, saying the network would pay any damage awards and adding that they had about three dozen similar cases pending. They considered mine a nuisance suit, filed by the John Birch Society in the midst of the heated presidential campaign between liberal President Lyndon Johnson and his conservative Republican opponent, Sen. Barry Goldwater.

The Birch Society brought its suit in Houston, Texas, assuming that was a likely place to find a conservative jury pool. Fortunately for me, the Texas judge's docket was full, so he transferred the case to Brooklyn, New York, which ended the matter after the Birch Society's lawyers failed to show up in court. The suit was dismissed. That experience taught me a crucial lesson: everything you say in a television news broadcast is subject to scrutiny and could bring on legal action. If you report something, you'd damn well better get it right.

With the presidential campaign in full swing, I was assigned to cover President Johnson's evening arrival at Chicago's Midway Airport, where a crowd of several thousand waited to greet him after he'd spent a busy day campaigning in the South. Microphone at the ready. I stood with other reporters at the ramp as Johnson emerged from the plane. Suddenly he walked over to me, grabbed my microphone and climbed onto the back of a truck platform to address the audience. He obviously thought my microphone was connected to a public-address system—dead wrong. It was connected to my camera, so not only were his shouted words lost on the crowd, they were distorted and unusable for television purposes.

The next morning I got a call from the Republican National Committee Headquarters in Washington. "We understand you were at the airport last night, and the president of the United States was drunk. Is that true?"

Old Lyndon, known to enjoy his bourbon and branch water, had certainly appeared in unusually high spirits, but I wasn't about to agree to such an insinuation. "Since I'm neither a doctor nor a police officer, I'm not qualified to comment," I replied. It was a dodge, but in the midst of a fiery presidential campaign I had no intention of putting my neck back on a partisan chopping block.

A week or so after Johnson's landslide re-election I was assigned to cover a Goldwater luncheon speech at Chicago's Blackstone Hotel. It was a cold, rainy November day, and when I walked out onto Michigan Avenue after his speech to hail a cab, there was Goldwater attempting the same thing, out in the rain alone.

Poignant and bizarre. Only three weeks before he had been a mere heartbeat away from leading our country, and now here he was in the same plight as me, unable to catch a cab in the rain. (Certainly the situation had its democratic aspects, but I believe our country should find a way to make use of anyone who places second in the race for the highest office of the land.)

A few months before that 1964 presidential election, the civil rights movement had taken a crucial turn with the launch of the Mississippi Summer Project. It was an initiative to register black voters in a state where only 6.7% of African-American citizens were registered—the lowest percentage of any demographic in the nation. Hundreds of college students, black and white, mostly from northern schools, flocked to Western College for Women in Oxford, Ohio, for training sessions sponsored by the National Council of Churches on how to register black voters, along with special classes in nonviolent techniques.

Three early graduates of the program, James Chaney, Michael Schwerner and Andrew Goodman—the first black, the other two white—vanished shortly after arriving in Mississippi and were widely presumed to have been murdered. Their disappearance heightened the activists' fears, yet staff and volunteers moved ahead resolutely with the summer campaign.

NBC News executives decided to do a one-hour documentary on the three missing civil rights workers and I was sent to the Ohio college to interview their friends and report on the training program. I found the young volunteers scared but determined to go to Mississippi to fulfill their mission. They were also well aware that doing so might cost them their lives, and I admired them greatly for their commitment while wondering if I too had the courage to act on my convictions regardless of the cost.

The television program, especially controversial in the South, raised public awareness about the three missing civil rights workers and spurred the federal government to investigate the case more vigorously. Not until August did FBI agents find the bodies of

Chaney, Schwerner and Goodman buried in an earthen dam. The three had been arrested by Cecil Price, a Neshoba County sheriff's deputy, then released from jail only to be stopped again and turned over to a Ku Klux Klan mob who shot them dead.

Three years would pass before those accused in the case were brought to justice in the famous 1967 "Mississippi Burning Trial." Deputy Price was sentenced to six years in prison, while another defendant got four years. The story would be made into a motion picture in 1988, and eventually, in 2005—the 41st anniversary of the crime—Edgar Ray Killen, a KKK member and part-time preacher, would be convicted of manslaughter in the three deaths and sent to prison for the rest of his life.

*

After my first year in Chicago I was assigned to anchor *The NBC News Chicago Report*, a local, hour-long television news program broadcast at 5 p.m. Even though my new responsibilities limited my time for reporting, I enjoyed anchoring the news as it gave me editorial input as to what stories we would cover.

It also meant working with and learning from several great television reporters, including Floyd Kalber, whose 10 p.m. broadcast dominated Chicago television news for years. Floyd was a no-nonsense broadcaster who hated the chatty, happy-talk news format that had pervaded local news programs around the country. He was a man of great integrity. Once while driving home from work Floyd was stopped by a Chicago policeman for speeding. When the officer recognized Floyd, he refused to give him a ticket until Floyd threatened to report him to the chief of police if he didn't. That was Floyd.

Len O'Connor was another of those great Chicago broadcasters. He too had a no-nonsense style, was dedicated to the truth, and was absolutely fearless, particularly in his efforts to expose Chicago mobsters. Once I heard a crash in the hallway just outside my office, followed by a shout from Len: "And take your goddamn jelly with you!" I made it to my door in time to see Len chase one of the city's most notorious gangsters down the hall to the elevator. The mobster had brought Len a jar of his mother's homemade jelly as a peace offering, with the hope that Len would go easy on him in his nightly commentaries. No chance.

Len was so fearless, in fact, that I often wondered why he didn't end up dead in a car trunk or wearing concrete overshoes at the bottom of Lake Michigan. When out-of-towners saw him deliver his nightly commentaries on television they must have wondered how a guy like that ever made it in broadcasting. He was fat, mumbled, and wore a perpetual scowl—far from the TV-newsman stereotype. All the same, Chicago viewers respected and loved him.

A few months into my new anchor job I experienced the first of many perks of appearing on television for an hour every day. To celebrate their wedding anniversary, my mom and dad flew to Chicago, where my sisters Pat and Audrey joined us. I made reservations for us to have dinner and see the show at one of Chicago's top hotels. There the *maître d'*, who recognized me from television, gave us the best table in the house and even persuaded the show's star, Ray Bolger, to come over to our table and sing his signature song, "Once in Love With Amy," to my delighted mom, whose name just happened to be—Amy. I was so proud.

Being recognized from television can also have its downsides. Sent to cover a home-invasion robbery at an apartment house on Chicago's Gold Coast, I walked in and insinuated myself among a bunch of detectives as they questioned a maid and other servants whom the armed robbers had tied up. I was getting plenty of juicy inside information when one of the detectives spotted me.

"Palmer, what the hell are you doing here? GET OUT, NOW!"

So much for incognito journalism.

One of the most painful episodes during my time in Chicago was an interview with a single mother on the South Side who had just lost her third son to the Vietnam War. Filmed as she sat with me on a couch in her living room, she described her anguish at losing first one, then another, and finally the last of her children. After the interview I went back to the station, turned the film over to a producer for editing, and didn't see the final version until it appeared on the air. With the program underway, I introduced the interview from the anchor chair and watched the studio TV monitor as the mother spoke, her face streaming with tears.

"I've lost my babies, Mr. Palmer. I've lost all my boys. Tell me, what am I gonna do now?"

At that abrupt ending to the edited interview, the director, Tony Verdi, switched back live to me in the studio, replacing the mother's face on the monitor with mine. Swamped with the emotion of her plaintive appeal, when I opened my mouth to speak not a word came out. At that, Tony, seeing my plight, switched immediately to a commercial and strolled calmly out to my anchor desk.

"Look, John, we run 12 one-minute commercials in this hour-long program—twelve. So take as much time as you need to regain your composure. Take all 12 if you need them."

After a couple of minutes I was able to continue with the newscast, chagrined at having lost my composure, yet in the days that followed mail poured into the station. The interview had affected viewers as profoundly as it had affected me.

*

In the summer of 1966 after his successes in the South, Dr. King took his civil rights movement north to Chicago. He and his aide, the Reverend Ralph David Abernathy, moved into a slum apartment on the South Side to demonstrate their solidarity with the poor. But King soon discovered that Mayor Daley was no Bull Connor, the Birmingham police chief who'd played into King's hands by turning police dogs and fire hoses on black demonstrators. Daley was far more subtle. He viewed King and his band of followers as outside agitators and enlisted as his allies many of Chicago's black leaders who were beholden to him. Abernathy would later write, "We received a worse reception [in Chicago] than we ever encountered in the South."

Their mission, Dr. King declared, was to rid the city of the real estate discrimination that kept black residents from getting mortgage loans. Real estate discrimination in Chicago was, as Taylor Branch wrote in his book *At Canaan's Edge*, a rough and floating target. Not enshrined in law, the discrimination had nevertheless been established through thousands of individual decisions made by brokers and landlords. While King argued that racism in Chicago was more pernicious than in the South, in the end he was outflanked by Daley, who made frequent promises that were soon forgotten or ignored.

That summer I accompanied Dr. King on many of his marches and demonstrations. Once when Dr. King was posting a list of demands on the door of the cardinal's residence he noticed me standing nearby and remembered our times together in the South.

"Brother Palmer," he said, "what brings you here to the frozen North?"

"You do, Dr. King," I replied.

"Well, up here it's going to be a much harder row to hoe."

My most memorable time with Dr. King that summer came when he and his followers staged a huge open-housing march through Marquette Park on the city's Southwest Side, an area populated by Polish-Americans and other first-generation Americans of Eastern European origin. Chicago police lined both sides of the street as King and his fellow demonstrators marched shoulder to shoulder past the modest but well-kept bungalows with their manicured lawns, dodging bottles and enduring chants of "Go home, nigger!"

At one point we heard a loud BANG, and Dr. King dropped to one knee thinking he'd been shot. It turned out to be an inch-long firecracker thrown at his feet. Forever burned into my memory are the cruel tauntings and jeers of that crowd as he regained his composure, held up his head again, and marched on. The famous

Dr. King had shown fear, and the crowd responded. He was human after all.

With so much going on around me, Chicago was an interesting and busy news town. But the nation's big story remained the war in Vietnam, and I wanted to report on it from the scene. So in July I wrote a memo to Reuven Frank, president of NBC News, asking to leave *The NBC News Chicago Report* and my local reporting duties to cover the war, arguing that a year or so of full-time reporting from Vietnam would benefit both NBC and me. In the memo I described myself as "30 years old, unmarried, healthy and anxious to be where the action is." After Frank approved my request, I got a series of immunizations and tidied up my affairs, all set to join the network "boys" in Vietnam.

My enthusiastic plans were quickly derailed, however, by a management change at NBC News Chicago. The new general manager trumped Frank's decision and blocked my transfer.

"Listen to me, Palmer," he said. "You have the number-one early-evening news program in Chicago. If you go away for a year, then come back, nobody in this town will remember your name or your face. Your leaving would damage your career and would cost the station a lot of revenue, and we can't have that."

Sorely disappointed, I figured that with human nature being what it is, there'd be other wars to come. A prophetic conclusion, as it turned out.

*

Not long afterward I was involved in one of those unscripted moments that happen more often than we would like in television news. On a holiday—I forget which one—Illinois Sen. Paul Douglas was scheduled to give a speech on Chicago's North Side, in Lincoln Park. My cameraman and I got there late and had to set up on the balcony of a building across the street from the dignitaries' platform. Luckily, we found a loudspeaker mounted on the balcony, so we taped our microphone beside it to pick up the senator's amplified remarks.

Right off we ran into a problem. Any time a bus or large truck passed along the busy street between our position and the platform, it totally obscured the camera shot. We vowed to make do. I marked a paragraph on the senator's prepared text and told the cameraman to be sure to have the camera rolling during that part of the speech. When Sen. Douglas reached that section of the text, the camera was indeed rolling, but another bus briefly blocked our view. After the speech we packed up and headed back to the station, where I turned over the marked text and film of the event to an editor, not suspecting anything was wrong.

An hour later on the air, I introduced the news clip from Sen. Douglas, then listened in horror as my cameraman's voice overrode the senator's: "Oh, God! Here comes another fuckin' bus!"

The balcony mic had picked up the cameraman's spontaneous complaint. Numb with fear, I managed to finish the newscast, and to my surprise the station got no more than 25 or 30 calls of complaint. Most viewers and listeners probably figured they'd imagined it, because nobody would say such a thing on television.

Still more Chicago news was generated that summer of 1966 by a 25-year-old drifter named Richard Franklin Speck. Late one July evening he knocked on the door of a two-story townhouse occupied by student nurses from nearby South Chicago Community Hospital. High on drugs and reeking of alcohol, he brandished a pistol at 23-year-old Corazon Amurao when she opened the door, promising, "I'm not going to hurt you." After tying her up, he moved through the house, rousing five other student nurses from their beds, and tying them up in their rooms. Three more student nurses came home during the next hour, only to be bound as well and lined up on the floor. Speck then raped, stabbed and strangled the eight bound women. In the meantime, fortunately, Corazon Amurao had managed to hide. Because Speck lost count of the number of women in the house, that lone young woman escaped her eight housemates' fate.

My cameraman and I stood on the sidewalk outside the townhouse the next morning with a group of other reporters as Cook County Coroner Andrew Toman showed us a layout of the house with the location of each body marked. We were studying his diagram when a newspaper reporter suddenly grabbed it and ran, not stopping until he reached his paper's composing room, where the diagram was quickly copied and put on the front page. Afterward the reporter returned the diagram to the coroner. He was questioned by police, the newspaper apologized, and the whole thing was forgotten. Chicago journalism is a highly competitive enterprise.

The student nurse murders launched the greatest manhunt in the city's history, and NBC Chicago cancelled all leaves for reporters, editors and camera crews. For several days my television crew and I staked out the Raleigh Hotel on the chance that Speck might return to the place where he'd stayed shortly before his killing spree, but he never showed. Then, a few days later, I had just finished anchoring the late Saturday night news when I got a call at home from the news desk: "We have a tip that Speck may be at a flophouse on West Madison Street. Here's the address."

I hotfooted it to the Madison Street location, where the night clerk led me to a dank second-floor cubicle furnished only with a blood-stained mattress and a blood-spattered copy of the *Chicago Tribune* headlined "NATIONWIDE MANHUNT FOR SPECK." The clerk told me the man who'd rented the cubicle had just been taken to Cook County Hospital after slashing his wrists. I made it to the emergency room just as they were wheeling him off to surgery. In the operating room the doctor wiped the dried blood from the man's arm, a tattoo appeared: BORN TO RAISE HELL. It was Richard Franklin Speck.

Tried and sentenced to death for the eight murders, Speck got a reprieve when the Illinois Supreme Court ruled capital punishment unconstitutional. He was then resentenced to consecutive life terms totaling more than 400 years but died of a heart attack in prison, after serving 19 years.

*

In the predawn hours on a Sunday a few months after the Speck murders, another sensational crime captured headlines in Chicago and across the nation. Someone broke into a 17-room Tudor villa in the wealthy lakeshore suburb of Kenilworth, crept upstairs to a bedroom, and stabbed a pretty young woman named Valerie Jeanne Percy to death. She was the daughter of Charles Percy, a self-made millionaire who would later become a U.S. senator from Illinois.

I covered daily briefings on the case at the tiny Kenilworth Police Department, which hadn't handled a murder case in 75 years, and additional briefings at the Percy home by family friend Jay Rockefeller, later to marry Valerie's twin sister Sharon and win election himself to the U.S. Senate from West Virginia. The police had little physical evidence to go on—just a shattered windowpane, the killer's bloody palm print on a banister and a footprint in the sand on the beach. A forensic psychiatrist told reporters, "The facts so far . . . indicate that the murderer knew Valerie and that he went to her home for the purpose of murdering her."

I viewed the body with Coroner Toman at the Cook County Morgue, who pointed out that she'd been stabbed more than a dozen times. Hundreds of detectives were brought in to work on the case, and thousands of people interviewed. The crime was never solved. To this day, the Percy family lives with the horror of that night and not knowing who took Valerie's life.

*

That gruesome summer did include one far lighter event: the Beatles' arrival in Chicago, the first stop on their American tour, to play a sold-out concert at the International Amphitheatre. When I showed up for a news conference before the concert, security guards frisked me half a dozen times before letting me into the young celebrities' crowded hotel room.

A few weeks earlier John Lennon had said in an interview for a London newspaper, "We're more popular than Jesus." Reaction in the southern part of the United States was intense, ranging from Christian radio stations banning Beatles songs to protests by the Ku Klux Klan. Their Chicago news conference was standing room only.

I found a spot on the floor down front as Lennon dealt with questions about his comment by declaring that his remarks had been "taken out of context." After John, Paul, George and Ringo then answered a host of silly questions about girlfriends, favorite movies and the like, I left thinking that their music was far more interesting than its creators.

*

Casualties continued to mount in Vietnam, and three-time World Heavyweight Boxing Champion Cassius Clay, who had changed his name to Muhammad Ali, refused induction into the army on the grounds that he was a Muslim minister and therefore qualified as a conscientious objector. In early 1967 Ali was convicted of violating the Selective Service Act, barred from the ring and stripped of his title, although the U.S. Supreme Court ultimately reversed his conviction.

At the height of the draft controversy Ali provided me with one of the funniest moments of my Chicago years. I went to the South Side motel where he was staying to ask for an interview. He came to the door in shorts and said, "Sure, set up your camera in the parking lot. I'll be out as soon as I get on some clothes."

Ten minutes later he emerged ready for the interview, and as the two of us stood next to each other in front of the camera, I had barely begun my questions when Ali grimaced as if in great pain.

"Stop! Stop!" I shouted at the cameraman, then turned to Ali. "What's the matter, Champ?"

"I need to take a leak," he said.

"Fine. We're not under any deadline. You go on in and take care of it, we'll start over when you come out."

"No," Ali said doggedly. "I want to do the interview now."

So I restarted the interview, and once again Ali appeared to be suffering. A second time I broke off my questions. "Look, this is crazy. There's no reason for you to be miserable. Go to the bathroom. We have plenty of time."

Stone-faced, Ali said, "If you want this interview, go ahead and ask your questions, now." His hands hung loose at his sides.

I stood close to him again and was starting the interview for the third time when I felt something run down the side of my leg. "Hey!" I yelled, and jumped back.

The big man laughed so hard he had to sit down on the pavement. After psyching me out about his supposed need to urinate, Ali had dribbled a handful of BBs down my trouser leg. I joined in the laughter wholeheartedly, knowing I'd been had in a big way.

Years later when the champ was in Atlanta to light the Olympic Torch I had an opportunity to shake his hand. Impaired by his Parkinson's disease, he didn't speak, but when he gave me a smile and a wink I thought maybe he remembered me as the victim of his long-ago practical joke.

*

Eventful 1967 brought yet another summer of unrest to Chicago, along with many other cities and towns across the country. Comedian and civil rights activist Dick Gregory staged daily downtown marches and ran for mayor against Richard J. Daley. On the previous Thanksgiving Day, when he began a hunger strike to protest the war in Vietnam, he'd weighed more than 280 pounds and smoked and drank heavily. When he finally broke his fast forty days later, incredibly, he weighed just 97 pounds.

After an interview with Gregory one Friday afternoon when I mentioned that I was catching a plane for New York City, he said, "I'm going to New York too. Sammy Davis opens at the Copacabana tonight. Why not join me at our table?"

I couldn't resist his invitation, and that evening as we watched the show, Sammy Davis, Jr., dedicated his performance to Gregory. "You went to Mississippi," Davis said. "You were in Watts. You've been on the front lines of the struggle for justice."

Gregory leaned over and whispered to me, "That's nice, Sammy feels guilty for not being active in the movement."

After the show Gregory invited me to join Davis in his tiny second-floor dressing room. I went along to find the famous song-and-dance man in his underwear, devouring fried chicken. When Gregory introduced me as a reporter from Chicago, Davis blurted, "Oh, God. He'll write, 'The nigger was eating fried chicken in his shorts.'"

Gregory reassured him that I was a trusted friend, and we later joined Davis in his stretch limo for a tour of Harlem nightspots. Somewhere along the way actress Kim Novak joined our group, and we ended the excursion having breakfast at Manhattan's Brasserie—an unforgettable glimpse of New York nightlife for this Tennessee boy.

PHOTO GALLERY

1936–1968

John and his mother, Amy Boughton Palmer, Kingsport, Tennessee, 1936

John and older sisters Patricia and Audrey at Orchard Court, Kingsport, Tennessee, circa 1945

Fishing on Cherokee Lake, Tennessee, circa 1947

1723 Orchard Court, the Palmer home in Kingsport, Tennessee

Palmer Family fishing trip (l–r) Guide, Spencer Palmer, John, Patricia, Amy and Audrey Palmer, Guide - Boca Grande, Florida, circa 1949

First Place Dobyns-Bennett Debate Team, circa 1952

Northwestern University Theatrical Production, circa 1954

John working hard to get the interview, circa 1964

Getting the sound bite from presidential candidate Senator Barry Goldwater, 1964

Interviewing Secretary of State Dean Rusk, circa 1966

Walking the picket line for AFTRA strike in support of technicians, Chicago, 1967

Interviewing presidential hopeful Senator Charles H. Percy, 1968

6

RACE STRIFE AND SPACE

ALTHOUGH CHICAGO HAD more than its share of civil rights strife in 1967, the unrest there couldn't compare to the violence in Detroit, where after five days of rioting 43 people lay dead, 1,189 had been injured and more than 7,000 people had been arrested. Detroit's troubles arose from multiple political, economic and social factors, including police abuse, lack of affordable housing, economic inequality, black militancy and rapid demographic change.

The Detroit violence had subsided a bit when Black Panther Party leader H. Rap Brown, famous for proclaiming that "violence is as American as apple pie," scheduled a speech at a rally outside a Detroit supermarket. My television crew and I came to cover it, accompanied (fortunately, as it turned out) by an off-duty Chicago policeman hired as our driver and courier to get the film back to the station.

Brown was late in arriving, and the crowd of several thousand grew restless. People passed around liquor, and fights had begun to break out when a group of black men suddenly appeared on the supermarket roof and began pelting the crowd with bottles and empty glass gallon jugs. All of us on the ground tried to dodge the missiles, and my crew and I managed to avoid being hit, terrified by the *swoosh* of those heavy jugs flying through the air. Our prudent courier told us to get back in our rental car and leave, but we'd traveled only a few feet when the crowd attacked us. We rolled up the car windows and locked the doors as some assailants sprang onto our car roof and jumped up and down until they flattened it while we hunkered down as low as possible inside. Then they started breaking the windows.

I thought we were done for when a black face appeared outside my window. He held a revolver in his hand and yelled, "I'm a Detroit police officer! When I count to three, get out of the car and follow me!"

He wasn't in uniform, but he was our best, and only, hope. At his count of three we unlocked the car doors and tumbled out into the street as he fired three shots in the air. The crowd moved back, and he shoved us up the steps of a house about 20 feet away.

"Get inside, lock the door and go to the basement!" he ordered, then stood on the porch warning the crowd that he had three bullets left for the first three people who tried to rush the house. From our hideout we soon heard welcome police sirens signaling the arrival of reinforcements, and after the crowd was finally dispersed we emerged to climb back into what was left of our car and head for the airport. The Hertz Rent-A-Car agent's face when we pulled up in that battered, caved-in car made me thankful I'd initialed the insurance box on the rental agreement. The news story we were able to salvage from our ordeal was far from spectacular, as during our time in Detroit we'd been too concerned with our own survival to film much of what was taking place.

*

Chicago's snowstorm of the century, the Blizzard of '68, was a humdinger. In a two-day period, 23 inches of snow fell. Michigan Avenue and the Outer Drive looked like parking lots. Commuters unable to make it home spent several nights camped out in their cars or, if they were lucky, snagged one of the few available hotel rooms. Passengers at O'Hare Airport were stranded. Sixty deaths would be attributed to the storm, mostly heart attacks from shoveling snow.

Bad as it was, the storm nevertheless afforded some welcome relief from the previous months' murders and racial strife. With streets and highways impassable for ordinary vehicles, we covered the city by helicopter and 4WD trucks. Our station stayed on the air around the clock, broadcasting nothing but news about the storm.

It was an exhausting time for reporters, crews and editors, and several months later the station showed its gratitude for all the late hours and hard work by hosting a dinner dance for its employees. By then, NBC technicians and reporters, including me, happened to be on strike, but NBC Vice President Bob Lemon sent a telegram to each of us saying we were all still welcome to attend. The next day the *Chicago Tribune* ran a story about the evening headlined "NBC PEACOCK WAS PROUD OF HIS BROOD LAST NIGHT." An accompanying photo showed me dancing with Isabelle Mrozik, a non-striking employee who filled in as a newscaster during the walkout. The strike lasted a couple of weeks, and when it ended I was happy to leave the picket lines and get back to reporting the news.

*

Months later when I looked back to those Detroit riots I saw that they were only forerunners of the violence that would sweep Chicago and much of the country again in early April 1968, in the wake of Dr. King's assassination. Not long before, the charismatic leader had delivered his famous "I Have a Dream" speech in Washington, D.C., raising the hopes of millions. But when news came of his murder, predominantly black sections of more than a hundred cities erupted in grief, rage and rioting. Thousands of federal troops and National Guard soldiers had to be called out to restore order—often impossible to achieve until the fury abated.

Chicago's violence centered in the black ghetto on the West Side. Mayor Daley blamed the rioting on outside agitators and told Chicago police to shoot to kill. At our television station, reporters and camera crews were issued gas masks and bulletproof vests, because police, firemen, reporters and camera crews were drawing indiscriminate sniper fire. Looting of liquor, furniture and clothing stores often continued even with reporters and cameras present. I had never seen such disregard for property and lives. The sale of guns, ammunition and flammable liquids was banned. It was a terribly dangerous and frightening story to cover. Smoke and tear gas hung over the area for days. The smell got into our clothing and our hair. We covered the rioting and looting using only available light, as bright television lights at night would have exposed reporters and crews to even greater danger.

When it was over, nearly three dozen West Side blocks lay in ruins, and scores of mostly black-owned businesses had burned to the ground, although some escaped looting after their owners scrawled "Soul Brother" on their windows. Before it was over, 11 people—all black—had been killed, more than 500 injured and thousands arrested. Property damage was in the millions of dollars.

The situation was different in Indianapolis, however, where Robert F. Kennedy learned of Dr. King's death minutes before a presidential campaign appearance. In addressing the political rally, Kennedy asked the crowd to lower their campaign signs. He said,

"I have some very sad news for all of you, and, I think, sad news for all of our fellow citizens, and the people who love peace all over the world; and that is that Martin Luther King was shot and killed tonight in Memphis, Tennessee."

Kennedy went on. "For those of you who are black and tempted to be filled with hatred and mistrust of the injustice of such an act against all white people, I would only say that I can also feel in my own heart the same kind of feeling." Referring to his older brother, the late President John F. Kennedy, he said, "I had a member of my family killed by a white man." He ended his remarks by asking the crowd to go home and say a prayer for Dr. King's family. That night and during the days and nights that followed, Indianapolis remained free of violence.

When NBC News asked me to anchor Dr. King's funeral I welcomed the assignment. The mourners' outpouring of grief for this man, who had been both praised and vilified during his lifetime, was moving and painful to watch. It was another situation where I wished I could have been a participant rather than a detached observer and reporter. Although I didn't know Dr. King well, I had spoken with him dozens of times during interviews and demonstrations, and I admired his courage and dedication to justice. It was a heartbreaking occasion.

*

In Chicago on the night of June 5, 1968, I stayed up late to watch the returns of the California presidential primary. Robert Kennedy won, putting him well on track for the Democratic Party's presidential nomination. I watched him address a rally in the ballroom of the Ambassador Hotel in Los Angeles, then turned off the television and went to sleep, as I had an early morning network radio broadcast. At 5 a.m. I got up, dressed, and walked the four blocks to the Merchandise Mart to prepare for my five-minute network *News on the Hour* broadcast.

On my way up in the elevator, an elderly cleaning woman with a bucket and mop joined me. "Isn't it terrible about Bobby Kennedy?" she said.

All I knew at that point was that he'd won the primary, because I'd seen him on television greeting his triumphant supporters. "Why, no," I said, "I don't think it's terrible at all."

She stared at me, incredulous, shook her head, and got off on the eight floor, while I rode on to NBC's studios on the 19th.

The moment the elevator doors opened I heard the NBC radio network up and running—very unusual at that early hour. Then I heard a reporter's voice: "Kennedy still clings to life with a bullet in his brain." Shocked, I realized what the cleaning woman had meant. After nearly 40 years, I still wish I could see her again and explain.

Kennedy died the next day, and I had to keep a long-scheduled appearance at a school in northwest Indiana. I'd planned to talk about life as a news reporter, but on hearing that Kennedy had visited that same school just months before, I tossed out my prepared remarks and led a discussion with the students about the murdered senator's life, his opposition to the war in Vietnam, his crusade for social justice, and this latest tragedy befalling his family. When it was over there wasn't a dry eye in the auditorium, including mine.

At his slain sibling's funeral Sen. Edward Kennedy, the last surviving brother, gave a memorable eulogy. "My brother need not be idolized, or enlarged in death beyond what he was in life, to be remembered simply as a good and decent man, who saw wrong and tried to right it, saw suffering and tried to heal it, saw war and tried to stop it."

*

The deaths of Dr. King and Robert Kennedy—both opponents of the Vietnam War—helped fuel the feverish activities of anti-war demonstrators who flocked to Chicago that August for the Democratic National Convention. The city prepared weeks in advance for the convention, training police in controlling the tens of thousands of activists expected to descend on the city. Once again, we reporters, photographers and camera crews pulled out our gas masks and bulletproof vests. Barbed-wire barricades went up. All police leaves were cancelled. Fifteen hundred Army troops and 1,000 Secret Service agents were brought in. My camera crew and I were one of five NBC teams assigned to cover the demonstrations.

It was Sunday, Aug. 25, when the violence began. After anti-war organizers tried and failed to get permits from the city to sleep in Lincoln Park and demonstrate outside the convention site, they set up camp in the park anyway. Police moved in at dusk with tear gas and billy clubs to clear them out. Many protestors were injured, along with 17 reporters and a number of police officers. Throughout the convention, unfortunately, police viewed all of us in the press as enemy combatants.

At midweek came the worst day of protests, dubbed "The Battle of Michigan Avenue." A large group of demonstrators was stopped when they tried to march to the convention site, and the media captured graphic scenes of violence as police moved in with tear gas and batons. Innocent bystanders, reporters, even doctors offering medical help were beaten severely. I was standing on a corner of Michigan Avenue when police officers, enraged by the demonstrators' taunts, dashed past me into the Hilton Hotel coffee shop and began beating patrons.

More chaos erupted inside the convention hall. When Sen. Abraham Ribicoff, a Connecticut Democrat, shocked the convention by saying, "With George McGovern as president of the United States, we wouldn't have Gestapo tactics in the streets of Chicago," Mayor Daley erupted in anger at that and shook his fist, yelling "FUCK YOU!" The mayor later denied using that word—but he said it. NBC News checked and rechecked the videotape to make sure. In the end, Hubert Humphrey won the Democratic nomination easily, although he would ultimately be defeated by Richard Nixon.

The commission later set up to investigate the actions of

Chicago's police during that convention week would describe the violence as a police riot, but Mayor Daley, true to form, disagreed and gave the police a pay raise.

That Friday morning after the convention ended, as the conventioneers were packing up to go home, NBC's *Today* closed its program with a five-minute video montage of the week's events. Viewers were treated to scenes of Chicago police beating handcuffed demonstrators as they were led to waiting paddy wagons, while a recording of Frank Sinatra singing "Chicago, My Kind of Town" played over the scenes of violence. Many months would pass before relations between the press and Chicago police returned to normal.

As for me, after six years in Chicago, I thought it was time to test my journalistic mettle in New York. My request for a transfer didn't go over well with management at the local station then either, because my one-hour daily news broadcast was leading the market in its time slot.

Fortunately, having my contract up for renewal gave me some clout. After a trip to New York and an interview with the news director at WCBS, word got back to NBC in Chicago, and through the good offices of Russ Tornabene, a top NBC News executive, a deal was worked out with NBC New York. And so the winter of 1969 saw me off to the Big Apple.

*

New York City is not the first locale that comes to mind when a reporter thinks about covering space travel, yet that's how it worked out for me. A chance encounter with Bob Priaulx, the producer-director heading up NBC's coverage of the Apollo space program, led to my assignment as a reporter and co-anchor for six Apollo launches, including man's first moon landing and, later, the tragic explosion of the space shuttle Challenger.

My first New York assignment was anchoring the 7:25 a.m. and

8:25 a.m. local news cut-ins during the *Today* show for WNBC-TV, after which I spent the rest of my day out in the city covering stories for the station's main newscasts at 6 p.m. and 11 p.m. One morning during my first month there, I was leaving for an assignment when I spotted Priaulx in the hallway, introduced myself and expressed interest in space reporting.

He said, "What do you know about the Manned Space Program?"

"Not much, but I can learn real fast."

My candor must have paid off, because later that day I returned to my office to find my desk piled high with reading material about the Apollo space program, complete with hundreds of pages of diagrams and technical details on U.S. plans to land a man on the moon. Bob Priaulx was no slouch at moving things along.

In fact, I got lucky, because at the time many network television reporters and correspondents either didn't understand space exploration, didn't like it, or thought it was far too technical to bone up or report on. On the other hand, three prominent correspondents were already out there leading the way: Frank McGee of NBC News, Walter Cronkite of CBS and Jules Bergman at ABC. And there were others who made their own important contributions to space reporting, including Roy Neal, Jay Barbree, Chet Huntley, David Brinkley, Hugh Downs, John Chancellor, Jim Hartz and Tom Jarrell.

The Apollo launch pads were at Cape Canaveral—later known as the Kennedy Space Center—but once any space flight got underway, the handling of it then passed to Mission Control at NASA headquarters just outside Houston, Texas. Regardless of the two official space flight facilities, though, at the start of the new era the networks considered New York City operational headquarters for their space coverage. All three constructed mock-ups of the spacecraft and lunar lander in their New York studios.

NBC converted Studio 8H (now home to *Saturday Night Live*) into a huge space port with millions of dollars' worth of simulators, the idea being that if a difficulty with the actual spacecraft arose, a reporter could simply walk over to the mock-up and point to and describe the problem.

During those early months I spent countless evenings studying and memorizing facts about the Apollo program, including late-night visits to the Studio 8H mock-up. Everything about it fascinated me—so much impressive technology coupled with the stark drama of every flight that put human lives on the line.

The race to the moon had begun in earnest long before. I was still in college in 1957 when the Soviet Union launched the world's first artificial satellite into earth's orbit. Called Sputnik I, it spurred the United States to enter space exploration in a big way. The U.S. program, unlike the military-controlled Soviet space program, was under civilian control, and NASA gave all three commercial television networks access to every space mission and its entire cadre of astronauts. While U.S.S.R. cosmonaut Yuri Gagarin had been the first man in space, our own country's up-front media coverage of the Apollo program helped build public support to such an extent that an American hero, John Glenn, soon became the first American to orbit the earth. And before his tragic assassination President John F. Kennedy pledged that America would achieve a manned lunar landing before 1970. We would see that pledge fulfilled.

My own coverage of space exploration kicked off in December of 1968 with the launch of Apollo 8, one of its aims being to orbit the moon and photograph proposed Apollo landing sites. After the launch I went to Denver's Gates Planetarium, where scientists had designed a revolutionary television-telescope system that could scan the surface of the moon and relay pictures back to earth. The marvelous result was that, on Christmas Eve of the same year, live pictures of Apollo 8 orbiting the moon with Astronauts Frank Borman, James Lovell and William Anders on board flashed onto television screens in living rooms all over America.

When I returned to my hotel late that evening to find carolers singing in the lobby, rather than thinking I should be at home somewhere with family, I remember thinking how lucky I was to have witnessed such an amazing once-in-a-lifetime event. The times, and with them my career, were moving too fast for me to muse on any home life I might be missing at holiday times. The Apollo 8 crew completed its successful mission in January, and I soon anchored a welcome home ceremony for them at New York's City Hall, following the traditional tickertape parade up Broadway.

Two months later I was at Cape Canaveral as part of the NBC space coverage team for the launch of Apollo 9—the first manned flight of the lunar module that, within a few more months, would land a man on the moon. Immediately after the launch, a charter flight took me, along with Frank McGee and other correspondents, producers and technicians, to the Johnson Space Center in Houston and Mission Control. It was a pattern that we would repeat, and while Frank, a seasoned correspondent whom I greatly admired, had mastered the complexities of space travel, he hated air travel so much that it took three hefty martinis to fortify him for every one of those Cape-to-Houston flights. During actual NASA space flights Frank, assisted by his knowledgeable producer Gene Farinet, occupied the anchor chair for many hours at a time in a masterly job of coverage.

Our NBC space team lived and worked in a motel across the street from the Space Center, broadcasting from a rooftop studio. In space exploration's early days public interest in the subject was so great that we broadcast hourly reports on the astronauts anytime they were in space. Here's a sample of one of those broadcasts during the Apollo 9 flight:

"I'm John Palmer, NBC News. For astronauts McDivitt, Scott and Schweickart, this Sunday is a day of rest. They had a breakfast of eggs, juice and toast, and are planning a series of photo experiments this afternoon over the southwestern United States. Experts will analyze the photos looking for new mineral resources and food-growing areas—a new dimension for space exploration. That's the latest from Apollo 9."

One off-duty Saturday afternoon I sat with Frank McGee in the NBC office suite watching a pro football game when a photographer appeared at the door. Frank reacted with lightning speed, knocking a beer can from my hand and shouting to the stunned photographer, "GET OUT!" His reaction shocked me until he explained that some weeks before we arrived, at an NBC party around the motel swimming pool, a news photographer got a shot of NBC anchor Chet Huntley shoving a piano with a scantily clad lady perched atop it into the deep end.

After he'd kicked the photographer out, Frank grumbled, "That piano episode was more than enough bad publicity for NBC News. I figured this guy was here for a follow-up."

The Apollo 10 flight that followed Apollo 9 served as the dress rehearsal for man's landing on the moon, with a run-through of all aspects of the lunar-landing mission exactly as it would take place, except for the actual touchdown. The mission took eight days, including time for a simulated moon landing.

(Frequent launch delays caused either by inclement weather or various technical problems were common with the Apollo program. We had all done our homework, and since some of those delays lasted several days, we made the most of our free time by playing volleyball or enjoying barbecues on the beach, plus an occasional round of golf. During one such delay Bob Priaulx and I slipped off to a local links, and I was driving our golf cart on a hillside overlooking a small lake when the cart tilted sideways. Rather than let the cart roll over entirely, I drove straight down the hill toward the lake, and before I could take corrective action, in we went. The cart floated for a few seconds then settled in about five feet of water. As I groped underwater for the off-switch, Bob shouted, "Forget that! There's alligators in here!"

He didn't have to say it twice. We swam to shore as fast as we could, dragging our golf bags behind us. I've never seen someone look so disgusted as the club professional, when he saw us walking back to the clubhouse wringing wet with no golf cart in sight.)

In July of 1969 as Apollo 11 prepared to lift off the launch pad at Kennedy Space Center for man's first moon landing, I was vacationing in Ireland and had stopped at a little roadside pub. A dozen or so farmers had come in from their fields to watch the launch on television, and at the moment the spaceship cleared the tower, a grizzled old fellow stomped his mud-caked brogans on the wooden floor and shouted, "That's Johnny's rocket! That's JOHNNY'S ROCKET! Go! GO! *GO!*" Our late president's Irish kin had surely remembered his bold pledge.

Back in New York four days afterward, I recalled that scene for viewers when I broadcast live from Times Square as Commander Neil Armstrong set foot on the moon and uttered those famous words, "That's one small step for man, one giant leap for mankind."

Of course Armstrong was the man of the hour on his return to earth, with a New York welcome reminiscent of Charles Lindbergh's 1927 homecoming after the first solo trans-Atlantic flight less than 40 years before. Broadway could scarcely contain the crowds' excitement for the tickertape parade, then a formal welcome at City Hall, and I was thrilled to anchor both for NBC News.

Media coverage of such a history-making mission and its aftermath continued for some time, so that one evening in my reporting I made a passing reference to the moon rocks Armstrong had collected. Watching from home, Reuven Frank, then president of NBC News and a prolific memo writer and wordsmith, wrote me this memo: "During the *11th Hour News* on Sunday, July 27, you said that study of the rocks would be completed 'after the danger of decontamination is past.' I don't think that's what you meant." Believe me, any time you goof on the air somebody's ready to let you know.

As soon as Armstrong returned home from a worldwide tour each major network was asked to choose a correspondent for a one-on-one interview. I got the nod for NBC News and had my first question ready: "What did you say to the many audiences along your tour?"

Armstrong's answer stays with me to this day, because I hope I've done my best to live by it.

"At every stop, I had the same message. If you do your best, try your hardest and live your dreams, you, too, can reach your own moons by achieving your own goals in life."

But then he surprised me, because his eyes filled with tears as he went on. "There was only one place where I couldn't bring myself to say those words—Bangladesh. I had never seen such poverty in my life. I simply could not hold out false hope to those people, who seemed to have been forgotten by the world."

In November 1969 Apollo 12 completed another perfect mission, landing a second man—another American—on the moon. The NASA program continued to grow in many important respects until the space shuttle, on the drawing board even before that first moon landing, made its first flight in 1981, the Columbia. Twenty years after Yuri Gagarin first orbited the earth, the viewing public had grown so accustomed to space travel that the subject actually seemed mundane—until January of 1986. But I'm getting ahead of myself.

*

The call came shortly after 2 a.m. on a Monday morning about three months after I had moved to New York to anchor and report the news from NBC's flagship, WNBC-TV. The caller was from *Today*, and Frank Blair, the show's long-time news anchor, had called in sick.

"We'd like you to anchor the news later this morning," the voice said. "You can go back to sleep now, and we'll give you a wake-up call in a couple of hours so you can be here by 5 a.m. to prepare for your four newscasts."

I sat up in bed, instantly wide awake.

Go back to sleep? That was a nonstarter. *Today* had an audience of about five million people, and this was my first crack at such a big opportunity with the network. My first thoughts were of my mom and dad, both of whom had passed away, wishing I could call them and tell them to tune in when the program came on. I spent the next two hours laying out my clothes, pressing the shirt I planned to wear, selecting the right tie, all the details. When NBC's wake-up call came I was ready to walk out the door. As I hailed a cab outside my Manhattan apartment at 34th Street and 3rd Avenue, I told myself, "This is a big deal, Palmer. Don't screw it up."

That morning in 1971 the *Today* hosts were Hugh Downs and Barbara Walters, both of whom greeted me warmly. But at one point, Barbara turned to Hugh and said, " I'm so sorry Frank won't be here this morning, so we could all be together." I was devastated, but the show must go on, after all, so I did what I was supposed to do. During my first newscast at 7 a.m. I began perspiring so profusely that the floor director, Jim Straka, had to move in and wipe my face every time I was off-camera.

When my second newscast ended, Joe Garagiola, one of the most popular members of the cast, saw my distress. He walked over, put his arm around my shoulders, and said, "Hey, John, I just talked to my mom in St. Louis, and she says you're doing a great job." Joe may not have been a good liar, but I've never forgotten his kindness. I guess things must have improved during my last two newscasts that morning, since I was invited back about a dozen times later in the year to sub for Frank. And 11 years later, after reporting from overseas and the White House, I would return to *Today* to anchor the news for the next seven and a half years.

*

During those intervening years the world would see many historic changes, and if the changes in my own life couldn't be called historic, they were certainly vital ones for me. After New York I would spend six months in Israel, make another pass through Chicago, then go on to Beirut and Paris. Assigned in 1979 to Washington and the White House, I at last met the peerless woman I couldn't live without, and, mindful of my dad's advice, I married her. Saving the romantic details for another chapter, I'll say here only that in time, after Nancy and I made our home together, we were blessed with a trio of delightful daughters. The far-ranging bachelor newsman would finally settle down to family life, although until it happened I couldn't imagine the great happiness it would bring.

✳

New assignments continued to come, and I had joined the *Today* show as news anchor when from my third-floor office at NBC News in New York on the morning of Jan. 28, 1986, I watched the launch of the space shuttle *Challenger* on a closed-circuit television feed from the Cape. By that time even the networks had become so blasé about space coverage that the launch wasn't carried live on the East Coast. Only NBC on the West Coast took it live, preempting *Today*, which aired in its usual time slot but on Pacific Time.

After my regular morning *Today* show stint the network had asked me to stand by for bulletin duty because Tom Brokaw and the other two top network anchors, ABC's Peter Jennings and CBS' Dan Rather, were at the White House for a briefing on President Reagan's State of the Union address, scheduled for that night.

About an hour before the launch was to take place a copy boy brought me a thick packet of AP and UPI wire-services stories on the *Challenger* to bring me up to speed in case something happened that would require me to go on the air. Scant moments remained before the launch at 11:39 a.m. EST I called in a cautious question to our central news desk.

"I don't expect anything to go wrong, but in case it should, where do I find a hot camera?"

A hot camera is one that's ready to shoot. Since President Kennedy's terrible assassination when correspondents had difficulty finding one, I thought the fifth-floor news desk always kept one turned on and ready, but I needed to make sure. The desk editor confirmed it.

"Come up here. The bulletin camera's ready to go."

Challenger with its seven crew members lifted off the pad as I reached into a desk drawer to retrieve my IFB, the earpiece all correspondents use when broadcasting live in the studio to hear both the program and simultaneous updates from the producer in the control room.

Suddenly, 73 seconds into the flight, *Challenger* exploded, etching an eerie cluster of white contrails across the deep-blue sky. At that moment no one knew what had happened—only that it had to be catastrophic.

I sprang to my feet and ran up two flights of stairs, then slowed to a fast walk as the old broadcasting adage came back to me: never go on the air when you're out of breath, especially not to deliver a bulletin. I jumped into a chair in front of the hot camera near the news desk and plugged my earpiece wire into a console just in time to hear the announcer say, "We interrupt our regularly scheduled program to bring you this bulletin from NBC News in New York. Here is NBC News Correspondent John Palmer."

Gulp. At that second the red light atop the camera lit up and I was on the air. All I could say was what I knew, and that was precious little.

> There has been a problem with the space shuttle *Challenger*, just launched from the Kennedy Space Center, with seven astronauts on board. There appears to have been a major malfunction. Here, now, is the videotape of the launch, as we listen live to Mission Control in Houston as they try to determine what happened.

It was clear to me, as I'm sure it was to most viewers, that the spacecraft had blown up and that the astronauts couldn't possibly have survived. I didn't say so on the air, because I was acutely aware that one of the astronauts aboard was Christa McAuliffe, a schoolteacher from Concord, New Hampshire, whose students had gathered in an auditorium to view the launch. I could only imagine how horrible it had to be for them to see the explosion, just as it must have been for all seven astronauts' families and friends assembled at the Cape.

Somehow I carried on to anchor the first two hours of our coverage, figuratively flying by the seat of my pants and gathering facts piecemeal as they came in until I turned the anchor chair over to Tom Brokaw in our Washington studio. From time to time all through that afternoon and evening I relieved Tom, so that it was nearly midnight when I arrived at home on Barrymore Lane in Mamaroneck, New York.

Nancy and our girls were away visiting family in Washington, and the house was dark. Exhausted, I walked dejectedly up to the porch, where I spotted a tray of food on the top step, left by a caring neighbor with this note: "Watched you on television hour after hour on this tragic day and I know you didn't even have time to cry like the rest of us. Enjoy your dinner." With that I sat down on the steps and finally let my tears flow, after one of the most painful days of my career.

Scheduled to deliver his State of the Union address at the Capitol that night, President Reagan had planned to open his remarks with a tribute to the fallen *Challenger* astronauts until House Speaker Tip O'Neill got wind of his intention and set him straight:

> If the president of the United States comes to the Capitol tonight, he will deliver his State of the Union address in the dark. Members of Congress will be home grieving with the rest of America."

His annual address appropriately postponed, President Reagan then delivered an eloquent speech from the Oval Office instead. At its end he quoted from the poem beloved by many pilots, "High Flight" by Royal Canadian Air Force Pilot Officer John Gillespie Magee, Jr., who was killed on Dec. 11, 1941:

> We will never forget them, nor the last time we saw them, this morning, as they prepared for the Journey and waved goodbye and slipped "the surly bonds of earth" to touch "the face of God."

While covering the space program interested and excited me, my main job during my New York City years of 1968–1971 was reporting and anchoring the news for NBC's flagship station WNBC-TV. After a few months covering fires, shootings and politics, the station manager asked me to co-anchor the *11 O'Clock News* on Saturday and Sunday nights with Bob Teague, a television reporter who had plenty of experience. Before we began our dual-anchor newscast Bob and I spent a day together at his country house in Pound Ridge, New York, getting to know one another and discussing the kinds of stories we thought deserved more attention—health, the environment, race relations and business and government ethics.

I learned a lot about Bob during that day-long session, but I learned even more after a mutual friend suggested I read Bob's book, *Letters to a Black Boy*, which he'd written with his infant son Adam in mind. Its subject was life as experienced by a black man growing up in America. It was an angry book, and Bob was an angry man—understandably, in view of the slights and outright prejudice he had experienced.

One chapter written by his wife, an accomplished ballet dancer, was titled "The White Dinner Jacket." It tells of the time Bob, at her urging, bought a white dinner jacket to wear on a vacation in the Virgin Islands.

> . . . That evening he put on the new jacket; and off they went arm in arm, to the palm-roofed dining pavilion of her

> dreams. It was dimly lit, a small hurricane lamp flickering on each table. The palms swayed to Calypso music. The scene was quietly festive, like a painting slowly coming to life. There were the newly arrived pale people from the States, anticipating tomorrow's sun and next week's tan. The stage was perfectly set for her beautifully jacketed husband to enter and take his place in her dream. Several white couples converged behind them in the dining room entrance. Suddenly, a bill was pressed in to her husband's hand. A man whispered confidentially, with the greatest of urgency, "A good table for my party, if you would." Her husband, hand extended, stared at the bill. A second bill was placed on the first. The man leaned forward as insistently as before. "I know you can take care of it," he whispered. "Please." She and her husband stood looking at each other, stunned momentarily and speechless. Later they would laugh about it, but at the moment of comprehension they could not. The brown headwaiter glided toward them, beckoning. Her husband pressed the bills back into the insistent one's palm, saying evenly, "You've made a mistake." As they turned to follow the headwaiter, only she noticed the crimson flush that swept the insistent one's face. Her husband undoubtedly was too occupied with his own complex emotions, which registered not at all through the coconut-shell brown of his features. She loved the way her husband looked.

Although Bob and I occasionally had a drink together after work, we were not social friends, yet our dual-anchor format worked well. We never had a serious argument, only occasional differences about which story should lead our newscast.

A year later I was assigned to anchor the *Sixth Hour News*—WNBC's daily early-evening news broadcast. We had an all-star cast including veteran New York reporter Gabe Pressman, Gene Shalit with his popular movie reviews, Dr. Frank Field doing the weather and famed athlete Kyle Rote reporting on sports. The program was a strong number two in the market. Nevertheless, the higher-ups at WNBC thought a bigger-name national correspondent as anchor might bring in a bigger audience, so in the spring of 1971 the station announced that veteran NBC News correspondent Sander Vanocur was replacing me as anchor of the *Sixth Hour News*.

Until then my career had all seemed to be going my way, and my first experience of being dropped from a news program came as a terrific blow. My dad happened to be in New York City that weekend and did his best to console me, telling me how as a young man during the Depression he got fired when he had a wife and child to support.

"Look at it this way, son," he told me. "You're single, with your whole life ahead of you." In short, stop feeling sorry for yourself. Although my contract had another year to run, I decided to resign and go skiing in Europe as I pondered my next career move. But just before I was due to leave another of those blessed strokes of luck came my way when NBC News President Richard Wald spoke to me at my farewell lunch.

"John, how would you like it if NBC News paid for your ski trip to Europe?"

I was gun-shy. "What's the catch?"

"I want you to leave immediately, tomorrow, and stop off in Israel for a month or so. We've just made a change in correspondents there, and we'd like you to fill in for a while."

I knew then I'd be a fool to refuse. I left the next day on assignment as the NBC News correspondent in Israel for what turned out to be a six-month stay—long after the snows had melted in the Swiss Alps. Fortunately, I enjoyed my time in Israel, covering a variety of stories, and my first exposure to the Middle East evolved into a lifelong fascination with that part of the world.

*

My stay in Israel came to an end that fall when Bob Lemon, general manager of the NBC-owned station in Chicago, offered to double my salary if I would come back to Chicago and co-anchor my old program with Jim Ruddle, who'd taken over when I left. I accepted and soon concluded that Chicago had a "second city" inferiority complex relative to New York City, because to counter the impression that I'd originally left for greener pastures in the Big Apple, the station spent several hundred thousand dollars to persuade Windy City viewers that I was a loyal Chicagoan. Their advertising agency even had me pose for a photo with the lions in front of the Chicago Art Institute captioned "John Palmer is as much a part of Chicago as the Lions."

I tried co-anchoring with Ruddle but quickly realized it was not fun. The truth of the matter was I simply felt I'd been there and done that and it was vividly apparent that Jim was not thrilled at my return. Yearning to get out of the studio and back to covering stories, I was off and out on the road again any time my bosses would let me go.

*

On the night of June 9, 1972, torrential rains over the eastern Black Hills of South Dakota produced a deadly flash flood that roared though the town of Rapid City. Over a six-hour period nearly 15 inches of rain fell, taking the lives of 238 residents and stranding thousands. The destruction included 1,335 homes, scores of businesses and 5,000 automobiles, with damage in the hundreds of millions of dollars.

On the morning after the disaster NBC News chartered a plane to take me, producer Ted Elbert and our television crew to Rapid City to cover the devastation. By the time we arrived the water level had dropped, leaving stark evidence of the horror that had left the community in the dark just hours before. Drowned corpses hung amid the branches of trees. The only sound breaking the town's haunting silence was a lone railroad-crossing signal protruding from a receding sea of murky water, still flashing red, its bell wildly clanging. Rescue efforts had begun, and residents struggled to recover even though most of the town had no electricity and, ironically, no water. It truly was a case of water, water, everywhere, and not drop to drink.

Ted and I and our crew registered as the only guests at a small motel on the outskirts of town. With no running water, each evening after we completed that day's television report—run on *NBC Nightly News* for a week—we used the motel's small swimming pool as our private bathtub. As word of our improvised spa got out and dozens of rescue workers and homeless residents flocked to join us in our "bath," the motel pool's water soon turned every bit as murky and contaminated as the surrounding floodwaters and we had to abandon our daily lather-up and scrub-down.

We ended our coverage, gratefully, after a week, and drove to Denver to catch a flight back to Chicago. We decided to treat ourselves to first-class seats. After checking in at the counter I strolled onto the plane, took my seat, and was on my second Scotch before I noticed that Ted Elbert, who'd stood behind me in line, wasn't on board. The flight crew was just closing the door for takeoff when Ted came storming aboard, in an absolute snit.

"Can you believe this? They took me into a room and strip-searched me, just because I have hair on my face."

"No, Ted," I said, "it's not your goatee. It's because you smell so damn bad."

I had no idea how I made it through. Maybe it was the aftershave I splashed on.

They say a flash flood like the one that hit Rapid City in 1972 comes once every 500 years. Even so, the residents of that resilient community not only rebuilt but also took steps to make sure any subsequent flood that struck their area could never again have such devastating consequences. The city adopted a flood-plain management program, converted most of the flooded areas into large parks and installed a flash-flood early-warning system—a lesson many other flood-prone communities have yet to learn.

*

The following year NBC sent me out to South Dakota again, this time to cover a story that would become as infamous as the Siege of Wounded Knee, where, in 1890, the U.S. Army's 7th Cavalry had massacred more than 150 starving Sioux.

The modern-day uprising of 1973 began when a few hundred members of the Oglala Sioux tribe, bolstered by leaders of the radical American Indian Movement, took over the notorious massacre site. Major grievances had spurred the Indians into action: deplorable conditions at the nearby Pine Ridge Indian Reservation, federal violations of Indian treaties and corruption on the part of their own Indian leaders.

So on a wintry February day the protestors, led by Russell Means, occupied the tiny hamlet of Wounded Knee and proclaimed it the Lakota Nation—their own sovereign territory and no longer a part of the United States. This initial gesture of protest quickly turned into one of the largest armed conflicts in the United States since the Civil War. Military units, U.S. marshals, and FBI agents surrounded Wounded Knee for a siege that turned out to last more than two months, cutting off electricity in the dead of winter and doing everything possible to block food supplies.

Numerous firefights took place, and several Indians were killed. After a U.S. marshal was shot and permanently paralyzed, the already inflamed situation burst into an international story. All of us reporting from Wounded Knee on the day-to-day events were glad to discover how well the Indian occupiers knew the value of publicity. Eager for exposure of their grievances, they made our job far easier by welcoming into their compound anyone there to cover the story: network reporters, camera crews and newspaper reporters from around the world.

When we weren't encamped with the Indians at Wounded Knee, most of us stayed at a Pine Ridge boardinghouse, and I was there one morning when a Russian reporter for the Soviet newspaper Izvestia arrived. He'd been granted special permission by our State Department for travel outside Washington so he could cover the Indian takeover. Unsure what to make of him at first, I couldn't wait to see how he fared after he announced over breakfast, "I am here to cover the white man's oppression of the Indians." When he asked to hitch a ride with to me to Wounded Knee, I said, "Sure," and off we went.

At the FBI checkpoint, the Russian showed his State Department document and got waved though ahead of me, but when he arrived at the Indians' checkpoint and displayed those same credentials it was another story. The Indians handcuffed him and led him away on the spot. Apparently he hadn't been briefed on the nuances of the situation, namely, that the Indians had declared themselves a sovereign nation where U.S. State Department documents were not only irrelevant but an affront to their cause.

Inside the compound later I asked revolt leader Means what had happened to the Russian.

"I locked him up," he said bluntly.

It took considerable argument on my part to persuade Means to release my Russian colleague, finally winning him over after I made the point that he was there "to tell the world the story of Indian oppression in America." At length Means unlocked a storage-room door and set the bewildered Russian free, upon which he beat it back to Washington without writing a word about the Indian takeover.

If you've ever been to South Dakota in February, you know about those excruciatingly cold nights. On one such night as wind-whipped snow blanketed the compound, those of us inside could hear military armored personnel carriers revving up their engines. The Indians took this as a sign that the government troops were about to overrun their compound and gathered their forces for a preemptive attack, until television came to the rescue. Our cameraman, using his night-vision lens developed for the Pentagon during the Vietnam War, saw that the Army troops were simply rocking their armored personal carriers back and forth to keep the steel treads from freezing-up in the bitter cold. Although the Indians didn't stand down, they did temporarily relax.

After 71 days, the Indians surrendered and the Siege of Wounded Knee was over. For those who'd taken part in the uprising, those militant weeks had afforded them a sense of freedom. The siege also marked the waning of nationally publicized confrontations involving the Indian activist movement. When the siege began, unemployment on the Pine Ridge Indian Reservation was at 40 percent; today, sadly, more than 35 years later, it stands at 80 percent. From the beleaguered Indians' point of view, their effort seems to have accomplished nothing.

*

Two years into my second anchoring tour in Chicago the station's new general manager, Lee Schulman, asked to see me one night after the program in his 20th floor office. He wasn't there when I walked in, but my friend and immediate boss Ed Planer, the station's news director, was. Right away I saw the pained look on his face.

"This isn't good, is it, Ed?"

"No," he said, "It's not good."

Then Schulman strode in to deliver the *coup de grâce*. "Blow of mercy," the French term means, and that's what it eventually turned out to be. I stood up, shook his hand, and left.

Ed told me later that after my departure Schulman told him, "You know, this is terrible. Now Palmer has to go home and tell his wife and kids he got fired."

"No, he doesn't," Ed reassured him. "John's single."

At that Schulman said, "That's even worse. He'll be alone."

Maybe Thomas Wolfe was right—you can't go home again. Even so, I still regard Chicago as one of the best cities in the world in which to live and work, especially for a journalist.

Dick Wald, President of NBC News, came to my rescue. In short order I was off to Lebanon to begin a two-year stint as Beirut bureau chief and Middle East correspondent for NBC News, assigned to cover the Arab world.

7

HAVE TRENCHCOAT, WILL TRAVEL

ONE DAY A scorpion wanted to cross the Jordan River but couldn't find a bridge, so he asked a nearby frog for help. "I want to cross this river, Frog," he said, "but I can't swim. Will you carry me across on your back?"

The frog's eyes bulged even wider than usual. "Are you crazy? You'd sting me, and I'd drown!"

"Think about it," the scorpion said. "I'd be foolish to do that, because if I stung you we'd both drown."

"That seems logical," said the frog, so he agreed to carry him to the other side. But when they were barely halfway across, the scorpion plunged his venomous stinger straight into the hapless frog's back.

As the frog felt his life ebbing away, he croaked, "Scorpion, why did you do that? Now we will both die."

As the scorpion slipped under the water, he called out to the frog, "Don't you know? This is the Middle East."

Every journalist or diplomat who has ever worked in that part of the world must have heard that Arab version of the age-old fable. I first heard it shortly after arriving in Lebanon during the summer of 1973, sent to cover the Arab world for NBC News on my first major overseas assignment. In the months that followed, anytime the often-confusing events in the Middle East mystified my colleagues and me, the lesson of the scorpion and the frog—that the rules of logic don't always apply—passed for an explanation when we could find no other.

Often called "the Paris of the Middle East," Beirut in 1973 was a city with dozens of outdoor cafés, trendy nightclubs, a temperate climate and a liberal lifestyle that attracted Western tourists, Texas oilmen, journalists, spies and wealthy Arab investors. On my first day there, sipping a rum punch on a balcony of the luxurious St. George's Hotel overlooking the Mediterranean as a colleague briefed me on the region's current intrigues, I felt sure I'd landed in paradise. And paradise it was, for a while.

A week after my arrival in Lebanon, my driver, Antoine "Tony" Aoun, who was to become a friend, confidant, and often protector, drove me to an elegant garden party high in the mountains overlooking Beirut. On the way, we first passed a camp where thousands of Palestinian refugees lived together in squalor, many of them in shacks made out of cardboard or sheets of scrapped tin.

The region's stunning contrasts became even more vivid as we climbed into the mountains thousands of feet above Beirut and drove past the luxurious villas and summer homes of rich Lebanese and Arab sheiks. At the villa where the party was held, the

Japanese lanterns that festooned my host's manicured lawn also framed a spectacular view of the city and the gleaming Mediterranean below. Under the lanterns' festive light lavish tables displayed more delicious food than the guests could consume in a month. I enjoyed the hospitality but could not erase the troubling images I'd seen on the drive up the mountain.

Later that evening during a political discussion with my host and some of his friends about the conflicts and tensions in Lebanon between Christians, Muslims, Palestinians and other quarreling factions I found it impossible to keep my opinions to myself.

"I've only been here a week, but as far as I can tell Lebanon has no middle class. All I've seen are the very rich and the very poor, and I don't think that situation can last. One of these days the have-nots will rise up."

My host smiled knowingly. "All Western newcomers think that at first, but you will see. Despite our differences, we all get along."

Less than two years later Lebanon erupted in a vicious civil war that was to last 16years, cost tens of thousands of lives, and virtually destroy the city once so favorably compared with Paris. But I'm getting ahead of myself. I would have two other wars to cover first.

On Oct. 6, 1973, I was hanging pictures in my Beirut apartment when an urgent call came from my boss in London. "John, turn on BBC Radio," he said. "You're about to become a war correspondent."

Tuning in to learn that Egypt and Syria had launched a coordinated surprise attack against Israel, I left hanging the pictures for later. I spent the next week camped out at a checkpoint on the road to Damascus, trying to talk my way across the Syrian border. Finally permission for me and my television crew to enter the Syrian capital came from the Ministry of Information. At first we weren't permitted to accompany Syrian ground troops battling Israeli forces on the southern front, but our hotel rooftop in central Damascus provided a great view of the air war as Israeli Phantom Jets bombed the Syrian Defense Ministry and other buildings and engaged in dogfights overhead with Syrian MIG-21s.

We never knew what the next twenty-four hours might bring. One night a Ministry of Information official rousted us from our beds and drove us to a dingy makeshift operating room to watch Syrian doctors treat a severely injured Israeli pilot. His plane had been shot down over Damascus, and the pilot survived by bailing out, breaking both legs and suffering deep gashes across his chest and thighs when he ejected from his aircraft. The Syrian government, apparently stung by Israeli charges that their captured pilots were being tortured and even killed, wanted Western reporters to see for themselves that Israeli prisoners were being well cared for. We watched as a doctor in a white blood-spattered coat set the broken legs and sewed up the wounds while a nurse held a kerosene lantern.

I asked the groggy, moaning pilot how the Syrians were treating him.

“Pretty good,” he said in broken English, “for a guy who was bombing their capital.”

(After 10 days under the close supervision of Syrian military officers we were allowed to accompany Syrian troops battling Israeli forces near the city of Kunitra on the Israeli border. Through borrowed binoculars, I peered across the lines looking for my NBC colleagues covering the battle from the other side but recognized no one.)

Up against the Syrian military’s strict censorship, as American journalists we were particularly suspect because of U.S. support for Israel. These Syrian censors often struck the most innocent of sentences and phrases from our copy, so to get around that difficulty I wrote one script for their eyes, then recorded a different script as the sound track for our film. Tony would then drive the complete package of film and sound track over the border to Beirut to be flown to London, after which the full report went by satellite to New York for broadcast.

Many nights, if a knock came at my hotel room door I sweated bullets, certain the Syrian police had discovered my scam and had come to haul me away. As time passed with no repercussions, I concluded that the Syrian Embassy in Washington wasn't monitoring U.S. television news from the front and felt freer to report all that I saw and heard.

It was a short war, ending after 17 days when the U.N. Security Council called for a ceasefire just as Israeli forces were about to crush Egypt's Third Army, surrounded and stranded in the desert. Nevertheless, the conflict set the stage for a historic U.S.–brokered peace agreement between Egypt and Israel, and in the months that followed I took up residence at the Cairo Hilton to cover Egyptian President Anwar Sadat and his ongoing pursuit of peace.

*

It was while I was on a tour of Middle Eastern capitals, familiarizing myself with my new territory, that Richard Nixon's presidency came to an end. I had left Washington in the middle of the Watergate Congressional hearings that summer but had closely followed developments as the committee reviewed the transcript of a secret tapes made, at Nixon's behest, in the Oval Office. One tape revealed that six days before the June 1972 Watergate break-in, Nixon had tried to use the Central Intelligence Agency to block the FBI's investigation into the burglary. That was the "smoking gun" that connected Nixon directly to the burglary, a fact he had long denied.

And on Aug. 9, 1974, Nixon's presidency ended in the shadow of that scandal. Americans saw it all on television—the helicopter on the south lawn of the White House, Nixon's final victory salute, and then the departure of the only president in American history to resign. With no satellite TV in Egypt, I joined several dozen American tourists crowded around the Reuters wire-service machine in the lobby of the Cairo Hilton as we took turns reading aloud the running reports from the White House. The teletype machine, clacking out paragraph after paragraph at rapid-fire speed, was our only connection to the historic events unfolding at the White House.

"Nixon is now walking toward the helicopter. He's going up the steps. He turns and salutes. President and Mrs. Ford are waving goodbye. The door is closed. The engines are revving up. Now the helicopter is lifting off. The helicopter has now disappeared into the clouds and President and Mrs. Ford are walking back into the Executive Mansion."

As President Ford said a few minutes later, "Our long national nightmare is over." Many non-Americans in the lobby of the Cairo Hilton that day expressed amazement that our president had been forced to resign simply because he obstructed justice and lied to the American people. An Egyptian employee of the hotel said to me in bewilderment, "Don't all politicians do that?" It was a sad time, but I also felt a sense of pride that our political system had worked. The leadership of the most powerful democracy in the world had changed hands without a shot being fired.

*

Barely settled in my new role as Middle East correspondent for NBC News, I promptly faced further challenges. After weeks of failing to arrange an interview with Sadat through official channels, my frustration drove me to a more creative approach. I rented a limo and talked one of our producers into donning a black suit so he could serve as my chauffeur to Sadat's summer palace a few miles up the Nile. When palace guards stopped our car at the first checkpoint I rolled down my window and, running my words together, mumbled, "JohnPalmerAmericanNBC."

Even to me it sounded like "John Palmer, American Embassy." My ruse had the desired effect, for the guard also seemed to think that was what I'd said. The same strategy worked at the next two checkpoints; then we were inside the palace compound.

Ushered into a large reception room where I took a seat in a big leather chair, I did my best to conceal my nervousness. The cup of tea brought by a servant only added to my unease. After 15 minutes, big double doors at the far end of the room opened and in strode a tall, confident, smiling President Sadat, followed by two aides. As I rose and shook his hand, his smile dissolved into a look of concern; he was probably wondering the reason for this unscheduled visit from a representative of the U.S. Embassy. Was there some urgent matter that needed immediate attention? After some confusion as to who I was and for whom I worked, Sadat again flashed me the engaging smile I soon came to know quite well.

"I admire your American spunk, Palmer," he said, "but no interview. Only a little chat."

What a lucky beginning for me. My American spunk led to a relationship that produced a half-dozen exclusive interviews with the Egyptian president, broadcast on NBC News during an especially critical period of negotiations between Israel and Egypt. Sadat was already coming to understand the power of the press and the special importance of television, which probably helped to grease the skids for me. (He talked willingly to the press, as a cartoon of the time illustrated. It depicted briefcase-carrying diplomats standing with ears cocked behind a group of reporters, trying to hear what Sadat was saying to the journalists to find out his thinking.)

As we came to know each other better and Sadat came to trust me, we often met at his summer home on the upper Nile, where we would sip orange juice and talk informally, without camera or microphone, about the Middle East and world politics. Over time I was privileged to see a side of this courageous man that most of the world never knew. One evening he invited me to come by for what he always called "a chat," and we watched the television news together. Cairo television carried a report that night about a blind newsboy whose newspaper stand had been vandalized and his money taken by thugs. Incensed, Sadat ordered his aides to find the boy immediately and bring him to the palace. An hour later, we heard screaming sirens as a police escort arrived with the frightened youngster in tow and delivered him to Sadat. The trembling boy, dressed in a dirty T-shirt, torn brown pants and worn sandals, was on the verge of tears.

The president spoke to him in Arabic, and as he did so an aide came close to translate quietly into my ear in English. "Don't be afraid," Sadat was saying. "I intend to make sure you get a better newsstand at a busier corner than the one you had before."

Still not sure what was happening, the boy managed to mumble "Shucron," "thank you" in Arabic, before devouring the cheese sandwich and orange juice offered by Sadat's butler.

As aides then led the youngster away Sadat turned to me. "I wish I could help all Egyptians like that. Our country is just too poor. That's why we need peace with Israel, so Americans will come here and invest. Then things will be better."

During one of our chats Sadat suggested that I become his press secretary. This startling proposal took me by surprise, but I managed to come up with a quick answer. "Mr. President, an American spokesman is the last thing you need. Your critics would crucify you."

He waved away my objections. "Oh, I would keep you in the background. You would be unofficial, behind the scenes. Just for consultations, you know."

Flattered, I briefly considered the offer, but in the end no matter how much I admired Sadat and believed in his cause, I couldn't forget that scorpion and that frog. Middle Eastern politics would likely always be so volatile that abandoning my career as a reporter to become Sadat's advocate could prove an extremely shortsighted move.

In more than one of our private off-the-record conversations Sadat told me that he fully expected to be killed by any one of a dozen Arab groups that opposed his 1977 visit to Israel and his decision to enter into a separate peace agreement with the Jewish state. His wife had always been fearful that he'd lose his life, as she told me when I interviewed her in the garden of the presidential palace in downtown Cairo. One of the pleasures of my association with

Anwar Sadat while he was Egypt's president was getting to know charming Mme. Jehan Sadat. An elegant and extremely good-looking woman, the day I interviewed her in the private garden she was wearing a yellow pantsuit, an outfit she would never have worn for Arab television. She and her husband were very geared to the American audience, because Sadat knew he couldn't think of bringing his country out of poverty without American investment. In order to reach the Americans to make any headway, he had to make peace with Israel, because American business wasn't about to go in there without peace between the two countries.

It was Mme. Sadat who gave me the behind-the-scenes story of the 1953 coup that had overthrown King Farouk. Preparations for the coup were in place, masterminded by Gamal Abdel Nasser with the help of supporters including Anwar Sadat. Sadat, then a military officer, was scheduled to be the point man in charge of assuming control of nationwide communications once the coup began. He and all the others knew that in a *coup d'état*, taking over communications to proclaim your victory is probably the most important element for success, and he was ready. The conspirators had a code of some sort to signal the moment to act, a few words as simple as "The moon is blue."

The Sadats were then living in a village outside Cairo, and one evening after Sadat had taken his daughter a movie, a messenger showed up at the family's door. Handing Mme. Sadat a note, he said, "This is an urgent message for your husband. Please give it to him right away." The message was "The moon is blue." But Mme. Sadat, worried that the coup would fail and that her husband would be killed, tore up the note.

When the movie ended Sadat wandered out into the streets and saw people running and shouting. The coup was underway. Shocked, he rushed home, ran in the house, exclaiming to his wife, "I can't believe he left me out! I was to take over radio and television!" Sadat had his lieutenants in place to manage the whole thing when the signal came, but after he didn't report in, Nasser had to send somebody else to handle it. At first Sadat was crushed, believing he'd been passed over, until Mme. Sadat confessed what she'd done.

"The message came for you," she told him, "but I thought the coup would fail. In fact, it may yet fail. I tore up the note and threw it away in fear for your life."

When she told me the story years later I asked, "What was his reaction? Wasn't he terribly upset?"

She laughed. "I cannot repeat his words to me, either on American or Egyptian TV."

When all was explained, however, Nasser understood and forgave him. Nasser assumed the presidency and continued in that position for about 11 years until he died of a heart attack. An Arab nationalist and great friend of the Soviet Union, Nasser had played the U.S.S.R. against the U.S. and had gotten the Soviets to build the Aswan High Dam, the greatest dam in the history of the world at that time. Scores of Russians came to Egypt, and Egyptians traveled to the Soviet Union. The Soviets sent the Egyptians military equipment and provided them with training, while at one point, according to Nasser, our own CIA tried to bribe him with two million dollars in a suitcase crammed with $100 bills. He claimed he accepted the money and used it to build a tower in Cairo that became known popularly as the CIA Tower. After Nasser's death, Vice President Sadat took over.

Sadat knew what a great risk he was taking in his peace-making efforts, fully expecting to pay with his life. I've often thought it takes a lot more courage to make peace than it does to make war. After Nasser's cultivation of the Soviet Union, many in his country were upset with Sadat. They didn't like his reform policies, or his attitude of cuddling up to the West, and most of all they detested his intention to make peace with Israel. He knew all too well that the Egyptian fundamentalists, the Muslim Brotherhood, would never sit still for that. They believed that while Israel held one inch of Arab land—Palestinian land—no Muslim should give up the fight, and they still believe that today. Some in Egypt would settle for the current boundaries, some would like to go back to the boundaries of 1948, and some won't tolerate the idea of the state of Israel anywhere in the Middle East.

Aware of his vulnerability, Sadat had plenty of bodyguards, and after President Nixon lent him some Secret Service personnel to train his own people, the newly trained bodyguards suddenly looked like U.S. Secret Service agents, all in dark suits and dark glasses with that little plastic tube protruding from one ear to facilitate communications. Everyone knew how dangerous Sadat's trip to Israel would be, and the American agents tried to prepare Sadat's bodyguards as best they could for the risk, but they encountered a major frustration—Egyptian courtesy.

Upper-class Egyptians are very cultured people, highly sensitive to propriety. I found that out for myself in the Arab world and especially among Egyptians, who are polite almost to a fault. Whenever I made some request, regardless of what it was or how outlandish, people would never deny me outright. Rather than telling me, "You're out of your mind! You can't go there! That's a secret military installation," they would just say, "We'll check and you come back tomorrow." To them, saying no seemed far too abrupt, too impolite.

The Secret Service trainers sent by the U.S. government ran into a similar difficulty in their efforts to ensure protection for Sadat. They tried to persuade the Egyptian bodyguards that they must do everything and anything to protect their president, even if it violated the Arab code of propriety, but it was an uphill battle. For instance, they tried to train them always to keep their suit coats unbuttoned, so they could get to their sidearms instantly. But the Egyptians, terribly conscious of decorum in the president's presence, considered it disrespectful to appear in his presence with their jackets unbuttoned. Time and again, the Secret Service guys would look over to see those coats buttoned up. You'll never see a U.S. Secret Service agent with his coat buttoned. I'm not sure they ever convinced the Egyptians to follow their example.

Sadat did a great many things to foster prosperity for Egypt.

He created the free port of Alexandria and did all the right things economically to lure American investment and big companies into the country. Making peace with Israel was his objective, not necessarily because he believed in his heart it was the right thing to do, but because he knew it was the only way to get his people out of poverty. And that was his number-one objective, even if it seemed a hopeless one.

True to his prediction, Sadat was eventually murdered as he reviewed a military parade on Oct. 6, 1981, gunned down by four hardline Arab assassins, members of the Egyptian Islamic Jihad organization who had infiltrated the Egyptian army units in the parade. Back in the U.S., by then as a White House correspondent with NBC, I was terribly saddened when I heard the news, and reported on White House reaction to the murder with a heavy heart. I had lost a friend who happened to be a world leader, a man I greatly admired. To me Anwar Sadat is still a hero, for in the face of savage opposition from other Arab nations and organizations he dared to commit himself to the peace effort, while other Arab leaders, like PLO leader Yasser Arafat, selfishly worried about their own careers and did little to relieve their people of the burdens of conflict and poverty.

When I had time to reflect on my friendship with Sadat, I understood that I had become too close to the subject I was covering. Not good for a journalist, because emotions cloud judgment and erode the independent point of view—the basis of responsible reporting. Even so, I feel privileged to have known the man so well and to have witnessed his courage and vision at firsthand.

*

Meanwhile, as tensions between various political and religious factions in Lebanon intensified, U.S. support for Israel in the 1973 Arab-Israeli War had spawned a new crisis on the home front. Arab members of the Organization of Petroleum Exporting Countries

(OPEC) announced they would no longer ship oil to any nation that had supported Israel in the conflict. The resulting oil shortage and quadrupling of U.S. gasoline prices led to long backups at the pumps. As the lines grew longer and tempers flared, Americans took a fresh interest in the Arab world—especially such oil-producing countries as Saudi Arabia and Kuwait.

In the face of changing world events, NBC News with its usual dispatch sent me along to the Persian Gulf to cover the political and economic implications of the oil crisis at its source. One of my reports featured a new golf course under construction in Saudi Arabia. Because growing grass in a waterless desert is obviously impossible, as a substitute the Saudis sprayed the sand with thousands of gallons of crude oil, of which the kingdom has an endless supply. When hardened by the sun, it provided a firm playing surface. Back home, Americans frustrated by the prolonged oil and gasoline shortage found this story shocking in the extreme.

While covering an OPEC summit in the conservative Persian Gulf state of Qatar, NBC cameraman Ken Ludlow and I ran into a minor crisis of our own. The Qatar customs officials were starting to inspect the dozen or so cases of equipment we had brought along when Ken pulled me aside in anguish, perspiration pouring down his face.

"John, we're in trouble."

"How so?" Everything seemed fine to me.

He jerked his head toward an ominous sign on the wall:

ANYONE BRINGING ALCOHOLIC BEVERAGES
INTO THE COUNTRY SHALL BE SUBJECT TO
THE PENALTY OF FLOGGING.

Then I got it. Ken must have brought along his favorite alcoholic beverage—beer. He whispered, "I stashed a case of St. Pauli Girl in with our equipment." To make matters worse in this conservative orthodox Muslim country, every can carried the portrait of a shapely half-naked woman. Surely cause for a few extra lashes.

When a customs agent suddenly stopped the conveyor belt moving our baggage through the X-ray machine we held our breath. "What is this?" he demanded. On the screen we could see the same thing he saw—the outline of twenty-four metal cans.

I said, as casually as I could, "They're cans of chemicals to develop our television film."

Right away Ken picked up the drift. "If you open the box and expose the cans to light, it will ruin the chemicals, and then we can't cover your summit for American television."

That customs agent had never worked in the broadcast world, because if he had he'd have known we were shooting video, not film, and therefore needed no processing chemicals. He conferred with another official then nodded and waved us on through. That night after dark Ken wrapped his case of St. Pauli Girl in a blanket, carried it down the back stairs of our hotel, and buried it in the sand. At least that's what he told me.

*

Back in Lebanon the central government was growing weaker by the day. Chronic feuding between Christian and Muslim factions festered like an open sore, and when Chairman Yasser Arafat of the Palestine Liberation Organization (PLO) took up residence in Beirut, his move heightened the unrest. Sporadic episodes of violence broke out between various militia groups, while war loomed on the horizon in another part of the Middle East.

I was vacationing in Greece when I spotted a startling newspaper headline: PRESIDENT MAKARIOS DEAD. The man in question was, of course, Archbishop Makarios, president of the eastern Mediterranean island of Cyprus, part of my territory. Resigned to my holiday's premature end, I phoned my boss at NBC News headquarters in London to have my expectations confirmed.

"Get to Cyprus as fast as you can," he said. "Charter a plane if necessary, but get there!"

Off I went to Cyprus to join Peter Jennings of ABC News, Karsten Prager of *Time*, and other Beirut-based colleagues. We soon discovered that the newspaper story was wrong. Makarios was not dead, only in hiding in the mountains after a military coup.

I stayed on to cover whatever stories might arise, and one evening we were having a few beers at the Ledra Palace Hotel on the "green line" that separated the island's Greek and Turkish sectors when we heard reports that the Turkish fleet was on its way to Cyprus with an invasion force. Would Greece and Turkey—two NATO allies—actually go to war over that small island? Most of us discounted the possibility until we awoke at dawn the next morning to the sound of rifle and machine-gun fire as thousands of Turkish paratroopers dropped from the sky. In the Middle East less than a year, I was now covering my second war.

And what a strange war it turned out to be. By day, with other reporters, cameramen and still photographers from all over the world, we covered the fighting, then repaired at dusk to the comfort of our hotel, crowding into the bar each night to hash over the day's experiences. One particularly shocking development had to do with a hangover of British influence in Cyprus—driving on the left side of the road. The invading Turkish tank commanders, accustomed to driving on the right side back home, refused to change their ways in Cyprus and appalled us by flattening mile after mile of automobiles, most of them fortunately unoccupied.

One memorable day a Greek Cypriot employee at our hotel drew me aside to say that Turkish Cypriots had carried out a massacre in his tiny village, then buried their victims in a shallow grave. It sounded like a story worth tracking down. Early the next morning I appropriated a couple of shovels from the hotel basement and drove with Jim Hoagland of the Washington Post to the village. The report appeared to be true, because an old man led us to a concrete building, one wall of it pocked with bullet holes and freshly whitewashed, and at the wall's base was a large plot of freshly turned earth.

"At least two dozen bodies, they buried them where they fell," the old man said. "They lined up all the men between the ages of fourteen and seventy and shot them on the spot."

Talk about hands-on journalism. Jim and I began to dig but soon grew wary when several cars drove slowly through the deserted village, their occupants watching us from a distance. Were they just curious, or had they something more sinister in mind? Shirtless and sweating under the hot August sun, we dug faster. As each shovelful of dirt came up, dozens more horseflies swarmed to the bottom of the deepening pit, drawn to the sickening stench. After about an hour my shovel struck something soft, and further digging revealed the abdomen of a man. A few feet away we uncovered a hand, then a leg.

That was enough. We jumped in the car and sped away, then telephoned U.N. officials about our discovery. Jim's piece made the front page of the *Washington Post*, while mine was NBC's lead story on *Today*.

After Greek Cypriot snipers began firing on our hotel from rooftop positions, the building came under return fire from Turkish rockets. I needed no persuasion to take cover with other journalists in a hallway. Over the noise of combat, a young woman reporter from London asked *Time*'s veteran combat correspondent Karsten Prager, "How can you tell the difference between incoming and outgoing fire?"

"You can tell by the sound—" he was saying when a rocket pierced the hotel's outer wall and exploded, collapsing the ceiling and showering us with debris and plaster dust.

Everything was quiet for almost a minute before Prager broke the silence. "That, young lady, was incoming."

Waves of laughter echoed up and down the darkened hallway. Cypriot civilians who had also taken refuge in the hotel must have wondered what was so funny about a direct hit by a rocket, or for that matter about the war. The conflict in Cyprus ended as wars generally do, with hundreds dead, thousands of displaced refugees, and a divided country.

That April of 1974, as most Americans' attention was shifting from the Middle East to Vietnam with Saigon on the brink of falling to the Viet Cong and North Vietnamese, Beirut was still my home base. By then the crisis on my doorstep was so superheated that the city, and in fact all of Lebanon, was about to explode into all-out war.

Until something crucial happened, I was free to travel to Cairo to meet my visiting bosses from New York and London. The day was a warm one, and we were finishing a pleasant lunch at an outdoor café in the shadow of the Pyramids when I turned on my short-wave radio as I frequently did to catch the latest news from the BBC.

The lead story pulled me up short. It wasn't about Saigon, but about Beirut, where the smoldering hostilities had finally burst all bounds, with a ferocious gun battle outside a suburban Beirut church between Palestinians and Lebanese right-wing Christian militia.

My lunch companions told me, "We'll get the check. You grab the next plane back to Beirut."

That violent clash was the match that ignited an inferno. For 16 years afterward sectarian strife would engulf Lebanon, leaving another country in ruins and tens of thousands maimed or dead. The reminder of my time in the Middle East would be spent covering that nasty civil war.

During home leave later that year I dropped by NBC News headquarters in New York to see my greatly admired acquaintance, anchorman David Brinkley.

"Frankly, John," David told me, "you're out there in Lebanon risking your life every day to cover a war that nobody here really gives a damn about. Your combat reports, good as they are, serve mostly to separate commercials on our program."

I was crushed, but I appreciated his honesty. After that I was a lot more careful with my crew—cameraman Ken Ludlow and soundman Shibley Simann—as we covered the daily gun battles in Beirut's violent streets. We agreed on a few rules for covering the fighting, the chief one being never to go into a street battle on our own. We would go only in company with fighters from one side or the other. One group firing at you was bad enough, but getting caught in the crossfire was a thousand times worse.

We put considerable effort into building relationships with all the militia commanders—the Christian Phalange Party, Shi'a and Sunni Muslims, PLO fighters and other Palestinian splinter groups. The various militias would either give us a pass (usually a piece of paper with the scribbled signature of their commander) or an escort. Dozens of armed roadblocks impeded any movement through the streets, each one manned by a particular militia group among the many. Whenever we approached any one of these roadblocks, as we did daily, we had to rummage frantically through our pockets to retrieve the correct pass, for grave consequences could ensue if we produced the wrong one.

We had our favorite escorts, and the Muslim one was Selem, a black-haired 16-year-old dressed in military fatigues who always wore an engaging smile. Selem was leading us with his fellow Sunni Muslim fighters through the bullet- and bomb-scarred streets near Beirut's hotel district when he warned us about Phalange snipers on the roof of the nearby Holiday Inn. At an intersection close to the hotel, he told us, "Now, go, but crouch low, run fast, one at a time, and zigzag as you cross the street!" I went first, followed by Ken and Shibley. The last in line, Selem had just started his run when we heard the loud crack of a rifle shot and the sickening thud of a bullet striking a human body. We turned back to see the boy already in shock from a bullet in the upper back and bleeding profusely from a softball-sized exit wound in his lower belly. All we could do was drag him into an alley, where his comrades stuffed his kerchief into the gaping hole, loaded him in the back of a pickup truck and raced six blocks to American University Hospital.

I was determined to follow, but his fellow combatants said no, one declaring, "Gunmen at the hospital won't give you a chance to explain." The rest of that day young Selem stayed foremost in my mind. When night came, I phoned the hospital and was told that Selem had died.

During those dreadful days Ken, Shibley and I had an agreement that if any one of us ever considered a particular situation too dangerous, we would immediately withdraw. That happened more than once. We'd stationed ourselves on the roof of an abandoned building one morning to film machine-gunners as they battled fighters firing rocket-propelled grenades from a concealed perch across the street. For that part of my report, known in the television news business as the "on-camera close," I crouched behind a wall and had begun speaking to the camera when cameraman Ludlow's face alarmed me. One of his eyes was peering through the viewfinder, while the other half-closed eye kept twitching. His mouth hung wide open, as was Shibley's, to lessen the chance that concussions from the grenades would rupture their eardrums. For once the insanity of what we were doing pulled me up short. I stopped talking and told them it was time to leave.

Month after month as the various groups went on battling for control of the city we expanded our personal rules of combat coverage. We decided that whenever possible we would limit our coverage of the fighting to morning hours. Doing so made sense, because our film had to be aboard Middle East Airlines Flight 201 to London by noon so our reports could make the satellite to New York in time for the evening news. This change also limited our exposure to the hazards of street fighting and gave us the much-needed restorative of a quiet lunch, as we rarely had the stomach to eat before going out to cover what we referred to as "boom boom." Afternoons were taken up making contacts with news sources and planning the next day's coverage.

One evening my girlfriend, Karen Brown, and I were in the living room of my second-floor apartment when we heard a commotion outside. I looked out the window to see 20 or so armed men jump out of a truck and run into our building. With no idea of who they were or what group they might belong to, I barricaded our door, told Karen to hide in a closet, turned off the lights and telephoned Squad 16, the Beirut Police Department's paramilitary unit.

The officer who answered said, "How many are there?"

I whispered, "About two dozen, and they're armed to the teeth."

"Oh, that's too many. We can't handle that," and he hung up.

I was angry but not surprised. Beirut's police and even the Lebanese army were no match for the thousands of marauding gunmen who seemed to own the streets. In the darkness I kept watch, and a few minutes later the intruders left the building with a blindfolded man in tow. It was the Lebanese businessman who lived upstairs. When they shoved him into their truck I felt sure we would never see him again, but two days later I met him in our stairwell.

"Welcome back," I said. "I'm glad to see you're all right."

Something that passed for a smile flickered over his lips. "Oh, everything's fine, no problem. It was just a business misunderstanding." He hurried on up the stairs to his apartment and quickly closed the door.

It was like that in Beirut. People often used the civil war as a pretext to cover acts of revenge against neighbors or business competitors. When a grocery store down the block from my apartment was blown up, the neighbors suspected a competing grocer whose store was across the street.

As the lawlessness continued unchecked we saw even greater acts of violence. In broad daylight in the center of Beirut I witnessed the most wanton act of killing I have ever seen. A group of black-clad, ski-masked Christian Phalange Party gunmen lined up about a dozen Muslim laborers from Syria against a building and methodically machine-gunned the lot.

Badly shaken, I must have shown the distress on my face as I ran down the street and into the lobby of the St. George's Hotel. Monsour Brady, the dapper concierge, looked alarmed. "My goodness, Mr. Palmer, whatever is wrong?"

I told him I had just seen a dozen innocent people killed simply because of their religion.

Brady, a Lebanese Christian, shook his head sadly. "Oh, when are my people going to stop killing each other?"

I leaned closer. "It was Christian militiamen who did the killing."

At that Brady's face hardened, and his cold reply has stayed with me for years. "Well, Mr. Palmer, those Christian fighters must have had good reasons for doing what they did."

If that well-educated man could justify such a senseless act in his own mind, I saw little hope for his country.

*

Of course we welcomed any lighter moment, such as the time sniper fire pinned down me, my crew and our driver Tony in a parking lot. During a lull in the shooting we decided to make a break for it. Tony was always a snappy dresser, and as the four of us took off running as fast as we could, his prized new Gucci loafers went flying through the air.

"Tony!" I yelled. "Your Guccis!"

Without breaking stride, he yelled back, "MEESTER PALMAIR, FUCK THE GUCCIS!" For weeks afterward that phrase was our rallying cry.

On another occasion with my office partner Phil Caputo, then a reporter for the Chicago Tribune, I spent a night on a Beirut hilltop with Christian militiamen who were firing mortar rounds at a Muslim-owned car dealership in a valley about half a mile away. They fired a dozen rounds before finally hitting the showroom, which burst into flames and brought cheers from the fighters around us.

Caputo had been a Marine captain in Vietnam, and he could hardly contain himself. "These guys are so incompetent!" he fumed. "It should take three rounds at most. You bracket a target with one round to the right, then a second one to the left. The third should be right on target!"

When Caputo was later shot in both legs at a checkpoint and had to be flown back to the States for medical treatment, I was sorry to see my friend go but envious that he was getting out. Later, Phil wrote *Rumor of War* about Vietnam, and several other best sellers.

*

When Jordan's King Hussein invited a group of reporters to come from Beirut to Amman for lunch we were glad to accept. As we sat at the table with the king and his secretary of defense, they recalled the days when Yasser Arafat had been in Jordan with his troops making war on Hussein. The king at that time had lost control of his own capital, with the Palestinians in control of checkpoints around the city, even stopping Jordanians to ask for their papers. It was the Jordanians' country, but the Palestinians had essentially taken it over after being tossed out of their territory on the West Bank. Some were then living in refugee camps, though many more lived in the capital city of Amman.

The king's palace was high on a hilltop, and he recounted one incident when his situation had become almost untenable. Hussein was a graduate of Sandhurst, the British military school, and after he began to crack down on the Palestinians he was reviewing his troops when fighting broke out, so he retreated into the palace to leave his troops to fight off the attackers. At one point with the palace entirely surrounded, he recalled that the shooting got louder and louder while he tried to read quietly indoors.

At that point in the story he turned to his secretary of defense. "Mr. Secretary, tell these gentlemen about our conversation at the time."

The secretary looked embarrassed. "I'd rather not, Your Majesty."

So King Hussein said, "All right, I'll tell it. Aides were coming to me periodically with updates on the situation, and at one point I asked one of them, 'How would you appraise the military situation?' And the official said, 'Very grave, Your Majesty. There is doubt that we can avoid being overpowered. You should think of getting out.'

I asked him, 'Do you say the situation could be termed very grave?' 'Oh, yes, indeed, Your Majesty. Very grave.' So then I said, 'Would you further state that it's downright shitty?'"

We all laughed uproariously. The secretary of defense hadn't been willing to repeat the word in the presence of the king even thought Hussein himself had used it.

On another occasion I was interviewing Hussein as we walked outside that hilltop palace inside a low wall, with the city of Amman down below. I noticed that his bodyguards seemed agitated about something, so I paused in my questioning.

"Your Majesty, is something wrong here? Your bodyguards seem very concerned about something."

"They're worried that we're too close to the wall." The guards were signaling that he should move away from the wall, because he could be seen from below, and somebody with a 'scoped rifle could shoot him.

One amazing aspect of being in the king's presence was that no one would ever turn his back on the royal person, just like in *The King and I*. Whenever a servant came into his presence, upon leaving that person would back out, making bows as he walked backward all the way across the room. Hussein was so Americanized that I found the persistence of this practice odd.

He had a wife who was American by birth, though of Lebanese descent. His beloved first wife had been unable to produce an heir, so he built her a house on the palace grounds and for dynastic reasons married Queen Noor, the former Lisa Halaby, daughter of Najeeb Halaby, who was John F. Kennedy's secretary of transportation.

*

A few weeks before my assignment in Beirut ended, the NBC News program *Meet the Press* came to the city to tape an interview with PLO leader Yasser Arafat. Palestinian security guards blindfolded all of us—members of the panel, cameramen and sound technicians—then drove us around the city for an hour before leading us into a dingy apartment where we did the interview.

Shibley, our soundman, was always our group's worrier, and as the interview ended and we were preparing to leave, he insisted that we have individual snapshots taken with Arafat.

"We can keep them in our wallets, in case some PLO guys try to give us a hard time."

He had a point, so we did as he suggested. My photo showed a smiling Arafat with his hand on my shoulder. Two weeks later that picture would save my life.

After a day of covering the fighting in the south the crew and I were on our way back to Beirut when, at a checkpoint just blocks from our office, two gunmen stopped our car. We had been stopped many times, but right away we saw that this time was different.

One of the gunmen was clearly in a rage. He examined our passports, then shouted in English, "You, the American"—waving his gun at me—"get out of the car!" I wasn't about to argue. I stood outside the car to put my hands in the air while Ken and Shibley slouched down in the back seat. The two gunmen got into a loud and furious discussion in Arabic. I figured they were talking about me but had no idea what they were saying. With far better Arabic than me, Shibley would understand, so I asked him, "What's going on? What do they want?"

He lowered his head and in a calm, quiet voice said, "John, they say they're going to kill you." The two were Palestinians, Shibley said, and the enraged one's wife and two children had been killed the day before when Israeli warplanes dropped American-made bombs on a refugee camp.

Before I could think of anything to do the two Palestinians ordered Tony, at gunpoint, to drive away with Shibley and Ken, leaving me to their mercy on the otherwise deserted street. I have never been in a tighter spot.

They motioned me to walk ahead of them to the end of an alley where several naked, blood-spattered bodies lay, presumably earlier victims of their rage. They then grabbed and tore my shirt, forcing me to take it off along with my trousers. For once I understood the true meaning of the words "scared stiff." Every muscle in my body was taut. Of the myriad images that raced through my mind, the paramount ones were of my mom and dad back in Tennessee. They always worried so much about me, and now this. I was the most frightened I've ever been in my life.

With my face to the wall and hands over my head I kept repeating, "*Sahaffee, sahaffee*"—the Arabic word for journalist. It seemed to make no difference to the two Palestinians. Then I thought of the Arafat photo.

"I'm a friend of Abou Amar!" I exclaimed, using Arafat's *nom de guerre*. Urgently I jerked my head toward my trousers lying on the ground. "Look in my wallet, the picture!"

As one of the men went through my wallet and retrieved the photo I remembered Arafat's smile, his friendly hand on my shoulder. Would it do the trick?

On seeing the "proof" of my claim the two launched into another loud argument in Arabic, and I prayed they were arguing about the trouble they could bring on themselves by killing Arafat's "friend." One gunman appeared to be arguing for my release, while the other seemed determined to kill me in revenge for his terrible loss. The debate raged on until the first man moved close to me and said in a low voice, "Pick up your things and run as fast as you can."

I scooped up my wallet and trousers and without looking back ran out of the alley, down the street, across a park, then three blocks to my office. Ken, Shibley, and Tony, waiting on our office balcony, waved and called my name when they saw me, while Lillian, our office secretary, shocked at seeing me in such a state of undress, simply covered her eyes as she cried with happiness.

That night I called my boss in London. "It's time for me to leave Beirut." I prayed he wouldn't disagree.

"You're right, John. I just hope you won't find your next assignment too rough."

"I hope I won't either. Hell, it can't be much worse than this."

The smile in his voice carried over the long-distance lines. "NBC News wants you to make plans to move to Paris."

What a relief! Leave battle-torn Beirut for the City of Light!

Unfortunately, finding my replacement took much longer than expected, so several weeks after my scheduled departure date had come and gone I sent NBC headquarters in London a telex: NEXT WEEK I SHALL LEAVE BEIRUT, EITHER FOR PARIS OR HOME TO TENNESSEE. IT'S YOUR CALL.

A few minutes later the machine clacked out the reply: PALMER, YOU ARE "GO" FOR PARIS.

But I couldn't get out of covering one last street battle, and as chance would have it, the fighting broke out on the very day when movers were to pack my belongings for shipment to France. Aware that returning to my apartment that day would be too dangerous, reluctantly I called the movers and directed them to pack up everything and ship it by air, since the Beirut port had gone up in flames weeks before.

I still felt a little shell-shocked myself when I joined my furniture in France a few days later to discover that the movers had packed and flown to Paris the entire contents of my Beirut apartment, including my landlord's stove and refrigerator. NBC paid the very expensive freight bill with no complaints, and I never heard from my Beirut landlord. I was just thrilled to have traded "the Paris of the Middle East" for the real thing.

8

CITY OF LIGHTS

My first challenge in France was the language, which at times I thought might be an insurmountable one. Although I have a pretty good ear for accents and voices and consider myself a fair mimic, the grand old French grammar nearly defeated me. I'd had a little high school French, but because my teacher was not a native speaker I emerged from those classes with an East Tennessee accent, and I never studied French again until I got to Paris. The *Comédie française* had nothing to fear from me.

Finding a place to live turned out to be far easier than mastering the language. My girlfriend Karen had come with me from Beirut to Paris, and we found a fine apartment with a unique inside balcony on Rue Passy in the desirable *6eme arrondissement* near the Museum of Man. With housing taken care of, I quickly felt the need of linguistic help, so I engaged a very pleasant and competent tutor named Sylvie. She could not have been nicer, charming and agreeable, but like some European women then, she washed her hair only occasionally and didn't use deodorant. I had to keep reminding myself, You're in Paris, John. Get over it.

Because Europe and most of Africa was easily reached from Paris, NBC was forever sending me to cover some far-off story. My stay to cover it might be short, or it might be quite long. Nevertheless, determined to persevere at my French, every night that I was at home I had Sylvie come to my apartment to help me make some headway with vocabulary, pronunciation, and grammar *à la française*. I did pretty well on the first two, but after being away on some lengthy assignment I'd come back to Paris to find that every verb tense but the present had flown clean out of my brain.

Sylvie did her best with me, even on the night when, after seven weeks in Africa, I came back to the apartment in a rage. On my way home I'd stopped at a *boulangerie* for bread, then at an *épicerie* where I saw some small sacks of turnips for sale. In a beer garden once I'd seen Germans peel, slice, and salt raw turnips to nibble with their beer, and the idea appealed to me—a bite of turnip, a sip of beer. I waited my turn to be served then asked in my hesitant French for a sack of turnips. Seeing a price of "16" posted, I held out 16 francs.

The little Frenchman behind the counter drew himself up, eyes wide. "*Mais, monsieur, c'est trop cher, même pour les Américains!*" The French people waiting in line behind me all laughed. Dumb American, paying the huge sum of 16 francs for something that cost 16 centimes! It made me furious. I was still fuming when I came back to the apartment to find Sylvie waiting for me, and I really unloaded on her.

"YOU FROGS!" I yelled. "I've had it UP TO HERE"—pointing to my chin—"WITH YOU! I try to speak your blasted language, and the minute people hear my accent, they switch over to English so they can improve theirs. I'm really trying, dammit, and still I get ridiculed!"

"John, John, what in the world has happened?"

I told her about trying to buy the turnips and getting laughed at. Sylvie listened patiently then said, "Well, I'm sorry that's happened to you. But there's one thing you must always remember, John. The French are just as mean to each other as they are to Americans!" At that I had to laugh, and we got down to work on our lessons.

Not everything in Paris was such a struggle. During my third year based in Paris, a marvelous-sounding invitation landed on my desk at the NBC bureau, so I accepted right away. Baron Rothschild—Grand Prix race-car driver, screenwriter, theatrical and film producer, poet, head of the famed banking dynasty and one of the most successful winemakers in the world—was inviting me and a bunch of other journalists for a weekend at his Chateau Lafitte-Rothschild winery near Bordeaux in southwest France. Well, who wouldn't accept that? He even sent a chartered plane to fly us down. Thinking only of the pleasure of it, I didn't stop to wonder why in thunder this famous Frenchman would be inviting me on such a jaunt.

Off I flew with the others on a Saturday morning to be served a lovely brunch as soon as we arrived. That afternoon we toured his *caves* and were treated that night to an elegant seven-course dinner with top-drawer vintages, as delightful as anything could be. Not a word was mentioned about the purpose of the occasion, only a cordial welcome from the baron to the nice reporters who'd been kind enough to come down from Paris. All of us were having the time of our lives, finally struggling up from the dinner table about 11:30 or 12 after a great deal of heady wine.

Next morning we had a tour of the vineyards, learning a great deal from the baron's experts who showed us all the processes involved. Then came the luncheon, with more of the very best French cuisine, a wonderful first course, then the entrée, more delicious wines, a delicate dessert—almost too good to be true.

It was only as we lolled in our chairs feeling extremely fat and happy after that superb lunch that the baron made mention of someone's plans to install an oil refinery not far away, which he *knew* we would understand as a great tragedy for his beautiful wine-making enterprises.

Light slowly dawned in my wine-fuddled brain. This was why we were here! He wanted this bunch of tame journalists to kill any likelihood of that oil refinery becoming a reality. One more stage in my education on the topic of Everybody Wants Something. You'd think I'd have remembered Governor Vandiver's dinner invitation back in Georgia, when I had been on the air just a few weeks. It should have worked the same way with the baron, but I wasn't smart enough to recall the lesson.

And the weekend wasn't over. After Sunday afternoon lunch the baron told us, "Now we're going to play a little game. Here's the game. You go into the *cave*, where each one of you can select any bottle of wine we have in our winery. Watch out for the 1860 wines—they could be vinegar, or they could be the best wines you've ever tasted in your life! Maybe a 1942 would be a better bet for you, who knows? So go down there and look around and choose your bottle to take home with you."

I chose a 15-year-old Chateau Lafitte to take home, resolved to make it last for days back in Paris by rationing myself to tiny sips at a time. After we chose our bottle of wine and got ready to take the plane back to Paris we found a case of wine with each person's name on it—good, fairly recent stuff which we could keep for a year or two before drinking. And after we were bused to the airport we were served more of the same wines on the plane. Wow.

I knew NBC's rule that if you accepted any gift valued at more than $50 you needed to write it up and give the report to your boss, so I sent mine to London. My boss sent me back a teletype: "SOUNDS LIKE A WONDERFUL WEEKEND, THANKS FOR THE FULL REPORT. I HOPE THE MEMORIES WILL STAY WITH YOU FOR A LONG TIME, BECAUSE AS OF THIS DATE YOU WILL NOT

BE ASSIGNED TO COVER ANOTHER WINE STORY DURING THE REST OF YOUR TIME WITH NBC NEWS IN FRANCE."

Not that we did that many wine stories, because the country was virtually awash in the stuff. But it was a good lesson for me, to relearn the propriety of things and be reminded that the mere act of bringing to light what I'd done did not somehow cleanse me. A great lesson in the ethics of professional journalism. Do I regret the weekend? Not on your life.

I had taken part in an earlier wine event when I volunteered for a nighttime ride in a single-engine plane, one of a fleet speeding the year's first bottles of Beaujolais Nouveau from France to England. Our team was competing in the annual race to see who could get the first of the new vintage to a London pub before midnight. We crossed the moonlit English Channel at breathtaking speed, and the instant we landed at Heathrow, waiting confederates loaded those cases of wine and us into cars for a breakneck race with little regard for traffic signals through London's winding and foggy streets. When my group came in sixth, that was one race I was happy to lose.

Whenever my crew and I were on assignment somewhere in France away from Paris we always managed to put up at wonderful old *chateaux* that took guests overnight and served us fabulous meals. My French crew was terrific, but I never got used to their habit of always having wine with the midday meal. Never in the afternoon after they'd poured wine all around at lunch was I any good for work. Two glasses of the stuff would put me straight to sleep, and eventually I figured out I'd have to save the wine-drinking for the end of the day.

*

The African assignment that made me forget my French verbs had been in southern Zaire, to cover the trial of some mercenary soldiers. The courtroom scene struck me as bizarre—African barristers sweltering in English-style judicial robes, their jet-black faces topped by traditional white English-style periwigs. The English model of justice was still practiced in the country. But that didn't cut any ice for the mercenaries. The trial went on for weeks and weeks—almost two months—until the accused were convicted and one of the British mercenaries was sentenced to death.

Told to stay on to the bitter end, I was there to see one of them driven out to a soccer field where the executioners tied him to a post to face the firing squad. No more than 30 feet away from them, we reporters saw his face and heard whatever they said. When the command was given, the rifle squad lined up along their mark, raised their weapons and took aim, waited for a count of "1, 2, 3" and fired. The victim slumped against his bonds, then he opened his eyes and look around. Incredibly, the firing squad had missed their target; he had merely fainted. As the chief executioner walked over to him, the victim opened his eyes blearily and said, "Wha' hoppen? Wha' hoppen?" At that the executioner drew his pistol, pointed it at the man's head, said, "This is wha' hoppen" and shot him dead. That was their kind of justice. Finally I was free to head for Paris again.

On another trip to Africa, my crew and I were in Kinshasa in the old Belgian Congo during the civil war and heard that the fighting was endangering some Belgian copper-mine workers in Kowezi. Told that the French Foreign Legion was coming in to rescue them, we left for Kowezi to check things out. General Mobutu, the corrupt tyrant who ran Zaire with U.S. support, fancied himself something of a pilot, and when some other journalists and I boarded a huge air cargo plane for the flight, there sat General Mobutu at the controls. I felt a little better to see a U.S. Army copilot, knowing he could take over. Mobutu invited us up to the cockpit during the flight to show us what he could do. Scary.

It took us two or three hours to get to Kowezi, where the only shelter we could find was some burned-out cars. So that's where we slept, my camera crew and I, in the back of a couple of burned-out cars. We found an old blanket to lay over the rusted springs for a makeshift bed, and at least it was shelter at night. Scouting around the next day we noticed some men, women and children hiding in the bushes, weeping. When we asked through our translator what had happened, they said another tribe had killed all their men and put them in a house down the road. To check it out, we went directly to that house and opened the door to find rooms chock-full of bodies, stacked shoulder-high one atop the other. It was the worst thing I'd ever seen, so hot, with flies everywhere, and already a horrible, horrible smell.

I told my cameraman, "You have to get these shots."

He shook his head. "This can never be used on the air."

"Of course not, Ken. But let's just document it, because this is an absolute massacre."

Dreadful or not, he took the pictures. In the light of these wholesale murders we figured the Belgian workers were in danger of suffering the same fate, which was why the French Foreign Legion was flying troops in. We watched their planes come in at an unbelievably low altitude, no more than 100 feet, paratroopers jumping out with barely enough time for their 'chutes to open and swing once before they stood on the ground ready to fight. They had to do it that way, for if those paras had jumped from a higher altitude and drifted slowly down, the fighters on the ground would have picked them off in the air. I'd encountered some pretty tough guys in the Middle East, but those Legionnaires were absolutely the toughest military outfit I'd ever seen. Shaved heads, sunbaked, tattooed—just tough. Thugs, you might say, but mostly young guys, and I knew that a lot of people joined the Legion to get out of prison. Those paras looked like they could handle anything the tribal fighters might dish out.

After Ken filmed the massacre I sent a message back to Kinshasa to our fixer who'd stayed there to receive our film and send it on to London. The message about it got through, and I did a story about how terrible the fighting was, Belgian hostages and all the chaos in Zaire, and sent it in. The next day New York sent back word that they planned to lead with our massacre story that night. Tragic though it was, we were gratified to have come up with a story from the depths of Africa that was ours alone.

Later that night as we bedded down in the car to try to rest, before I dozed off I tuned my radio to the BBC as I did every night. Immediately I knew our story was sunk, because the BBC was reporting that the greatest air tragedy in history had happened in the Canary Islands that very day. Two Super 747s, both on the ground, had crashed on the runway and burned, killing about 500 people. Ken heard it too, and we both knew our massacre story was gone. If it ever ran, it might have got 20 seconds or so, but it certainly never became anybody's lead story. The greatest tragedy in the lives of those poor Africans was a mere blip on the larger world screen.

*

While Africa had its share of warfare then and now, it was with the Arab-Israeli conflict still very much alive that two Palestinians and two Germans hijacked an Air France flight from Tel Aviv headed for Paris and took it to Entebbe Airport in Uganda instead, knowing that Uganda's President Idi Amin was sympathetic to the Palestinian cause. The hijackers declared that unless the Israelis released a number of Palestinian prisoners they would begin killing their own Israeli and Jewish hostages. In response, the Israeli government quickly organized and carried out a commando rescue mission with great skill and daring, killing all the hijackers and rescuing about 100 hostages. When the rescued hostages were flown to Paris, I went out to Orly field at 2 a.m. to cover their arrival and to my surprise spotted entertainer and talk-show host, Merv Griffin waiting for the plane.

I walked over to him. "What are you doing here, Merv?"

He told me that his producer was one of the hostages, and he had flown over to be there when his man was returned. Of course, there was much rejoicing when the beleaguered passengers emerged from the plane, with Griffin among the celebrants.

*

The rest of my Paris assignment also involved plenty of travel outside France, much of it in the Middle East. Around that time a U.S. Congressional delegation traveled to Egypt led by Speaker of the House Jim Wright. While they were there, the congressmen and their spouses were taken to see the Pyramids and the Aswan High Dam, all on Uncle Sam's tab. When the group arrived in Cairo for a meeting with Egyptian President Sadat, several reporters, including me, were invited to sit in. Before the session, a congressional aide asked me what would be a good question for Speaker Wright to ask the president, since the group had been out of touch for more than a week.

At that time the biggest news story in the world was a comment Sadat had made, I think to Walter Cronkite or Barbara Walters, that he would go to Jerusalem to talk peace with Golda Meir. So Wright asked Sadat if that was his intention, and Sadat said, "Yes, I will go."

When I reported the exchange my boss at NBC said, "John, are you sure?"

"Undoubtedly. The president of Egypt said in my presence, in answer to that question, that yes, he would go to Jerusalem." I also told them I'd given Jim Wright that question to ask.

Still dubious, my boss said, "You know we'll have to commit a million dollars in equipment, editing, material and personnel to cover this huge thing between Egypt and Israel. You better have this right."

I was scared to death. "Well, I heard Sadat say it, and I know how deeply committed he is to making peace. Believe me, tears were welling in the man's eyes when he said, 'I shall go to Jerusalem.' I know it'll happen."

And Sadat did go, to be met at the airport by Golda Meir. I stayed in Egypt that time without covering the meeting, but throughout that period I was in and out of the Middle East. I'd go back to Beirut to interview Arafat, somewhere else to interview somebody else, cover a breaking story in Amman, then fly off to Africa or wherever else I was sent.

One evening around 11 my boss called from London to tell me a British Airlines plane and a Yugoslav airliner had crashed in midair. "Forty minutes from now there's a flight from de Gaulle airport to Belgrade. You be on it."

I grabbed the suitcase, ran on into the Champs Élysées, jumped in a taxi, and rushed to the airport. With my ticket waiting for me and before the days of rigid airport security, I boarded the plane in short order. Although it was still nighttime when we landed in Belgrade, after I took a taxi to the crash site in a cornfield I could see pieces of planes and bodies lying all around—my first experience of the macabre reality of an air disaster. One plane had flown into the belly of the other, thousands of feet in the sky, and the second plane had come down three miles away. We stayed there until dawn revealed the side of the first plane's fuselage ripped away like a dollhouse, passengers inside still slumped over in their seats, dead.

Another assignment sent me to the Netherlands, where frustrated Moluccan immigrants had taken some schoolchildren and adults hostage. They were seeking fair treatment from the Dutch government and Dutch employers, because they were all holding down menial jobs for quite low wages. The child hostages were rescued first. Then we got a tip that the adult hostage standoff was also about to come to an end. I was in the field watching the building where the hostages were held when the police called out in every language they could muster, but chiefly Dutch, "EVERYBODY GET DOWN! GET DOWN!" Their hope was that the hostages would hear them and do as they were told before the police sprayed the place at head level with gunfire. Luckily the hostages heard them and complied. All the Moluccans terrorists were killed, and the hostages were set free. Afterward cots were set up at the high school gymnasium to provide a place to deal with people expected to suffer from the Stockholm Syndrome. Even though I'd already been there for a month and was desperate to get back to Paris, I was told to stay until all the dead were buried so I could tie the story up.

It was after such long-drawn-out trips that that my girlfriend Karen decided to leave. "We got together because we wanted to be together," she said, "then you go off time and again for six weeks that turn into two months. I'm not staying any longer." She had a point. Known as the guy who always had the suitcase packed at the office, I was ready to leave on a moment's notice. No wonder Karen decided she'd better move on.

*

It was Oct. 16, 1978, and a huge and impatient crowd filled floodlit St. Peter's Square in Rome. They were waiting for the announcement that signaled the election of a new pope, and when a plume of white smoke emerged from the Sistine Chapel's chimney, the cheers went up. A few minutes later Cardinal Felici appeared on the balcony to announce that a new pope had been named in the person of Cardinal Karol Wojtyle. Few in the crowd were familiar with the Polish prelate, and as I sat atop the colonnade fronting the square I heard murmurs, "*Schwarze, schwarze.*" Black, they were saying, he must be black. Some Germans in the crowd, recognizing that the new pope was not Italian, surmised he must be African.

Elected the 263rd successor to St. Peter at age 58, John Paul was the youngest pope in 132 years, the first Polish pope, and the first non-Italian pope in four and a half centuries. The new Pope John Paul also came out onto the balcony to address the assembled throng.

"I have come from a faraway country—far away, but always so close in the communion of faith," he said. When he went on, "I do not know whether I can express myself in your—in our—Italian language," the crowd roared with appreciation, and his next words won them over entirely: "If I make mistakes you will correct me." At that moment, he became the Italians' and everyone else's pope.

Within hours of his election, this modern-thinking new pope who spoke a number of languages conducted an international news conference in several of them, which sent Vatican bureaucrats scurrying to find out what he was saying. Over the next quarter-century he would travel to 129 countries on 104 trips, visiting and revisiting Poland, though never China or Russia. During his years in the Vatican Pope John Paul would, unlike some of his predecessors, create few new programs. Rather, he would seek to clarify and enforce Catholic doctrine, rather than reshape or expand it. The world soon recognized him as a strict theological conservative who attacked abortion and what he called the "culture of death" in general.

It was in June of 1979 that I had the opportunity to cover the Polish pope's first visit home to his native country after his election. Foreshadowing the wider challenge to communism that came a decade later, millions of Poles defied their communist government and turned out to greet him.

I first saw the man up close several months later aboard Papal One en route from Dublin to Boston, the first leg of his trip to the United States. His hands fascinated me: big, creased, workman's hands that swept the air in broad gestures. They were the hands of a man who'd once labored in a rock quarry, as a factory worker, who was an athlete and lifelong outdoorsman, a soccer player, camper, hiker. Solidly built and vigorous, he had a bullish neck and strong, if somewhat stooped, shoulders. He was 5-foot-10, we were told, and weighed 175 pounds, with close-cropped graying hair.

The first stops on his American trip included Boston, Philadelphia, New York and Chicago, all cities with significant Catholic populations where he drew extremely large crowds. Afterward he went to Washington and spent an afternoon with President Carter at the White House, celebrated Mass for 1,500 priests at St. Matthew's Cathedral and led another public Mass afterward on the Mall. Expected to draw as many as one million of the faithful, the Mass on the Mall brought out a far smaller number, and some of those present actually left early, apparently put off by the pope's homily with its stern admonitions against abortion and birth control. He remained unpopular among some American Catholics who favored contraception, ordination of women and allowing priests to marry.

That Mass on the Mall had major implications for me, although I didn't know it at the time. As we waited on the press platform for the event to begin I looked around for someone who might do me a favor and buttonholed an energetic young NBC employee. When I asked her to bring me a cup of hot coffee I hadn't the slightest idea that this person was to become my wife. But that's a story for later. I went my way, she went hers—for the moment.

When the Pope and his entourage left Washington to return to Rome, I took a shuttle flight to New York for a meeting with the new president of NBC News. For a year or so, I had been thinking of returning to the United States after six years overseas as a foreign correspondent. When my European colleagues would ask why I wanted to go home, I would often reply, "Because I miss Halloween." That was a silly answer, but I did miss American holidays, and while I had adjusted to living in the Middle East and in France, I yearned to return. I figured that after six years, you were either destined to remain an expatriate for the rest of you career or you went home. When I made my pitch to Bill Small at his spacious office at NBC headquarters in New York he gave me little encouragement. "You have done very well as an overseas correspondent. Why don't you stay there?" he said. "Besides, I just got here and I have a lot of things to do before I get around to shifting correspondents around."

Disheartened, I returned to Europe. Then, quite unexpectedly, just two weeks later, Small called me at my Paris apartment to say, "Palmer, I am calling to offer you the most prestigious job we have: White House Correspondent."

I was thrilled—so excited that I didn't even ask how much the job paid., "When do you want me in Washington?" I asked, to which he replied, "Yesterday."

*

It was Nov. 4, 1979, a beautiful, crisp day in Paris, when I walked the three blocks from my office up the Champs Élysées to the stylish Le Fouquet's restaurant for my farewell luncheon. After six years as a foreign correspondent for NBC News covering wars, insurrections, shipwrecks, summit conferences, hijackings and plane crashes, at long last I was going home.

My colleagues and I sipped champagne, swapped stories and speculated about my new assignment as White House correspondent before talk quickly turned to a major news development that had taken place in Iran earlier that day. Militant students in Teheran had taken over the U.S. Embassy, seizing dozens of Americans hostages. The stage had been set weeks before when Islamic revolutionaries overthrew Shah Mohammed Reza Pahlevi, further straining an already tense relationship between the U.S. and Iran. Militant students, unrestrained by the new revolutionary government, retaliated by taking over the embassy. This was such a big deal that I told the London-based head of NBC's European operations I was surprised he'd taken the time away from monitoring the situation to fly over for my going-away party. He smiled confidently and took another sip of bubbly.

"This is the kind of story that's likely to be over by the time a correspondent, producer and TV crew hit the ground in Teheran."

We had no idea then that this first major act of terrorism by Islamic militants against the United States would become a seemingly interminable ordeal for the hostages and for our country, or that it was a forerunner of far worse things to come.

On my first morning back in the States I gazed out of my Washington hotel window across Lafayette Park to the White House, where television correspondents stood on the frost-covered north lawn reporting the latest on the Iranian hostage crisis. I would soon join them, for both the American public and the entire Carter administration became quickly consumed by the horrifying impasse.

9

WASHINGTON AND ALL THINGS POLITICAL

I CAN'T SUM UP the White House gig any better than veteran television journalist Bob Schieffer did in his memoir *This Just In*, so I'll let Bob say it for me.

> Covering the White House is the most glamorous job in all of journalism and, in television, the most prestigious. It is

> the place where the networks assign reporters who have been put on the fast track, the testing ground for future stars, and it is the White House correspondent who generally gets more air time on evening news programs than all the other reporters, but I soon learned what other White House reporters knew: It was not always as exciting as it seemed from the outside and could sometimes be downright boring, a place where real reporting was sometimes all but impossible and where you had contact with the president and his staff only when they chose to see you.

Had I heard that comment at the start of my White House assignment I'm sure I would have said "amen" to the first part and ignored the second. It would take time to bring me face to face with the downside of the job, because when it began I was purely thrilled to be where I was.

During my broadcasting career it has been my good fortune to work for some of the best bureau chiefs and producers in the business, ethical men and women who cared very much about news content and who insisted that reporters keep their personal opinions and biases out of their reporting. Sid Davis, my bureau chief at NBC News in Washington, was just such a person. When I was first assigned to cover the White House for the network, Sid told me, "John, there will be long hours and a lot of travel, but anytime you don't pinch yourself as you go to work and walk through the Northwest Gate into the White House, thinking how lucky you are to be covering the beat, just let me know and I'll pull you out."

Anyone who has visited the White House press room is astonished at the cramped quarters. Everything you need to do your work is there—computers, phones, fax machines, television monitors—but reporters sit side by side, practically rubbing shoulders, in tiny little booths. It's very democratic. If one of us has a cold or the flu, we all get it. You quickly learn a great deal about the lives of your fellow cellmates. It's impossible to keep secrets, since conversation with wives, husbands and children and are inevitably overheard. We generally abided by the same rule as Las Vegas: what happens in the White House booth stays in the White House booth.

During my first White House assignment I shared the booth with Judy Woodruff and Bill Lynch. Later, at different times, I was joined in our NBC News cubicle by Andrea Mitchell, Emery King, Jim Mikaszewski, Claire Shipman, David Bloom, Brian Williams, David Gregory, Bob Kur and Campbell Brown—fine reporters all. Despite our close quarters, for the most part we worked well together, sharing sources and information. Often our professional lives were combined with social friendships, so that many became close, lasting friends of mine, as did others in the White House press corps, such as AP's chief correspondent Terry Hunt, the best deadline writer and reporter I've ever known.

I shared the NBC News booth with David Bloom for just two years before he moved on to co-anchor *Weekend Today* and then leave the relative comfort of the studio to cover the U.S. invasion of Iraq where, in short order, he became a familiar face and voice to millions of Americans. An embedded reporter with the U.S. Army's 3rd Infantry Division, on April 6, 2003, to everyone's great sadness, David died after suffering a pulmonary embolism at age 39. His death affected the NBC family like no other in recent memory, and 11 days after he died I wrote the following tribute, which I sent to his widow, Melanie.

> When older or retired television news reporters gather, they often lament the current state of the profession. We talk about how things used to be, about our commitment to ethics and hard work, about how much attention we paid to the facts, how hard we tried to keep our opinions out of the story, how we deplored the blurring of the lines between news and entertainment. We often wondered aloud if the new generation of television news reporters could measure up.

Well, the new kid, David Bloom, measured up and then some. His viewers knew that, and those of us who worked with him knew that. We watched in awe as David roared across the Iraqi desert heading for Baghdad, perched atop his specially outfitted tank, broadcasting live, night after night, day after day.

With desert sand in his hair and gesturing with his arms, he gave a human face to the war, and we marveled at his boyish enthusiasm and energy, his attention to the big picture while focusing on the personal stories of the soldiers in his unit. There were times, on and off camera, when he offered his satellite telephone to soldiers so they could make that treasured phone call home, as he did most every day to his wife Melanie and their three young daughters.

David's death was a shock, and it made us all better understand the terrible loss and pain that so many other Americans have known when dreaded news came from the battlefield in Iraq. He died not from a bullet but from a blood clot. I can hear him now, complaining. "John, isn't it ironic to go through all this and then die on the battlefield from a pulmonary embolism? Shit,who would have thought?"

David was a fine writer, but he had the maddening habit of reading his copy aloud as he wrote it to see how it sounded. "I write for the ear," he often said, "not for the eye." We often had to shush him, fearing the folks next door in the CBS booth would be listening and know what story we were working on. He was very competitive when he was onto a scoop. His eyes would brighten up, then he'd say, "We're gonna smoke the competition tonight." And he often did.

When things got boring at the White House, David had the uncanny ability to take an instant power nap. He'd fall fast asleep, sitting upright next to me in his chair, and wake up ten minutes later refreshed. It's a trait that must have served him well during the nonstop dash across the Iraqi desert with the 3rd Army as he reported live, on the air, hour after hour.

In one of his last reports David told us why he was there. "If we send young people to war, we ought to show the American people back home what it's like." And that was what he did until the day he left us.

As I learned my way around the Carter White House, some of those days were easy and some not so great. For anyone covering the presidency for a major news organization, as I was for NBC, I found out after a while that you could ask to see the president if you didn't abuse the privilege and if it wasn't a formal interview. I was working on an environmental piece and wanted to ask President Carter some specific questions about his environmental policy, so I went to White House Press Secretary Jody Powell.

"Could I see the president today or tomorrow, sometime this week? No more than six minutes? I'm working on a piece on the environment, and I'd like to be clear on his environmental policy. No shooting, not on camera, just a few quotes when he has a few minutes."

I was ready for Jody to say yes when he shook his head. "Sorry, John, not today. He's wearing his ass on his shoulder."

Had I heard him right? "I beg your pardon?"

Powell said, "I thought you were from Tennessee."

"I am. What's that got to do with anything?"

"You've never heard that someone's wearing his ass on his shoulder?"

"Never."

"Well, it means they're out of sorts. He's rejecting every letter that comes to his desk because of a smudge on the paper or a missing middle initial, so he's wearing his ass on his shoulder today. You know the first lady's out of town—she's been gone three days—and he's so accustomed to bouncing thoughts off her that he gets like this when she leaves. They're true partners. They talk on the phone while she's away, but for him it's not the same. If I were to let you go in there now it would not be a good session. I don't know how it'll be tomorrow, so let's put this on abeyance for now."

Even though I never did add the expression "ass on the shoulder" to my vocabulary, I now had a good idea what those who did use it meant.

Times were less stressful when the Carters' travels took us down to Plains, Georgia, that tiny town that was their home and site of their peanut business. Reporters and crews stayed in the Best Western motel there, because that was the best housing around. The press secretary, the press, even visiting dignitaries had to stay at the motel. When there wasn't much to report we'd organize softball games, usually the press against the Secret Service, which the agents always won because they were in such great shape and had such superb reflexes.

We generally had to deal with so many weighty matters that whenever I could I tried to inject a little humor into my dealings with the president. At one point in Washington someone had thrown a wild turkey over the White House fence that caused quite a stir. The Secret Service had to chase the bird all over the White House lawn with the turkey running like mad, agents in hot pursuit until they captured it. It was a topic of considerable amusement, so at the first chance when we were with President and Mrs. Carter I said, "Mr. President, did you ever catch that turkey?"

After I asked that question expecting some light-hearted answer Rosalyn Carter snapped her head around to glare at me. Her husband had already been in office long enough to incur a great deal of criticism, with people saying he'd lost his way and his approval rating dropping below 40%. She took my remark to imply that the president was the turkey. That was something I would never have insinuated, nor do I know any other reporter or person who'd say such a thing to the president. By then she was just so hypersensitive that she took offense at the slightest remark.

One Sunday we waited on the White House lawn for the helicopter to bring the Carters back from Camp David on one of those occasions when the president's brother, Billy, had done some notorious thing to upset the family. As the president emerged from the helicopter and began walking toward the Diplomatic Entrance to the White House, we all wanted to ask him about Billy. I knew that to ask straightforwardly, "What about Brother Billy?" wouldn't hack it.

Aware of our shared love of fishing, I waited until he came close to me to say, "Catch a lot of them today, did you, Mr. President?" At that he stopped and, like any fisherman, had a story to tell. He'd begun telling me about his catch, "I got this big brown trout—" when a cameraman behind me started filming. Then I said, "Now tell me about your brother Billy."

Those steely-blue eyes flashed fire, because I'd sandbagged him with the camera rolling. He couldn't just shoot me a dirty look and a hiss and walk away. He mustered up some answer like, "It's a family situation and it's being handled," and that was that. But afterward he was pretty guarded in his dealings with me. At least I'd gotten a comment from him, which was more than anybody else got. Later on when I tried a similar ploy, he gave me a glance that meant, We've been down this road before and this time I won't bite. The rest of the time he was in office he was wary of me, yet afterward I went down to his cabin in the Georgia mountains to go fishing and we had a good time. Even at that late date I managed to make another remark that didn't set well with him. I guess, as Flip Wilson used to say, the devil made me do it.

After a while we learned that sometimes when we'd thought President Carter was at that wonderful presidential retreat Camp David he'd actually slipped away to go deep-sea fishing off the Carolina coast or to some other spot, accompanied only by the Secret Service agents who never left his side. The press viewed that as not playing fair, because wherever the president travels a small group of reporters are supposed to travel with him. I understood his wanting to get away without an entourage, but by rights the press should have at least been given a statement saying "The president is in such-and-such an area today." Anything can happen, and we never forgot how Franklin Roosevelt died while having his portrait painted at the Little White House in Warm Springs, Georgia, as the press waited for him miles away at a picnic.

*

For me, the hostage story so lightly dismissed at that relaxed Paris *déjeuner* was one I would revisit time and again as I and other members of the White House press corps went about doing our jobs. Our coverage was to extend over many months of fruitless negotiations with authorities in Iran. The frustration felt by President Carter and members of his administration escalated as more and more time passed with no progress. Day in and day out the crisis dominated the news. Every night ABC News ran an hour-long special called *America Held Hostage*, a program that would eventually become *Nightline*. With each nightly newscast television commentators ticked off the lengthening days of captivity. Church bells tolled to remind Americans of their fellow citizens' plight.

Pressure began to build on Carter to take action. He first applied an economic squeeze by halting oil imports from Iran and freezing Iranian assets in the United States, then launched diplomatic initiatives to free the hostages, all to no avail. Contending that he had no time to spare for partisan politics, Carter then adopted what became known as the Rose Garden Strategy. He stayed at the White House and concentrated his efforts on anything that might release the hostages from their cruel predicament, even declining important political appearances that might have countered the efforts of Sen. Ted Kennedy, his rival for the Democrat Party's Presidential nomination, who was then campaigning hard in hopes of denying Carter a second term.

Those of us covering the White House didn't know it at the time, but just two days after the seizure of the U.S. Embassy in Teheran President Carter had ordered the Joint Chiefs of Staff to make contingency plans to rescue the hostages in the event they were put on trial and sentenced to death. With some modifications this would become the actual military plan put into operation by the Pentagon months later in a bold rescue attempt.

On the afternoon of April 24, 1980, the White House press office established an earlier lid than usual at 5 p.m., meaning there would be no more news briefings, press releases or statements issued that day. Glad to get home at a reasonable hour, I was reading in my Georgetown living room shortly before 10 o'clock that evening when the phone rang. The caller was Herb Brubaker, a desk editor at the NBC Washington Bureau. "It may have been a crank," he said, "but a guy just phoned about a lot of unusual activity at the White House tonight. You might want to check it out."

"Any idea who it was?"

"I wish I knew. The guy hung up without giving his name."

"Okay, Herb, I'll handle it." I then made what I viewed as a routine call to the press duty officer at the White House. "Anything out of the ordinary happening tonight?"

"I don't see anyone," he said, a reply that struck me as odd.

"You sure there's nothing unusual going on?"

He gave the same answer: "I don't see anyone."

At that my reporter's antennae went up. When you ask somebody if anything's going on and get such an evasive reply you'd best pay attention, and I did. I changed into a suit and tie, grabbed my IFB (the personal earpiece that allows television reporters to hear the control room while on the air), and drove the ten blocks to the White House as fast as traffic allowed.

I must have been operating on intuition, luck or a little of both. Whatever the impulse, heading for the White House that night was one of the best decisions of my career. When I showed my press pass at the Northwest Gate I knew my hunch had been right. A dozen government limos lined West Executive Drive, a dozen chauffeurs standing around waiting.

I spoke to the gate guard in as casual a voice as I could muster. "Gee, a lot going on here tonight, huh?"

"You bet," he said. "Everybody who's anybody. Head of the CIA, Joint Chiefs of Staff, people from State, they are all here."

I hurried up the White House driveway past the curtained windows of the West Wing executive offices to the press briefing room. The place was deserted except for two housekeepers cleaning up piles of newspapers and trash left by the dozens of other reporters who'd peeled out early along with me. Now I understood. That early closure by the press office was to avoid the chance of a reporter's premature discovery that something was up. The ploy worked, because we'd all cheerfully gone home oblivious of the drama playing out through the day down the hall in the Oval Office.

In the lower press office I found the duty officer I'd spoken with earlier from home, feet up on the desk, watching a basketball game on television. He turned in his chair, startled to see me. "What are you doing here? I told you I didn't see anything," he said.

I was furious. He had purposely lied to me, using the pretext of watching television so he could say he hadn't seen anyone.

Posted a few feet away at the door leading to the Rose Garden stood a Secret Service agent, a sure indication that the president was either in the Oval Office or somewhere else in the West Wing. Something big was definitely up. I resolved to stick around to find out what was going on.

After I took the ramp to Press Secretary Powell's upper-level office at a run I was surprised to find more than a dozen White House staffers crammed shoulder to shoulder into Powell's outer office. They were obviously trying to stay out of sight in case a reporter should wander into the briefing room and spot the staff still on the job at 11 p.m.

I knew many of them well and asked several what was up. "Nothing," they said, turning away, as if I had the plague. They'd clearly been there for hours, because I saw a stack of plates encrusted with leftover lasagna piled on a desk in the corner. The West Wing stonewall held firm.

Finally Rex Granum, a deputy press secretary and friend, walked over to me. "John, we have nothing for you on this."

By then I'd been around long enough to recognize the classic White House response from officials not yet in a position to disclose information, yet not wanting to lie to a reporter.

Still nobody revealed a thing. I remained the only reporter at the White House for what promised to be a long, frustrating night. I called Washington Bureau chief Sid Davis and told him what I knew, which was very little. There was clearly an international crisis of some kind, but so far I'd been unable to discover what it was.

"Keep working on it," Sid said. He then alerted network officials in New York, dispatched a television crew to me at the White House and sent reporters and crews to the Pentagon, State Department and the Capitol. Within a very short time all the bases were covered.

Now my anxieties set in. No matter how much I appreciated Sid's encouragement and tactical support, I'd been covering the White House for just under six months, and I began to worry that I might be misreading the gravity of the situation. All I could do was to keep questioning anybody I could find.

At one point a national security official intentionally misled me, claiming there was "a problem at the U.S. embassy in Bogotá, Colombia, that's been cleared up." I didn't buy it. Not a big enough deal to warrant this kind of a West Wing turnout.

As soon as Granum saw my frustration he called me into his office. "We may be a lot of things around here," he said, "but we're not liars, and you've just been lied to."

After more phone calls I finally learned it was a lot bigger than Bogotá. It was about the hostages from Teheran.

Half an hour later someone from the press secretary's office came for me, ushering me up the ramp to confront an angry Jody Powell. I'd never seen him so upset. He popped his challenge straight out: "What are you doing here, Palmer?"

"I know there's some kind of international crisis, maybe to do with the hostages in Iran. I'm the only reporter here, and if nobody will cooperate and give me information I'll have to go on the air with what information I have."

"You're a goddamn fool," Powell yelled, "if you go on the air from the White House and say there's an international crisis but you don't know what the hell it is!"

At that moment I got a break. A beacon of light splashed across the White House lawn just outside Powell's window. It was NBC cameraman Vo Wuynh setting up his camera and lights so I could go live from the White House lawn to the network, if and when I actually had enough information to go on the air.

I told Powell, "I'm going ahead to broadcast what information I have. You can watch it live in a couple of minutes when NBC News breaks into the *Tonight* show for my report, or you can open your window and hear me on the lawn."

It was a colossal bluff. Before I left his office I hedged. "If I decide to wait till you give me the official White House version of what happened, will you give me a 15-minute jump over other reporters on the story?"

Powell nodded in the affirmative and turned away. I hurried back to my press room cubicle for another call to Sid.

Sid echoed Powell. "You can't go on the air without knowing what the crisis is."

"I know. I know." But before I had time to say more I heard a loud knock at my door. It was Powell's assistant, saying Jody wanted to see me immediately.

I walked into his office a second time to find him standing at the window with his back to me. Assuming a calm I definitely didn't feel, I'd barely had time to take a seat on the couch when he turned and handed me a single sheet of paper.

"Read this. When you're done, you can ask me three questions—only three—and then get the hell out of here."

He was even more upset and angry than before. I took the paper and read as fast as I could. It was typed White House statement with several notations penciled along the margins:

> The President has ordered the cancellation of an operation in Iran which was underway to prepare for the rescue of our hostages. The mission was terminated because of equipment failure. During the subsequent withdrawal of American personnel, there was a collision between our aircraft on the ground in a remote desert location in Iran. There were no military hostilities. The President deeply regrets that eight American crewmembers of two aircraft were killed and others were injured. Americans involved in that operation have now been airlifted from Iran and those who were injured are being given medical treatment and are expected to recover. This mission was not motivated by hostility toward Iran or the Iranian people and there were no Iranian casualties. Preparations for this rescue mission were ordered for humanitarian reasons to protect the national interests of this country and to alleviate international tensions. The President accepts full responsibility for the decision to attempt the rescue. The nation is deeply grateful to the brave men who were preparing to rescue our hostages in Teheran. The United States continues to hold the government of Iran responsible for the safety of the American hostages. The United States remains determined to obtain their safe release at the very earliest possible date.

I was stunned. During the many months of preparation, this top-secret military operation to rescue the hostages must have been planned and rehearsed over and over. Yet not the slightest hint had ever leaked out.

When I finished reading Powell said, "You have about one minute to ask your three questions."

I was ready. "What was the equipment failure that caused the mission to be aborted?"

"A helicopter problem. Next question!"

"How did the eight Americans die?"

"An aircraft collision as they were pulling out. There was a fire. Last question!"

"When and exactly where did this happen?"

"A few hours ago, in the Iranian desert. I can't tell you exactly where. Now you're done."

I was getting up to leave when I saw tears in Powell's eyes. Tears not only for the tragic loss of life and failed rescue attempt, but also tears, I was sure, for the Carter presidency, which now faced a very difficult uphill battle if there was to be a second term.

As I moved toward the door Powell said, "I want you to hold off reporting this until I can call the wire services."

Well aware of the White House tradition that the first call-out on breaking news goes to the wire-service reporters before the television networks and the major newspapers get the word, in this case I felt that tradition didn't apply. I'd worked the story all evening, alone, at the White House.

"I can't hold off," I said. "I have to go with it right away." It was nearly 1 a.m., and the *Tonight* show was about to go off the air on the East Coast. The network would soon shut down for the night, leaving me no audience.

I reminded Powell of the deal we'd struck earlier—that if I held off going on the air until the White House could lay out all the facts of what happened, he owed me a 15-minute jump on reporting the story I'd sat on all evening. With a look that told me he'd accepted the inevitable, Powell waved me out the door.

My heart was pounding when I took my place in front of Vo Wuynh's camera and heard the announcer's voice in my ear. "We interrupt our regularly scheduled programming to bring you this special report. Here is NBC News White House Correspondent John Palmer."

While I had my scoop, the biggest of my career, my excitement was tempered by the awareness of what a tragic day this had been for our country, for a deeply disappointed president, for those who had died in the rescue attempt, for the families and for the hostages themselves who now faced an even more uncertain fate.

The rest of the story eventually came out. President Carter had aborted the rescue attempt after a sandstorm damaged three of the eight helicopters and, to make matters worse, a helicopter and C-130 transport had collided as they were evacuating the desert staging area. In his book *Keeping Faith* President Carter would describe this as "one of the worst days of my life."

*

The Democratic Party chose their nominee after a very close-run race between Carter and Sen. Ted Kennedy. Carter had so many strikes against his record in office that Kennedy came close to toppling him, and Kennedy had wanted it very badly. But in the end his party chose Carter as their candidate, and in Madison Square Garden at the Democratic National Convention once his renomination was assured, the president of the United States had to trot around that stage with no more dignity than a puppy dog to seize Kennedy's hand and raise it in the air for the traditional party unity shot. That's how ungracious Kennedy was about losing the nomination.

In spite of his absorption with the hostages, Carter knew that he'd have to hit the campaign trail to win re-election, so, reluctantly, he did. I traveled with him on Air Force One for many weeks during that campaign. The most memorable stop for me was Sullivan County, Tennessee, where I was born and reared, and before we landed I looked out the window to see the Dobyns-Bennett High School Band in their maroon-and-gray uniforms lined up at the airport to greet us. I felt so proud, seeing those school colors and that familiar band again. We journalists were about to leave the plane by the back door as we always did when a presidential aide came back. "John, the president wants to see you up front."

I went to the forward cabin to find President Carter waiting with a smile. "I understand this is your territory here."

"Yes sir, it is. That's my old high school band playing out there."

"Then come on and walk down the front steps with me today."

Whether anybody on the ground thought anything of it I don't know, but I certainly appreciated his kindness.

On that one stop in traditionally Republican East Tennessee our motorcade headed for the county seat of Blountville where Carter was to speak. It was drizzling rain, and fortunately somebody had thought to set up a tent. Now, where would you get a tent in a small East Tennessee town? Why, from the funeral home. They're the ones with tents. But when we drove up I was appalled to see the president taking his place behind a microphone under a tent flap with CARTER FUNERAL HOME spelled out on it. The photographers had already zeroed in, framing Jimmy Carter under the two words CARTER FUNERAL. When that picture appeared in a lot of papers across the country it was already apparent to most people that he was going to lose, so I can't imagine the funeral home tent contributed to his loss.

It was a short appearance, and CBS Correspondent Lesley Stahl and I soon were in the back seat of one of the cars for the return to the airport. Along the way city-bred Lesley commented, "Gosh, look at all these dilapidated barns."

I thought I'd provide a little rural education. "Those are tobacco barns. Can't you see the beauty in them?"

She stared at me as if I were nuts. "Beauty in a tobacco barn?"

"Sure. Look, there's another barn up that holler."

Lesley was really out of her depth in East Tennessee. "What's a holler?"

"It's a kind of little valley, and you'll see a lot of tobacco barns up in those hollers. They're truly a thing of beauty."

"Still look dilapidated to me. What do they put in there?"

"Tobacco, sometimes hay."

"But it's got all those holes in it, all those slats. The rain can come in."

I persisted. "It's an absolute thing of beauty, Lesley, all weathered and gray. Most of them may not be used any more, but they're still just beautiful in this lovely countryside."

In *The Wizard of Oz* Judy Garland got it right. Regardless of where you're from, there's just no place like home.

Finally Lesley gave in, at least enough to keep me quiet. "All right, I agree it's kind of charming. But there are so many of these dilapidated barns!"

Unbeknownst to either of us, our driver, from the local telephone company, had a tape recorder going beside him in the front seat. While I explained the beauties of rural Tennessee he was getting it all down on tape. Thank goodness I stood up as well as I did for my home country, because The Education of Lesley Stahl about a holler, a tobacco barn and why they're so beautiful later appeared in some local publication. I was glad I hadn't said anything I might have regretted when it came out.

*

Another painful episode of Carter's presidency was his decision not to allow the U.S. Olympic team to participate in the Moscow Olympics of 1980. The Russians had invaded Afghanistan, which was regarded as a sovereign country even if not a particularly reputable one and the president believed that stern consequences must follow such a blatant act of aggression. Some sanctions had already been invoked—withholding the sale of wheat and some other commodities—and he believed even harsher measures were in order. A great deal was at stake monetarily, particularly for NBC, which had the contract to cover the 1980 Olympic games in Moscow, for if no American teams took part, Americans were unlikely to watch the coverage.

Rumors had flown, although no one really believed the president would take such a major step as to keep the U.S. teams at home since American athletes had trained for those games for four years. Politics were not uppermost in any of their minds, as they, like most people, understood the Olympics as above politics. All of us in the White House press corps gathered in the East Room for a meeting with the athletes to hear what President Carter had to say about it.

I stood in the back of the room with the athletes in front facing the podium. When the president walked in and took his place, he told them: "I'm sorry it falls on you to take this burden of consequence, because you aren't involved in politics, and you've trained so hard. In fact, it breaks my heart to have to say this," and even from our place in the back of the room we could see tears welling in the president's eyes, "but you're not going to Moscow."

It came as a tremendous shock to everyone. Right away, you could see that he was absolutely intransigent on the point. No one spoke up or said a thing, because it was clearly a *fait accompli.*

We could hear some of the athletes weeping and see them wiping their eyes. It was a terrible blow, and many of them felt strongly that when it comes to the Olympics, the games should foster international good will, not be made a tool to penalize another country. As head of a democratic government the president didn't have the direct power to forbid them to go—that would be up to the Olympics Committee. Nevertheless he had real power to keep it from happening, because whenever a U.S. team goes to the Olympics the government provides considerable logistic support, and if the president withdraws that support, U.S. participation becomes essentially a nonstarter.

That decision didn't help Carter's image any either, but his presidency was already winding down and he didn't have much to lose.

I'm sure he did it because he thought it was the right thing to do, as military aggression should not be rewarded. On the other hand, many people thought that such punitive action was the United Nations' role and not the role of any one country. As for me, I was profoundly affected by seeing the president's tears and knowing what pain those athletes felt as well.

Afterward I got a call from an NBC executive asking about the president's decision. NBC had insurance, fortunately, with a provision that damages would be paid if the United States didn't participate, but the network would lose money all the same. Corporate NBC was the entity with the Olympics contract, and there's always a firewall between NBC News and the rest of the company so I was somewhat reluctant to take the call.

"Is this for sure?" the executive wanted to know.

I said, "You just saw it in television—the president of the United States said we're not going. Whether you agree with the decision or not, it's reality. No, I think President Carter meant what he said."

*

American voters may not realize that when you're first elected to the Senate or the House, you attend regular classes to learn how to do your job. Here's how you pass a bill, here's how to markup a bill, here's what happens then, here's where you get your postage stamps, here's where you get furniture from the furniture pool, here's how we choose who gets which office space. They teach it all to the newcomers in Congress, but there was nothing like that for the White House until 2004, when author Stephen Williams published a book entitled *How to Be President: What to Do and Where to Go Once You're in Office*. Such a book never existed when Ronald Reagan or his successors took office, and there were no classes for the incoming president.

In the Oval Office its on-the-job training, and every president has his own management style. Although he always kept himself at a distance, President Carter knew two or three hundred people who worked for him on a first-name basis, knew about their families, all the things that mattered to them. For a politician, that's an invaluable attribute.

He also knew what jobs those people did and could probably do them himself, if he had to, in a pinch. Deeply involved in the workings of the government though he was, he had difficulty delegating authority, which is the mark of a good manager. He couldn't help immersing himself in the nitty-gritty.

A story made the rounds about big disputes over who was to use the White House tennis courts on weekends. In the end, supposedly, Carter took the sign-up clipboard and put it on his own desk. "All right," he's alleged to have said, "Anybody who wants to play tennis will have to see me." If such a thing really did happen people would have viewed it as a waste of time on the president's part. Whether it's true or not, the story was told to me, and it's a good story that bears repeating. It certainly illustrates the fact that he was known for his micromanagement.

If Jimmy Carter were the captain of a ship that hit the rocks—he was a Navy veteran, after all—he'd probably be down below fixing whatever needed fixing, because he'd know that kind of detail and pride himself on it. In a similar situation, his successor Reagan would be up on the bridge, with no idea how the engine operated, whether it ran on diesel fuel or coal, or even why the boat floated. But he'd handle it in his own inimitable way. "Boys," he'd say, "there are rocks over on the right, and rocks over on the left. Now I want you to take it right down the middle." Reagan was so different from Carter—he was a big-picture guy.

*

The last stop of Carter's campaign tour was on the night before the election, in Seattle, Washington. After Carter made his final speech in an airplane hangar there, we all dashed out to board Air

Force One. It had been a grueling campaign both for the president and for those of us who covered it. Only later did Jody Powell tell me what had happened on the flight. While Carter was speaking in the hangar Jody had been on the phone with their pollster, who told him, "It's gone. It'll be a landslide. No chance." Incredible as it seems, the pollsters know these things before the first vote is cast, because their computers spit it out.

Relieved to be done campaigning, Carter got on the plane. "Well, that's the last one," he said. Within a few minutes Jody was calling him to give him the pollster's report, so Carter knew then that it would go against him, and apparently, in his forward cabin with just his aides, he wept on the trip back east. Now, I don't care what kind of president you are, I believe every president tries to do the best he can in office. If you did your level best and worked as hard as you could to be a good president, getting turned down after so much effort has to fall on you as a terrible blow. Carter had had so much working against him—double-digit inflation, hostages held in Iran, complaints about his isolation inside the White House, the Panama Canal turnover—it all added up. It was bad and he knew it.

We flew back to Georgia, landing at dawn on a rainy day, then took helicopters to a baseball diamond near his house in Plains. Rosalyn was there to meet him. Although he'd been given the bad news on the plane, apparently, the President had not called her with the bad news. Out on that field, when the two of them put their heads together and walked to an awaiting car that morning, you could tell that the pain of politics had really hit home.

She was more than hurt, she was truly angry. She'd wanted him to run again. In Mrs. Carter's eyes, you were either for 'em or agin 'em, no middle ground.

That night, after we were back in the White House, the president was severely criticized again after he went to the Sheraton Hotel to concede the election while the polls were still open in California and other western states. Many Democrats believed he caused other Democratic candidates in the west to lose because of his early concession speech.

Ronald Reagan was in the shower at his home in California when he was told, "The White House is calling, sir. The president's on the phone for you."

Carter was calling to say that he was conceding the election and congratulated Reagan.

The next morning Carter invited a select few of the White House press corps into the Oval Office for a brief chat before he left for Camp David. It was a poignant scene, the rejected president sitting behind his desk with his worn old briefcase atop it next to the light tan raincoat he often wore. His eyes were bloodshot, probably both from lack of sleep and many tears shed. I happened to look at his hands—Carter has extremely fair skin—and was shocked to see that the skin on their backs had absolutely worn through, all scabbed from shaking so many hands for months. It reminded me of a prizefighter whose hands must take terrible punishment. The difference was that Carter was expected to press the flesh with no heavy gloves to protect him. If it was that bad on the outside, what must he have felt like inside?

He spelled out for us all the things he believed he'd accomplished in his four years as president. One of the big ones was the Panama Canal. "It's their canal," he said. Reagan had campaigned about the canal, saying, "We built it, it's ours." But Carter said that while we'd had it for nearly a hundred years, it was in their country and their people had dug it with our money. He believed there were certain things that are right to do, and giving these people their canal was one of them. He also told us he was grateful that nobody had died in any war "on my watch."

After some further remarks he glanced out to see the helicopter waiting for him on the lawn and got up. "Well, it's time to go," he said. He started out with his briefcase and raincoat, then stopped at the door and turned back to us.

"I want you to remember, I'll still be around until January 20.

Don't forget, I'm still president of the United States. Until then I make the decisions, and I want you all to know and reflect on the fact." And with that he was gone.

After his November defeat Carter, with the assistance of Algerian intermediaries, launched a new round of negotiations that would eventually bring the hostages safely home. As soon as the United States released almost $8 billion in frozen Iranian assets, and just as President Reagan was taking the oath of office on Jan. 20, 1981, the nation rejoiced when the new Reagan White House press office announced the freeing of 52 hostages after a terrifying ordeal of 444 days in captivity.

All in all, the crisis had cost the United States millions of dollars and the lives of eight American servicemen, which damaged American prestige around the world. It all but paralyzed the final year of the Carter presidency and played a major part in Carter's reelection defeat.

When one president leaves office and a new one comes in, the transition comes at 12 noon on Jan. 20 while the new president is taking the oath of office. It's a marvelously impressive thing to see the way power is transferred in a democracy, without a shot fired. So simple, so beautiful, perfectly quiet and smooth. I noticed a carpenter taking the nameplates off the chairbacks in the cabinet room and putting new ones on, because a new cabinet was coming in. A new rug chosen by the new president was laid in the Oval Office. The Oval Office décor was changed in a few hours' time. People had cleaned out their desks and were going out to their cars with their arms full of personal belongings. Photographs of the Carters and their family had come down, and pictures of the Reagans and their family went up.

Two days after the White House changed hands I flew with former President Carter to a U.S. military hospital in Germany where he met privately with each of those 52 newly freed Americans whose plight had been his overriding concern for so many months. In spite of the Secret Service's strong objections he insisted on seeing the liberated captives alone. "I owe it to them," he said. The agents said, "But Mr. President, some of those people are extremely angry with you. Some may even want revenge. You may be attacked. Don't go in alone." He refused, because he felt that out of respect for all the hostages had suffered he ought to do and had to do it. A courageous act, in my view.

It was a tearful, yet joyful ending, undoubtedly one that Carter wished had come while he still held office. Would it have made any difference in the election? Who knows? So much of world history seems to hinge merely on timing.

10

ENTER THE GREAT COMMUNICATOR

I MET RONALD REAGAN in December of 1980, when NBC News assigned me to cover the president-elect's activities in California. Day after day, along with a dozen or so other reporters, I staked out his home in the Pacific Palisades section of Los Angeles, where we witnessed the comings and goings of potential cabinet appointees and senior staffers who would soon be household names. It was boring at times, but at least we were well supplied with snacks and cold drinks bought from an enterprising young neighbor lad who turned out to be George Burns's grandson. It was that kind of neighborhood.

Now and then Reagan would invite us in for a chat or to photograph him in his study as he worked on his inaugural address, writing in longhand on a large yellow pad. When he told us he'd just phoned to ask Malcolm Baldridge to serve as his secretary of commerce, he said Mrs. Baldridge had answered the phone, telling the president-elect that her husband couldn't possibly take the call because he was out in the corral breaking a horse. Reagan loved that.

"That man has his priorities straight!" Reagan said. "He's the right man for the job!"

An hour later Baldridge called back to accept and became one of the longest-serving secretaries of commerce ever, until his tragic death in a rodeo accident in 1987.

The day soon came when the Reagans had to leave their beloved California for Washington and the White House. For those of us watching the departure it was a poignant moment. As the two of them walked out of their home for the last time, a wistful look came over Ronald Reagan's face and he turned and stared at the front door for a full minute, deep in thought. Although that house was soon sold and they never lived there again, during his presidency the Reagans would frequently return to California, dividing their time between Rancho Cielo, in the hills above Santa Barbara, and the presidential suite at Los Angeles' Century Plaza Hotel.

*

In the early days of the Reagan administration the press had considerable freedom, invited into the Oval Office five or six times a day to photograph the president's meetings with all sorts of people, among them Sugar Ray Leonard, the prizefighter. Reagan said, "Come in, fellows, I want you all to meet Sugar Ray and Mrs. Ray."

At that Sam Donaldson burst out, "Oh, for God's sake, Mr. President, it's Mrs. Leonard!"

Reagan just laughed and said, "Well, there you go, Sam." He really liked Sam. Even though Sam was always yelling at him I think the Great Communicator had a great affection for him, and in fact Reagan's response to Sam typified his urbane dealings with the press.

Those first few months after Reagan took office Judy Woodruff and I were paired as White House correspondents for NBC News, and we often swapped off assignments. One week I did *Nightly News*, the next week Judy did it. We also alternated going out with the president, because whenever he traveled, a reporter from NBC, along with somebody from ABC and CBS, went too. Today, with so many networks, reporters have to alternate coverage in the press pool, but back then it was always either Judy or me for NBC.

The president was scheduled to speak to a group at the Washington Hilton, the kind of thing he often did when a big convention was in town. It was Judy's turn to go but I offered to make the trip if she had other things to do. "No, I'll do it, it's my turn," she said. So off she went. No matter where the president is in the world, at the White House we can listen to his remarks piped in live to our press booths, so I could hear his speech to report on it for radio if that was called for. So Judy was at the hotel with the president while I waited for the motorcade to return to the White House.

Suddenly, my phones started to ring and light up and I knew instantly that something had gone wrong. "What's going on? What's happened?" People were bombarding me with questions, and I didn't know a thing. Then I heard an excited voice: "There's a report of a shooting!" and running feet in the corridor. I turned on the television set to see White House Press Secretary Jim Brady lying motionless with his head in the gutter, bleeding and looking mortally wounded. As I went back to the booth to wait for Judy they replayed the shooting on the screen, and it was a horror.

My phone rang again. It was my bureau chief, Sid Davis. "CBS reports that Brady's dead. Can you match it?" That was his signature query—"Can you match it?"

"Good Lord, no, but I saw it on video. I saw the shot of it, and he sure looked it."

"Find out if he's dead," Sid said. "We're checking the hospital, but CBS reports he's dead. Find out."

I went running toward the press secretary's office and on my way there I met one of the president's old friends from the days of his California governorship and grabbed him. "Jim, Jim, tell me, is Brady alive?"

We at the White House had no idea at that point that the president had also been hit.

"John," Jim said, his voice dying away, "He's gone."

"He died?"

He nodded. "Brady's gone."

I was on the verge of running back to report to my boss when some intuition made me hold off. "How do you know that?"

Jim said, "I just heard it on CBS."

When I told Sid I couldn't confirm he was not pleased. "What? You can't?"

"Listen, there's nobody here I can talk to. The place is in chaos. Nobody's answering a phone, nobody knows what's happened, and the president hasn't come back."

I'm thankful I didn't confirm it, because Brady survived the attack, although severely wounded with brain damage. Ronald Reagan's friendship and loyalty to Jim Brady was such that after Larry Speaks took over as acting press secretary, Reagan kept Brady on the payroll. He was still officially the White House press secretary until Reagan left office.

We soon got the whole story. As Judy and the others on the scene reported it, I soon felt as though I'd been there to see it for myself. The president came walking out a side door of the hotel while reporters stood in the "press pen" 15 or 20 yards away, close enough for several of them to call out questions. The president was walking toward his limousine and waving when one of the reporters yelled a question. As Reagan turned to answer, a deranged young man by the name of John Hinckley, who had somehow managed to get into the press pen, pulled out a handgun and fired at the president.

Hinkley's act was entirely premeditated. Obsessed with the actress Jodie Foster, he thought he could impress her by shooting the president of the United States, so he came prepared with a gun and got in position to carry out the deed. It all happened in seconds, Hinckley reaching out with that handgun right over a cameraman's shoulder to fire at the president. One burst hit Jim Brady in the head. Another seriously wounded Thomas Delahanty, a District of Columbia police officer, and another struck Secret Service Agent Timothy McCarthy in the stomach. McCarthy, as agents are trained to do, had thrown out his arms and spread his legs to make himself the greatest possible shield for the president. If a shooter manages to get off a round, any agent in the line of fire is trained to take the hit as the president's last defense, and McCarthy took one. Another bullet hit the president's limo door, flattened, and slid sideways into his body within an inch of his heart. No one at that point even knew he'd been hit.

The president's personal agent is always armed, but his primary job is to get the president out of harm's way. He never pulls his weapon to shoot an assailant, leaving it to the other agents to fire back. It's the personal agent's job to grab the back of the president's coat, push his head down, force him to crouch low, and shove him into the back of the limo onto the floor. All of that Jerry Parr did just as he'd rehearsed it many times, then jumped in on top of the president. With the driver ready to roar away to return to the White House, within seconds the president was shouting angrily at Parr, "Get off me! Get off! You're hurting me! You're crushing my chest!"

Parr got off and helped him up onto the back seat, and when Reagan, still furious, opened his mouth to speak, rich red blood came gushing out. Parr knew that that bright red blood meant the president's lung had been hit. These dire possibilities have been rehearsed so many times that the agents know exactly what they must do and always know the location of the nearest hospital. So when Parr yelled, "George Washington University Hospital Emergency Room!" Secret Service headquarters alerted the hospital to be ready for them. They'd barely got the code out when the limo pulled up to the emergency room door. The president got out of the car, insisting he could walk in under his own steam, but he walked only a few steps before he collapsed.

Nobody had cellphones then, and the luckiest reporters were the ones who got to the nearest store or house first to commandeer a phone. On any breaking story, the first thing you always did was run to some nearby place and ask, "Will you hold this phone for me?" Money might change hands to make sure. Had Judy had a cellphone, she could have gotten word to us so quickly that within a minute or two, before the president even got to the hospital or a doctor saw him, the news would have been our all over the world. That's how it is in this business, electronic advances coming along all the time. As soon as you adapt to one and get accustomed to using it, something else comes along to take its place.

We heard afterward that President Reagan's sense of humor was intact even as he was being wheeled into the operating room. "I hope you're all Republicans," he said to his surgeons. And quite soon the viewing public got those first pictures of his familiar face and upright figure, looking spiffy even in his bathrobe with Mrs. Reagan at his side, both of them smiling and waving from a hospital window. All seemed well with the president, and he was happy to maintain that appearance. Only long after the shooting did we learn that the bullet in Reagan's chest had come within an inch of his heart, so close it could have been a fatal wound. It also caused an extremely dangerous infection, cleared up, fortunately, by treatment, and none of us knew that either.

One result of Hinckley's assassination attempt is that, from that day to this, presidents never go in and out of hotels within plain view. Instead, they enter and leave by a door to an underground garage, or if the hotel has no such entrance, by way of a canopy extending all the way from the building to the limo. Every precaution is taken to make sure the president won't be within range of a shooter.

*

Throughout his life, many people underestimated Ronald Reagan, and I think he counted on that fact and used it, often to great advantage. Many of his political opponents found themselves yielding to Reagan's charm and determination before they ever knew what had hit them. Reagan used his admirable people skills to great advantage with members of Congress. In his first year in office he was successful in getting legislation passed to stimulate economic growth, curb inflation and strengthen national defense, but at the cost of a ballooning federal deficit.

That first summer of his presidency, when he was still recovering from Hinckley's attempt on his life, he postponed his August trip to the ranch to lobby for passage of his tax cuts. Correspondent Andrea Mitchell, a member of our White House NBC News team, spent many hours in the broiling hot sun and the rain at the Southwest Gate of the White House, buttonholing congressmen as they left after a meeting with President Reagan. Although many of them had arrived strongly opposed to the president's plan, a good number left with smiles on their faces, saying they planned to take another look at the tax-cuts proposals. Some even proudly displayed the presidential cufflinks Reagan had given them. He got his tax cuts.

Over time I became quite fond of this particular president, who was such a likable and considerate guy. He was interested in people, he liked people, but he'd had kind of a rough start in office. His presidency took a pounding during his first two years, with high unemployment and a mushrooming deficit. Once, asked at a news conference about high unemployment in the country,

Reagan said he had just seen page after page of job offers in the *Washington Post.* It didn't seem to register with him that these were mostly hamburger-flipping jobs or other low-paying positions that wouldn't allow someone to support a family.

*

There was no better place to understand Ronald Reagan and his practical, down-to-earth manner than at Rancho Cielo—his California "ranch in the sky." The 688-acre ranch comprised a modest ranch house, a stable, several outbuildings and acres of hills and wide-open pastures. A helicopter pad and sophisticated communications van were the only presidential trappings allowed. Although Mrs. Reagan seemed to enjoy her time there, she never fully shared her husband's love for the rustic outdoor life, much preferring the comforts of the four-star Century Plaza and the closeness of long-time friends. A story went the rounds that once at the ranch she picked up the telephone and discovered a scorpion clinging to the mouthpiece, which could have had something to do with her preference for urban life.

Whenever the Reagans were at the ranch, usually in August, the White House press corps encamped at the Sheridan Hotel in Santa Barbara, where at 10 a.m. daily Acting Press Secretary Larry Speaks briefed us on the president's activities for that day. And brief, those reports were, offering such sparse nuggets of news as this: "The President and Mrs. Reagan plan to go horseback riding this afternoon. This morning the President is chopping wood and clearing brush." Little wonder that the Secret Service's code name for Reagan was "Rawhide."

In an effort to get some video of the presidential couple whenever they ventured outdoors together, news photographers took pictures using long lenses from a hilltop more than a mile away. Often the pictures were distorted by heat waves, but we aired them anyway as that was all we had.

While we saw little of the president during those August days in Santa Barbara, once every summer he hosted a party for the press. I think he enjoyed cultivating his rough-and-ready image, for he arrived on horseback at one of those barbecues, accompanied by a thundering cavalry of Secret Service agents. He had a favorite saying: "Nothing feels as good on the inside of a man as the outside of a horse."

During the Reagans' usual two weeks at the Century Plaza the president made occasional trips into downtown Los Angeles, trailed by a 10-car motorcade transporting his doctor, staff members, Secret Service agents, heavily armed police and two carloads of whichever network reporters were assigned to cover him that day. The last vehicle in the motorcade was always an ambulance. His trips included seeing friends, visits to an ear clinic and stopping at a retail establishment called The Meat Locker, where he selected choice cuts of prime beef. And then there was the Saturday he decided to get a haircut. I was one of three reporters who went along with him to his favorite downtown barbershop, and Reagan saw me standing behind his chair as the barber began to shear the presidential locks.

"I'm tired of people thinking I dye my hair," he said. "Now, John, I don't want you to take my word for it, or even the barber's word. Why don't you just gather up some of my hair from the floor here and send it to one of those fancy laboratories back East and have it analyzed?"

When I laughed, he said, "No, I'm serious."

"Mr. President, if you say you don't dye your hair, that's good enough for me. Besides, that's your business and no one else's." So no clippings went off to the "fancy" lab. More than once after that, the president would catch my eye and point to his full head of brown hair. "See, I still don't do it," he'd say, and as far as I know he never did.

*

In many ways Ronald Reagan reminded me of my dad. He had a good sense of humor, he loved to tell amusing stories and he could disagree without being disagreeable. He was anything but the "amiable dunce" a Washington lawyer, Clark Clifford, had said he was. It's true that he did delegate plenty of authority—perhaps too much—to his three top assistants, Jim Baker, Ed Meese and Michael Deaver. That was just his management style, because Reagan saw himself as the nation's leader or even its cheerleader, if you will, leaving details to others. He focused on the big picture: downsizing government, reducing taxes, restoring pride in America and facing down the Soviet Union through a huge build-up in military power.

He always used humor to great advantage. When asked about his relatively short 9-to-5 work day, he answered with a smile. "They say hard work won't kill you, but I decided not to take the chance." Then there was the famous audio check before his Saturday radio broadcast, when he ad-libbed: "My fellow Americans, I'm pleased to announce that I've signed legislation outlawing the Soviet Union. We begin bombing in five minutes." After a radio engineer and several correspondents heard those remarks, they were widely reported, yet presidential counselor David Gergen told me later he was sure Reagan knew exactly what he was doing—sending a message to his Republican political base that he was still the same conservative they'd put into office.

Reagan always loved a good story, and when one clicked with an audience he used it again and again. Many of his stories evoked the self-sacrifice of the American people, such as the World War II story of a B-17 pilot returning from a mission over Germany. When the aircraft was hit by enemy fire, the pilot ordered the crew to bail out, but before the pilot jumped himself, he took a quick tour of the burning plane and spotted his tail gunner, legs pinned against the fuselage. As Reagan told it, at that point the pilot unfastened and dropped his parachute, put his arms around the trapped tail gunner, and said, "Don't worry, son, we'll ride this one out together."

I heard the president tell that story half a dozen times, with never a dry eye in the room.

Eventually Lou Cannon, the president's superb biographer, asked Reagan how he knew what had happened if both the pilot and the tail gunner died in the crash.

"Good point," the Great Communicator said, and instead of losing a good story, he quickly adapted. The next time he told it, the co-pilot had witnessed what happened just before *he* bailed out.

President Reagan used another of his favorite stories to illustrate his optimism about life. It always brought a laugh from his audience, no matter how many times he told it. It's about a stable attendant who was cleaning out a stall. He kept digging and digging until someone asked him why he was still digging, since the stall was already clean. "Well," said the stable attendant, "There must be a pony in here somewhere."

One of President Reagan's most controversial decisions came in May of 1985, when his itinerary for a trip to Europe included a planned visit to a cemetery in Bitberg, Germany. After someone made the belated discovery that the cemetery was the burial place of hundreds of Nazi soldiers along with 49 members of Hitler's dreaded *Schutzstaffel*, or SS, many American Jewish leaders called on the president to cancel the stop, but he held firm, saying it was meant as a gesture of healing. The president's senior aide, Michael Deaver, had already gone out to Andrews Air Force Base ready to fly to Germany to ask Chancellor Helmut Kohl to withdraw the invitation for the cemetery visit when he got an urgent summons to return to the White House to meet with the president.

Deaver told me years later that Reagan was adamant. "Mike, I know where you were going and what you were going to do, but I intend to go through with my visit to the cemetery."

As it turned out, Reagan's speech on that occasion included some memorable words. "We who were enemies are now friends," he said. "In place of fear we have sown trust, and out of the ruins of war has blossomed an enduring peace."

In November of 1985 he took another big risk in attempting to establish a personal relationship with a prominent world leader, Soviet General Secretary Mikhail Gorbachev. Much to the horror of his closest advisors, who considered his approach naïve and dangerous, he reached out to Gorbachev anyway, and the result was a Geneva Summit between the two leaders and the beginning of a thaw in the Cold War.

While in Geneva the president stayed at the U.S. ambassador's residence where, despite the weighty matters of state he was dealing with, he fed the ambassador's goldfish faithfully every day. Just before the summit ended, when one of the fish was found dead, one of Reagan's top aides told me the president sent a staffer out to buy another goldfish that looked just like the one that had died. Reagan then left a note by the fish tank telling what had happened and expressing hope that the new goldfish would make up for the loss.

*

In the long run, I'm sure his aides never gave him enough credit for his skillful handling of the press. They might complain about his being "out of the box," meaning he wasn't following the program exactly as they thought it should be done. It was on a trip to Texas that I had a more personal experience of Reagan's expertise in dealing with the press. Jim Baker, the president's chief of staff, had invited him down to his ranch for a turkey hunt, and Mike Deaver went along. We of the fourth estate stayed at a motel in a nearby town but were always on the spot for any photo op or chance the president might make a few remarks.

The news story of the moment had to do with his National Security Advisor, Richard Allen, who had been accused of accepting unreported gifts from a Japanese journalist for setting up an interview with first lady Nancy Reagan. The gifts were said to be Seiko watches. People were talking about it, and it was turning into a minor scandal. The allegations were never proven, and the president hadn't yet asked for Allen's resignation.

On the day of the hunt we were all standing around as Reagan took his place in the passenger seat of Jim Baker's Jeep. Baker was driving and Deaver sat in back. As Baker cranked it up, I called out, "Mr. President! What about Richard Allen? Do you plan to keep him on the job?"

The president cupped his hand to his ear as though he hadn't heard me and just waved, at which point Baker gunned the engine so loudly that nobody could hear a thing. Reagan's people were like that, always seeking to protect him from the press. The effort was silly, because he was a big boy with eight years' experience as governor of California, and he could handle the press quite well. I got no answer to my question, and as they drove off in a cloud of dust the president made that familiar helpless gesture with his hands.

So on *NBC Nightly News* that evening I reported the story this way: "The president did not answer my question, apparently deciding to let his national security adviser twist slowly in the wind while he went turkey hunting."

The White House was furious, and when we got together for a little party that night, as we often did when the president wasn't doing anything and the lid was on, Acting Press Secretary Larry Speaks came over. "Palmer," he said brusquely, "that shot was below the belt."

"Larry, I asked the question, and the president declined to answer, so what am I left to conclude but that he'd decided to let his national security advisor twist in the wind through another weekend with no decision about his future?"

Speaks turned and walked away, ignoring me for the rest of the evening, but Ronald Reagan took a far more positive approach. I'd gone back to my motel room and was ready for bed when a knock came at my door. It was a White House courier: "President Reagan wanted you to have this." He handed me a large brown envelope, with an 8-by-10-inch color photo inside of me calling out to the president as he was driven away in the Jeep. The caption, hand-written by the president, read: "John, I truly couldn't hear your question today. If I had, I would have answered. Next time I guess we should use cue cards like they do in Hollywood. Warmly, Ronald Reagan"

What a beautiful way to handle the press! Sugar instead of acid. I've always kept that photo, because it meant a lot to me. I thought it was a class act, and in many ways he was a classy guy. A complete gentleman.

Later, Nancy and I were thrilled when the Reagans invited us to the White House for Sunday night dinner and a movie, with James Cagney and other well-known actors among the other guests. The dinner was held in the Red Room, eight tables or so. I was at the president's table, Nancy seated elsewhere. When the president entered the room, I was startled to see him in a sports coat that seem like it had once been a horse blanket—black and red checks, the loudest thing you ever saw, while the rest of us wore suits.

At dinner the president had his own personal waiter, and while he was never a big drinker, I noticed that every time the president took a sip of rosé wine the waiter refilled his glass to the brim. With his Hollywood friends around him he was enjoying reminiscing about his acting days, like the time in one of his earliest films when he was put in the back row of a troop of soldiers. The camera had to pan along the line for take after take, so Reagan, eager to make his mark, started scooping up dirt into a pile with his boots, and when it came to the final take he said he stood atop his dirt pile so his head was above the other men. With that engaging smile, he said, "That's the important thing in Hollywood, you know, being seen."

At that point I felt bold enough to tell a story about my grandfather. Granddad claimed that on an overnight train trip he'd had to combat bedbugs in the sleeping car, and he was so incensed that he wrote the president of the Pullman Company to complain. As he told it, he got a very nice, personal, and lengthy letter back from the vice president of the company, profuse with apologies and assuring him that the car had been taken out of service and thoroughly fumigated and refitted. Attached to the company's letter, unfortunately, was his original letter he had sent with a handwritten note at the bottom: "Send this guy Bug Letter #2." I was grateful when my story got a big laugh.

After dinner we were to go downstairs to see the film, and because reporters don't have the run of the Mansion, I didn't know where the movie theater was. I noticed Mrs. Baker, the chief of staff's wife, and Mrs. Reagan start down the hallway, so I just tagged along to the lower level until Mrs. Reagan turned to me. "John, you can go anywhere you like."

"Thank you, Mrs. Reagan," I said, and kept walking along with them and thinking that was a strange thing for her to say.

At that she stopped dead. "We're going to the ladies' room! Where are you going?"

Seeing my chagrin, she pointed to the library across the hall. "You can go in there."

A bit embarrassed, I walked into the library where a marine sergeant stood at attention in a corner with a towel over his forearm, in case any of us wanted to dry our hands after using the bathroom. The other person in the room, standing by the fire in his horse-blanket jacket, was the president of the United States. I walked over to him. "Thank you for this lovely evening, Mr. President. I'm looking forward to the film."

"So am I. You know, John, after you told that story upstairs about your grandfather and the bedbugs on the train, I had a story I wanted to tell, too, but there were ladies present."

I grinned. "Well, Mr. President, no ladies present now. What's the story?"

"I thought you'd be interested to hear it," he said. "I'll tell you, it's kind of a riddle. What do Jesus Christ riding into Jerusalem and a commuter on the Long Island Railroad riding into New York have in common?"

"I don't know, Mr. President, what do they have in common?"

"In both situations," he said in that memorable voice, "you're riding into town on your ass." He wouldn't tell it in front of ladies because of that word "ass." He laughed, and so did I, because it struck me as quite amusing.

When a little silence fell between us, to fill the gap I said, "You know, it's very exciting for me, being in this room. I've never been in the White House library, and I can remember as a kid listening to Franklin Roosevelt broadcast his Fireside Chats from right here."

Reagan's eyes got wide. "Really? Was it here? My goodness gracious!"

"Sir," I said, as if he should know, "it's your house!"

He nodded, smiling. "Well, I don't know everything about the place. But that's important, because I remember Fireside Chats. And to think we're standing right where Franklin Roosevelt made those broadcasts!" And of course, before he became a Republican, Reagan used to be a Roosevelt Democrat.

You could smoke just about anywhere then, even in the White House, and as the rest of the men came to join us several lit up. We had an after-dinner drink, then went two or three doors down the hall to the theatre. In the front row were easy chairs for the president and first lady and several of the actors featured in the film. Nancy and I were back in comfortable but less luxurious seats. When we realized that the film featured a scandalous shooting involving the architect Stanford White, I felt the tension in the room, knowing that Reagan had survived an assassination attempt and wondering how he could watch such a film. But he did watch it, as did we, and all went well. Afterward Mrs. Reagan could not have been more gracious, standing at the doorway and thanking us for coming.

I always thought Nancy Reagan got a bum rap. As everyone knows, she was desperately in love with her husband. As their published love letters reveal, they had one of the world's great love stories, and during my White House days their deep and lasting love for each other was quite apparent to me and others who often saw them together.

She is a very private person, however, even bashful. Once she was dedicating a statue in the White House Rose Garden when I noticed her hands shaking. Here was the wife of the president of the United States and a former actress, nervous about this little ceremony that must have been a new experience for her. After giving up her film career to be Ronald Reagan's partner, she always put him and his career first. I suppose most first ladies have their critics, and this one was criticized for her designer dresses, for replacing the White House china, for redecorating the family quarters, even for that famous worshipful gaze whenever she was at his side during a speech, looking adoringly up at him for long periods of time. I know she worried about him, and after he was shot she was terrified of losing him. At the time, she had good reason to fear for his life.

⁂

Thanks to President Reagan's frequent visits, I came to love California. While the Reagans were there vacationing we had little news to report, so it became something of a holiday for the press as well. My Nancy would go out with me to stay at the Sheraton in Santa Barbara, and we had great fun sightseeing and discovering the pleasures of California life. In the mornings in Santa Barbara the press would usually gather around 11 for one photo op with the president, who might receive a pair of boots someone was giving him or some other minor event, and we'd ask him a couple of questions. Then he'd say, "Fellows, go out and have some fun." So that's what we did.

A group of us were strolling along the beach there one night after a little too much wine, and our White House producer Jim Lee and I were carrying our shoes when we came across a giant sea lion that had beached itself. The thing must have weighed at least 300 pounds. We figured this creature needed to be helped back into the water, so we heaved and shoved trying to get it into the ocean, to no avail. The next morning when we convened for our daily press briefing, acting press secretary Larry Speaks said, "It pains me to have to make this special announcement"—this is still part of the official White House record—"but the Santa Barbara County sheriff notified me this morning that two members of the press corps were seen molesting a sea lion on the beach last night." He went on and on, making it sound utterly ridiculous. He went on to say that the sheriff planned to take action against the two journalists responsible, "who are at this time in this meeting, and you know who you are."

Traveling with the president to his vacation spots was always one of White House correspondents' perks, and I especially enjoyed a lovely trip to Barbados where the Reagans went to visit their Hollywood friend Claudette Colbert as President Reagan recuperated from the assassination attempt. We journalists were told we could bring our spouses on the charter flight for $100 round trip, so of course we jumped at the chance. At the time Nancy Palmer hated to fly, but Barbados was too good to miss. She took a couple of Valiums and wrapped herself in a blanket and sleep all the way. After our arrival we spent a couple of delightful weeks there on that tropical island.

With nothing to report on, some of us decided to try for a long-lens shot of the president swimming, maybe even showing the scar where the bullet had entered his chest. We had hardly gone out and planted ourselves behind some greenery near the beach when President Reagan came out of the house in his swim trunks and waded in. He still had the body of a lifeguard. A little later Mrs. Reagan came out and joined him for a swim. The Secret Service was close at hand as always, and afterward as she swam back to shallow water headed for the beach an agent must have told her journalists were watching. So word was sent to the house for an aide who came rushing down with a towel she could wrap around her legs as she waded out. Immediately I knew that we'd stepped over the line, intruding into these people's lives. Here was the president just recovering from a near-fatal bullet wound, and his wife so self-conscious that she wouldn't walk out of the surf without covering her legs. Sheepishly, we left, and I remembered that chastening moment for a long time.

*

President Reagan had a fairly well-known tendency to nap, which both he and we used to kid about. We were in the room at the Paris summit conference with all the leaders of the world around him when he dozed off. Then we learned why. Israel's invasion of Lebanon had kept him up all night as he tried to persuade the Israelis to stop what they were doing and get out, so his sleep deprivation shouldn't have surprised anybody.

He was also a bit forgetful at times. Whether it was an early indication of the Alzheimer's disease that finally overcame him I can't say, but it was another of those things we just knew to be so. His recently published diaries allude to his forgetfulness, so it was bothering him too.

After he left the White House and was known to be suffering from Alzheimer's disease, one of his aides who'd seen him recently told me a much sadder goldfish story. Reagan enjoyed goldfish and had a fish tank at home. Someone gave him a small plastic replica of the White House to put in the tank with his fish, and the person telling me about it said Reagan stared at the little house in the water for a while then said to his wife, "Gee, wouldn't it be great to live in a beautiful house like that?" What a tragic comedown for such a vital and larger-than-life man.

PHOTO GALLERY

1970–1981

WNBC New York Election Night with co-anchor Jim Hartz , November 1970

John interviewing Egyptian President Anwar Sadat, circa 1974

Reporting from Jerusalem, circa 1975

Covering conflict in former Belgian Congo, circa 1975

Escaping gunfire in Beirut during Lebanese Civil War, 1975

Reporting from Africa, circa 1976

Striking a pose in Russia, circa 1978

President Jimmy Carter faces the press the morning after losing re-election, 1980

VP George H. Bush congratulates John for receiving the Merriman Smith Award, 1981

John questioning President Ronald Reagan during White House press conference, 1981

Posing a question to President Reagan, circa 1981

John and wife Nancy meeting Nancy Reagan, 1981

11

THE GIFT OF A LIFE PARTNER AND ON TO *TODAY*

FOR A GOOD while after I married, at age 46, people used to ask me why I'd waited so long. I had a standard reply: "I *was* married—to NBC News," I was always ready to travel anywhere in the world to catch a good story. Whether it was a plane crash in Yugoslavia or a political coup in Africa, I tried to be there, and willingly.

I was also well aware of the hardship weeks on the road worked on reporters, producers, and crews who always had to leave a loved one behind. It could be especially painful for those with wives and children back home. During the two months that I was in Africa covering the mercenary trial, I'd seen a colleague from CBS News reading bedtime stories night after night to his son back in London from a pay phone in a dimly lit hotel stairwell.

When holidays came, Christmas or Thanksgiving or other typical family occasions, I did often ask myself what I was doing in some dreary hotel room, trying to read under a single bare light bulb hanging from a frayed wire. But no lonely wife was begging me to stay home, no sad children were crying for Daddy, so in that respect I felt fortunate to have stayed single. Never one to shun the ladies, I just didn't want to have to feel guilty for being absent from some then-nonexistent family. While those years on the road in Europe and the Middle East were exciting and fun and I felt lucky to have such a fascinating job, eventually my globe-trotting began to pall, and now that I know the fullest joys of being a husband and father, I feel even luckier to have had it all.

Taking the plunge into matrimony came about like this. As I mentioned earlier in the book, I first met Nancy Doyle in the fall of 1979 while covering Pope John Paul's visit to Washington. She does not recall that first meeting as one to cherish, claiming that I said only 10 words to her: "Hon, can you get me a cup of hot coffee?" Weary from travel, I must have sunk into a major fog, for Nancy is a beautiful woman.

Back to Paris I went, and soon afterward the hostages were taken in Iran, the day of my farewell party in Paris. A week later I reported to Washington to take up my new assignment as White House correspondent for NBC. Only after I returned to Washington did my vision clear enough to reveal what I'd missed before. I was new in my own job, and Nancy was a production assistant for *Nightly News* in the Washington Bureau. Running into her again seemed inevitable.

I well remember the day I stopped by the bureau to pick up my mail and got a good look at her. She was beautiful, sitting at her desk, laughing and talking animatedly with a group of colleagues. I was smitten, but when I asked my friend Bill Lynch about her, his reply was not encouraging: "Don't waste your time. She's living with a guy, and they'll probably get married."

In the days that followed Nancy and I talked often on the phone, mostly about work and what I planned to report on that day for the evening news. I didn't ask her out, no doubt fearful of rejection. But as time passed and she occupied more and more space in my brain, slowly my courage mounted. What was wrong with me, afraid to ask a charming woman for a date? Unconsciously I must have known that this woman was special, that once I took the plunge there'd be no turning back. Most middle-aged bachelors are well used to dodging marital ties, and I probably sensed what life had in store for me. Settle down? We'd see. In any case, I couldn't get her out of my mind.

In the end President Jimmy Carter came, indirectly, to the rescue. I was invited to attend a state luncheon for the visiting king and queen of Belgium, and beyond that, told I could bring a guest. Aha, I thought, this is the opening I've waited for. Whether she's attached or not, how can Nancy turn down an invitation to lunch with royalty at the White House? She couldn't, so in the early spring of 1980 she and I arrived at the Southwest Entrance to the White House for what I've always considered our first date.

We walked through the mansion's impressive entrance hall to join other guests waiting to be greeted by President and Mrs. Carter, who then introduced each guest to the king and queen. All was going well when suddenly a White House military aide, spiffy in his dress blues, approached Nancy, offered his arm, and escorted her to a seat in the East Room. Having just managed to snag this date, I wasn't about to let some other better-dressed guy beat me out. But when I tried to follow an usher stopped me.

"Sir, you're at table 12, over there."

What a blow! I'd covered many state dinners and luncheons as a reporter, yet never realized that invitees were seated apart from their spouses or guests. All I could do was accept the seat assigned to me and try to make myself agreeable to my table companions, while my eyes and my attention kept drifting across the room to Nancy. I'd never sat through such an interminable event. I was sure things were about to wind down once the president and the king exchanged toasts, but then came the entertainment—the president's young daughter Amy playing the violin. Groan. All in all, two and a half everlasting hours passed before I could break free.

My fellow lunchers must have been startled to see me leap to my feet and hustle over to recapture my date just as several men at her table handed her their business cards. "Now, Nancy, let's be sure to have lunch next week," one of them said just as I reached her side. Not if I have anything to do with it, I thought.

As she and I walked down the front steps of the White House toward Pennsylvania Avenue in search of a taxi I did my best to recoup my losses. "Listen, Nancy, this didn't turn out at all the way I'd hoped or expected. We hardly had a chance to exchange two words. How about pizza Sunday night?" Reluctantly, she agreed. Looking back, I guess pizza seemed like pretty second rate compared to a state luncheon at the White House, but I wanted to move things to a cozier level.

We shared that pizza, and soon afterward she broke up with her boyfriend and continued to share a place with Kerry Foley, her best friend. We had more and more dates until a trip together seemed like a good idea, so I invited her to go to Bermuda with me for a few days' break. She said sure, she'd like to go. What I didn't know then was that she told her parents, "Look, I'm going to Bermuda with this new correspondent I've been seeing, John Palmer." Fine, they said, have fun. "I'm telling you," Nancy said, "so you'll know about it in case I turn up missing and he turns out to be a serial killer or something." She still didn't know me well enough to trust me entirely, wondering if I'd been doing the same thing in every place I'd ever been all over the world. Fortunately she didn't confess her reservations to me. We went to Bermuda, and we had a grand time.

As the months went by we were dating each other exclusively, and over time my dad's matrimonial advice began to echo in my mind. I'd asked Dad how I would know when I had met the right woman. He replied, "You'll know it's time to marry when you can't imagine living without her." That was exactly where I was finding myself during those heady days. Eventually we decided it made more sense if she moved in with me, so that's what happened. We were still getting along just great, day in and day out.

The Carters had left the White House and the Reagans had moved in, and a year and a half after our first "non-date" at the White House, our romance was flourishing sufficiently that I felt ready to ask her to marry me. Remembering our earlier delightful time in Bermuda, I decided that would be the perfect place to propose and suggested we go there again. "I'd love to go," she said. After the reservations were made, to make sure I had everything lined up well in advance I boned up on diamonds, shopped around and secretly bought a beautiful engagement ring. Before we left I tucked the bill of sale into my bag for the benefit of Customs, wrapped up the ring, and put it in my pocket. I planned to give it to her on the last night of our stay.

We had great fun swimming and sightseeing on that beautiful island until the final day, when I made the nearly fatal mistake of chartering a boat for some deep-sea fishing. At first she said, "Why, yes, that's fine." Fishing has always been my passion, and I wanted to share it with my wife-to-be. She'd never been out in a boat with me before, and I was sure she'd be as crazy about it as I am. I quickly made a sobering discovery. Nancy did not share my love of fishing, and even worse, she detested being on the water in a small boat.

We'd traveled only about five miles out when she turned pale, then a sickly shade of green, and retreated to a bunk below deck. I went to her side and kept telling her the day wasn't turning out the way I wanted it to. Even though we already had lines out trolling, when I saw that things were going from bad to worse, I spoke quietly to the captain, unwilling to let my well-laid scheme be sabotaged.

"I hate to call off a day of great fishing, but you'd better take us back to the dock."

He shrugged. "It's your charter. We haven't caught the first fish."

"I'll pay for the whole day. Turn back anyway."

He turned the boat around grudgingly. Now, I can read a compass as well as the next man, and I saw that he was making a very circuitous route in reversing course. When I asked what he was doing, he said, "Hey, it's fine if you pay me for the whole day, but if I come back with no fish and the other captains come in with plenty of fish in their boats, anybody who sees I don't have fish is gonna say, 'Let's don't hire that guy for tomorrow, he has nothing.'"

"Believe me," I told him, "I know what I'm doing. I plan to ask this lady to marry me tonight, and if I keep her here throwing up all day, it'll wreck the evening for sure."

Then he understood and made straight for the dock. To my huge relief, five minutes after Nancy got her feet on dry land, she recovered completely in both body and spirit.

So instead of fishing we spent the rest of the day swimming and doing whatever else Nancy felt like until dinnertime, when we were seated under a spectacular starlit sky with a small orchestra playing soft music and candlelight flickering across the table. I couldn't have ordered a more perfect setting. We'd just finished dessert and were waiting for coffee when I reached for her hand and produced the ring I'd chosen with such care.

"Nan, honey, I'd like us to spend the rest of our lives together. Will you marry me?"

She just stared at the ring, her eyes big, then took it, not saying a word.

I'd expected jubilation, kisses, anything but silence. Finally I said, "Well?"

She blurted out, "I don't know, John. This is so sudden!"

I was shattered. "What d'you mean, sudden? We've been together for a year and a half!" We'd always had such a great time that I couldn't figure it out. We were so happy being together, living together, surely the natural next step was marriage.

And still she didn't put on the ring. "I'd like to think about it," she said.

Neither of us spoke while I struggled to salvage my pride and the situation. At last I said, "Then while you're thinking, would you please give me back the ring?"

She handed it back and I put it in my pocket. After another long silence she said innocently, "Did I say something to offend you or hurt your feelings?"

I did my best to sound carefree, sarcasm my only defense. "Oh, no, no! Most every Saturday night I propose to a different woman. I'm quite accustomed to being turned down."

We finished our dinner with occasional small talk about the weather, our aborted fishing trip, and other inconsequential things. Neither of us wanted to spoil our last night, so somehow we managed to set talk of marriage aside. We had our coffee, and I paid the bill for dinner. Before we went back to our room we had a dance together, with very little more to say to each other. Still nonplussed, I'd just had my first lesson in the mysteries of the female mind.

The next morning in the cab headed for the airport and our flight home Nancy turned to me. "Do you still have that ring?"

"Sure I have the ring."

So then she said, sweetly, "Well, if you give it to me I'd be happy to wear it."

Back at home we finally talked over what had happened. She told me that she'd considered marriage a mutual thing, as of course it is, and thought we should have discussed it together and agreed together to get married. To her, it felt like I had just come down from on high and deigned to propose. From my point of view, on the other hand, it was already a *fait accompli*, and a business-deal kind of discussion would have taken away all the drama and romance. A sentimental guy, I wanted to surprise her with the ring. For pity's sake, who else would I propose to? And who else would she want to live with?

Only in reliving those days for this book did I discover why she accepted my proposal that morning. Nancy has since conquered her fear of flying, but she hadn't licked it then, and she recently confessed that she'd taken a Valium that morning in Bermuda to help her relax for the flight. It made her *so* relaxed that she agreed to marry me! Humbling to think that our marriage and our three daughters are due to that one Valium tablet, but if it took a Valium to convince her, then three cheers for Valium!

We set a date and chose a place for our wedding, and as the day drew near Mrs. Reagan and Helen Thomas, doyenne of the White House press corps, gave a little luncheon party for Nancy at which they presented her with a pig-shaped purse, on the assumption that I was the pig Nancy would promptly turn into the proverbial silk purse. So it came to be that, on a clear cold Saturday afternoon in January, we were all set to be married in a ceremony at St. Alban's Episcopal Church in the shadow of Washington's National Cathedral. An hour beforehand I was at my Georgetown house getting into my tuxedo when the phone rang.

"This is the White House calling," a voice said. "I have a call for John Palmer from the president of the United States."

My first thought was that it was my best man, fellow White House correspondent Bill Lynch, pretending to be President Reagan. We all took pride in mimicking Reagan's voice, but Bill's version was by far the best. Fortunately I resisted the temptation to say, "Fuck off!" and just listened instead.

"John," came the familiar voice on the phone, "I'm out here in California on the golf course at the Annenbergs' place. They tell me you're about ready to leave for the church, so I just wanted to call, wish you well and tell you I hope you'll be as happy with your Nancy as I have been with mine."

The president then went on to describe, at length, his and Nancy Davis's wedding day 30 years earlier at the Little Brown Church in the Valley near Los Angeles, recalling the weather, the attendees and his best man, actor William Holden. Then I knew for sure that it was Ronald Reagan without a doubt, for no one ever enjoyed reminiscing more than he. Afraid I'd be late for my own wedding, I tried to interrupt the president several times during our conversation to thank him for calling, but he talked on and on and on. After he finally said goodbye I raced to the church, eager to tell Nancy exactly who had called to wish us well.

The next day we were off on our honeymoon to a ski resort in Vail, Colorado—a joyous, wonderful week. Already I knew in my heart that many more joys lay ahead. Dad had been right about getting hitched when you know you can't live without that peerless woman. What a lot I had to look forward to!

We had just arrived back home in Washington on Jan. 13, 1982, a bitter cold and snowy afternoon, when we heard scores of sirens and helicopters overhead. Every television station in the city was broadcasting the story. An Air Florida jetliner taking off from Washington National (now Reagan) Airport, had crashed into the 14th Street Bridge and then into the Potomac, killing 78 passengers, crewmembers and people on the bridge. Dramatic video showed survivors being plucked from the frozen river while others, tragically, disappeared under the ice. For Nancy and me, fresh from one of the most magical weeks of our lives, the day marked a jarring and painful reentry to the real world where both of us would continue to live and work.

When my time was up at the White House, President Reagan bid Nancy and me goodbye in a typically gracious way, inviting us into the Oval Office and making sure we posed for pictures with him as he presented us with a jar of his famous jellybeans bearing the Presidential Seal. He never missed an opportunity to show his thoughtfulness of others. As we left the White House for the last time, I remember clutching that jar of jellybeans in my right hand and holding Nancy's hand with my left, literally skipping down the driveway as if it were the Yellow Brick Road.

It wasn't that my years as a White House correspondent weren't wonderful and exciting, for as I've said before, any time you don't pinch yourself when you walk through that Northwest Gate, it's time to pull out. The tough part was always being on call, like a doctor, getting many, many 3 a.m. calls that meant you had to get up out of a warm bed and go. And the whole time I was up against such keen competition as Lesley Stahl of CBS and Sam Donaldson of ABC, first-rate journalists who could always show you up by getting to a story before you did. The day that I walked out that pressure was gone, and I felt immense relief. Yet years later I would be happy to return.

My *Today* show years began in the summer of 1982, when I was summoned to a dinner meeting at the swank Madison Hotel in Washington with NBC News President Reuven Frank and Washington Bureau Chief Bob McFarland. It was August, and much of Washington was on vacation, including McFarland, who came in from the beach for the evening. Frank had flown down from New York, and given those facts, I knew the meeting would be a crucial event. We ordered drinks and made small talk, my insides tight as a knot. Food was the last thing on my mind, and when our first course arrived, although the other two attacked theirs with gusto, I couldn't swallow a bite. I had to know what was up. Finally I took the plunge.

"Reuven, I know the president of NBC News didn't fly down to Washington tonight just to have dinner with me because I'm a nice guy and Bob didn't leave the beach and his family just for a fancy meal. What's up?"

They exchanged glances, and Reuven laid down his fork. "Okay, John, if you insist, I'll get right to the point. The sharing of news segments between Chris Wallace and Jane Pauley on the *Today* show hasn't worked out well. We'd like you to be the sole news anchor on the program."

My ears weren't deceiving me—he had really said the *Today* show. I was thrilled, excited, a little scared. After two and a half years at the White House I was ready to move on, and this promotion would mean moving to New York and the big leagues. My first thought was of Nancy, a native Washingtonian. What would she think? Married less than a year, we were expecting our first child.

Nevertheless I accepted the offer, pending Nancy's okay. She didn't let me down. When I called to tell her, she said, "Let's do it!"

So we were off to New York and one of my most exciting and challenging assignments with NBC. Beginning with high school and the days of Hugh Downs, Barbara Walters and Frank Blair, I'd always watched the *Today* show, and a time or two as a reporter in New York I had even subbed for Blair at the *Today* news desk, so I knew what the job entailed. Now I would be officially joining the program, which meant a great deal to me even though it was mired in second place in the ratings behind David Hartman and *Good Morning America.*

Since my friend Floyd Kalber from Chicago had succeeded Blair as news anchor on *Today*, I called to get his advice. He gave it, and it was blunt.

"Don't do it, John. Stay in Washington. Up there in New York they'll chew you up and spit you out."

Floyd was right, but seven years would pass before that happened, and I never regretted my decision to take the job.

Two weeks after that dinner at the Madison Hotel, I arrived in Manhattan with Nancy, whose pregnancy was now obvious, to take up residence at a hotel NBC had booked for us. It was not an auspicious start, and the kindest thing I can say about our lodgings is that it left much to be desired. The room's carpet was stained, and a pervasive odor suggested that the previous tenant had passed away and lain there unnoticed for days. That first look and sniff brought tears to Nancy's eyes. So, with *Today* show host Bryant Gumbel's support, NBC moved us uptown to the much nicer Wyndham Hotel, where we stayed for several weeks until we bought a house in suburban Mamaroneck. I learned about married life fast. If Nancy was happy, everybody was happy.

In many ways the *Today* show was like a family. Each weekday morning at dawn we all met in the make-up room and chatted about our children and what was going on in our lives while they made us presentable for the cameras. Sleep, or the absence of same, was often a topic of conversation, but none of us ever used the word "adjust" when talking about our sleep deprivation. Most of us used the word "cope," because each person dealt with it in his or her own way.

My daily routine was cut and dried. After going to bed around 10:30 or 11:00 p.m. I always got up at 3:30 a.m., shaved, showered and left for the studio at 4 a.m. Working the early shift at NBC does have its perks, one being a limo dispatched to your door every morning without fail. Rain or shine, my driver Morty Goldstein was always parked by the kitchen door ready to whisk me to Rockefeller Center over mostly deserted highways as I scanned the early editions of the newspapers.

Consensus among the cast was that NBC sent the car not out of concern for our comfort, but to make sure we didn't oversleep and miss the show. Weatherman Willard Scott sized it up for me:. "I guess you realize, John, they treat us like hookers. They send a car for us in the morning, but when they're done with us, we have to get home the best way we can."

In my case, it was usually the train back to our suburban home.

During those *Today* show years I tried not to nap in the afternoons, knowing it would make getting to sleep that night more difficult. But by Wednesday afternoon the sleep deprivation usually took its toll and a nap became inevitable. When Friday night rolled around Nancy and I often went out to dinner, but more than once she had to grab me just before my face fell into my dinner plate.

*

A couple of months after we settled in our baby was scheduled to arrive. After Nancy's due date passed, hardly a day went by that Bryant or Jane didn't ask on air, "John, any news about the baby?" When two weeks had passed, our executive producer Steve Friedman issued an embargo: no more on-air questions about the impending birth. Worried that things might not turn out well, Steve didn't want to let the baby watch become a big deal on the show. I understood, and Nancy and I had our own concerns.

Finally, the day did come. I was in the delivery room with Nancy that Friday afternoon, Dec. 10, when our first daughter arrived, and Molly's photo taken a few hours after birth aired the next morning on *Today*. During my seven years with the program Nancy and I were blessed with two more daughters, Carter and Hope. I suppose NBC is in our genes, for both Nancy and I are NBC alumni, and now grown-up Molly is a producer with *Today* in Los Angeles and Hope is researcher for *Today* in Washington. And Carter, who spent several months as an intern at *Saturday Night Live*, is currently a casting associate in Los Angeles.

As for our television ratings, all of us on the cast of the *Today* show—Bryant Gumbel, Jane Pauley, Willard Scott, Gene Shalit and I—were pleased to see the numbers gradually improve as we became more familiar and more welcome at America's breakfast tables. But the race still wasn't over. We were in an uphill contest against *Good Morning America*.

About this time a Hollywood producer approached me and asked if I would consider playing myself as *Today* show news anchor in a murder mystery, *The Mean Season*, which was being filmed in Florida with Mariel Hemingway and Kurt Russell. Participation in such a venture without approval from top management was contrary to NBC News policy, but when I approached Steve Friedman about it, he urged me on: "It'll be good for you and good for the show."

So I went for it. When the movie was released, I rushed a few blocks to a theater in Times Square to see myself on the big screen. I confess to sitting through three screenings of the film just to see my 18-second bit part.

A few days later, Tim Russert, an NBC News vice president and host of *Meet the Press*, stopped me in the hallway at NBC. "Am I crazy, or did I see you in a movie the other day?"

My heart skipped a couple of beats. I felt sure I was about to be fired for doing it, but much to my relief Russert just slapped me on the shoulder and said "Good job" before going on his way. I never heard any more about my sole venture onto the silver screen, and the movie wasn't a great success. All the same, after it was released on DVD in 2004, I forced our three daughters to watch it more than once.

*

As for Steve Friedman, he was an extraordinary executive producer, a hater of bureaucracy and a shrewd judge of talent. Always open to new ideas, he was loyal to his staff, even though his methods were a bit unorthodox. Steve's desk was never cluttered, and he made decisions about upcoming *Today* show segments on the spot. Whenever a producer came into his office to pitch an idea, Steve reacted immediately from the gut. "No," he'd say, "that won't work," or "That's good, go ahead and move on it." No pussyfooting around. Steve loved baseball and kept a bat in his office, a practice that could intimidate a producer who'd come to pitch his idea while Steve stood behind his desk swinging the bat.

Today show lore includes at least one legendary story about Steve. When he first took over the program, he noticed that anytime Bryant or Jane began speaking the audio engineer was late in switching on the appropriate microphone. To remedy matters, Steve told the engineer to put a piece of red tape on Bryant's mic and a strip of blue tape on Jane's, along with corresponding colors on the control-panel switches to make sure he always hit the right one.

When the problem persisted in spite of Steve's fix, he demanded to know why.

The engineer told him, "Because I don't have a color television monitor."

"Well, get one," Steve said.

"I'd like to, but the way things work around here, it would take NBC weeks to get around to bringing in a color monitor in place of my black-and-white one."

Undaunted, Steve said, "What if this one broke today? Couldn't you get a new one by tomorrow?"

"Well, sure."

Steve had his answer, and with one thrust of his cowboy boot he smashed the black-and-white monitor to bits on the spot. Once that story made the rounds, Steve found dealing with the network bureaucracy a piece of cake.

*

Vacation time was always welcome, and on a visit to Miami we joined some friends at a South Beach jazz club where we enjoyed the Latin music of flautist Nestor Torres and his band. A few days later I was chatting with Steve in his office and told him how much I'd liked their music. Steve jumped on my comment like a duck on a June bug. "Let's book him and his band on the show for next Friday."

"Hey, hold everything. I'm a news guy. No musical training." I didn't mention "The Marine Hymn."

"That's not important. If you liked him, so will our viewers."

The following week NBC flew Nestor Torres and his band to New York where we learned, to our great amazement, that his father was a substitute cameraman on our own show. So when it came time for Nestor's segment I introduced him on the air along with his dad, who had the pleasure of shooting his son's New York debut. Today Nestor is a Latin Grammy winner and successful recording artist with a national reputation.

*

I think it must have been 1984 when all of us at the *Today* show had to face up to something we'd long dreaded. We knew it was coming, the awful day when NBC's tech people descended upon us with computers and took away our faithful old typewriters, but we hoped they'd put it off as long as possible. That uncomfortable day came for me one morning when I arrived at 4:30 a.m. to begin preparation for my four *Today* show newscasts and panicked at the sight of one of those newfangled machines sitting on my very own desk.

Where, oh where was my typewriter? I felt physically ill when someone told me that every last one of them had been stacked unceremoniously in cardboard cartons and carried away like so much offal. Never mind that a technician well versed in the ways of computers was on hand to teach us this new way of doing things as we fought off panic and wrote those first newscasts without our beloved old friends. It was not the same. Relics of the past those typewriters might have been, but we depended on them, we knew how they worked, we needed them!

To allay our fears that the new computers might crash just before airtime and leave us helpless, one of the technicians who'd obviously taken a psychology course in college retrieved one old IBM Selectric dinosaur and set it up under a glass case with a hammer beside it, labeled BREAK GLASS IN CASE OF EMERGENCY. Whew. If all else failed, just knowing it was there gave us some sense of comfort. Yet in spite of our fears and my temptation to break that glass more than once, we somehow resisted ever using that hammer. As newsreels at the movie theatres used to remind us, time does march on, dragging progress with it.

By the time that safety net was removed a few weeks later, we were all able to use the computers quite well and write our copy much faster and more efficiently. When I look back today, I can't imagine how we ever managed to get along without the computer.

And yet . . . and yet . . . to this day, whenever I walk into a newsroom it's the silence that strikes me. I still miss the comforting clacking of those old typewriter keys.

*

Four years would pass before *Today* reigned supreme in morning television. In her book about *Today*, Judy Kessler quoted Steve's thumbnail summary of our cast: "Steve had his new team: street-wise in Bryant, everybody's sweetheart in Jane, the wacky uncle in Willard, the wacky cousin in Gene Shalit, and the man every mother wanted her daughter to marry in John Palmer." Whether it was true or not, the show was bound for success.

The *Today* show cast was and is its key to success. Co-anchor Bryant Gumbel was a hard worker who prepared meticulously for each interview. Some viewers found Bryant's interview technique overly aggressive, and while it's true he doesn't suffer fools lightly, I often wondered whether the criticism would be so sharp if he were white. It's been said many times, and I agree, that Bryant seemed completely natural, almost effortless in his role as host. He and I shared a fondness for margaritas and often talked about our fathers and how influential they'd been in our lives. We laughed a lot together, and he used to kid me unmercifully about putting mayonnaise as well as mustard on my hot dogs.

One morning, reading the papers as I always did while Morty drove me to work, I came across a Gumbel quote in *The Daily News*. In the article Bryant referred to *Today* as "my show," a comment I considered a bit egotistical. When I got to work I shot off an email to my friend and *Today* show news producer Jim Dick: "Did you see that Haig-esque comment by Bryant referring to the *Today* show as HIS program?"

My allusion was to the aftermath of President Reagan's being shot when Alexander Haig, then secretary of state, rushed into the White House Briefing Room to announce to reporters, "I am in control here." Haig had been under the erroneous impression that in the presidential line of succession the U.S. Constitution placed him first after the vice president of the United States.

At any rate, I'd no sooner clicked "Send" on my computer than I realized, to my horror, that I'd sent the message not to Jim but to Bryant himself. Panicked, I considered several options including sneaking into Bryant's office and throwing his computer through the window down to Rockefeller Center's ice rink. In the end I chose a less violent course with this follow-up email to Bryant: "The message you have just read from me, obviously, was not meant for your eyes. I trust it has not damaged our friendship."

He never mentioned the incident to me directly, but when I walked into the studio that morning he did give me a smile and a knowing glance. Several years later when I was leaving the show Bryant recorded a videotaped message that was played at my going-away party in which he said I would always be his friend and we could just keep that errant email to ourselves.

*

Then there was the case of the leaked memo—in this case, Bryant's. While hosting the 1988 Olympics in Seoul, Marty Ryan, by then the executive producer of *Today*, asked Bryant to send him a critique of the show, its content and its cast. With his usual straightforwardness and brutal honesty Bryant complied, warning that the memo was for Marty's eyes only, potentially explosive stuff. Few members of the *Today* show, including me, escaped his critical judgment, although we knew nothing about it at the time. Bryant wrote that my newscasts were not terribly well written, adding, "John doesn't make it a lot better and it looks like every other newscast anywhere and everywhere."

He complained that Gene Shalit's reviews were often late and that his interviews weren't very good. But Bryant's biggest target was weatherman Willard Scott, whom he accused of holding the show hostage to his assortment of whims, wishes, birthdays and bad taste. Nor did he spare Marty Ryan himself, nailing him for "a lack of guidance and a lack of willingness to stand on folks and make sure they do what's necessary." Bryant did, at Marty's request, withhold any comment on co-anchor Jane.

Five months later on the day NBC switched to a new computer system, a glitch left the memo out there for all to see. It was quickly duplicated on the Internet and picked up by the press, tarnishing the illusion for many viewers that the *Today* show cast was one big happy family. Public airing of the memo was extremely painful for all of us, including Bryant, whose critique had damaged the program he was trying to improve. Even Jane must have wondered what harsh opinions of her he had kept to himself.

*

A few times I found myself on the hot seat because of what I had said in one of my news reports, one of them after word came that Woody Hayes, the legendary Ohio State football coach, had died. He had compiled an amazing record of wins during his 28-year tenure at the university. I was at my *Today* news desk on March 12, 1987, preparing for my 8 a.m. newscast when reports of his death came across the wire. With little time to spare, I wrote a brief obit to deliver on the air and promptly set off a firestorm of Buckeye State resentment.

Here's how it read: "Woody Hayes of Ohio State University, one of the most successful coaches in college football, died today. He was a member of the College Football Hall of Fame and compiled an enviable lifetime record of 238 wins. But many people remember Hayes for an incident that cost him his job at Ohio State, in which he punched an opposition player in the throat after the player intercepted a pass along the Buckeye sideline."

The phones began ringing within minutes after I read that item on the air. I took a number of those hostile calls myself, all with basically the same complaint—I should not have mentioned the incident when Hayes's temper got the best of him. Several callers even suggested that if I ever visited Ohio, they would express their displeasure with me in more physical ways. Two weeks later I received a letter with a copy of a church bulletin from a Columbus minister who had devoted his entire Sunday morning sermon to people like NBC's John Palmer, who dwell on one unfortunate incident in the life of a great man who accomplished so much. Apparently hell hath no fury like the Ohio State football fans.

*

I first met film critic Gene Shalit while anchoring the early evening news on New York's NBC affiliate, long before he became a *Today* show star. An accomplished writer and critic with a phobia about live television, Gene showed great courage and determination in overcoming that fear, using his appearances on the New York affiliate as a proving ground and going on afterward to become one of the best-liked and most successful members of the *Today* show cast. With his infectious laugh, Gene is a favorite with the public as well as with fellow members of the cast, past and present.

Willard Scott was probably the most widely recognized one of us. Whenever I traveled with him, people greeted him everywhere—on the streets, at airports, at sporting events. Dining out with Willard was a memorable experience because other patrons would wave from nearby tables and send over bottles of wine and champagne.

Willard suffered from a severe fear of heights. Acrophobia, it's called. He readily admitted to it and would talk openly about it. Whether he was telling the truth or not, he recounted for the rest of us how he cured himself of it by a method I wouldn't recommend to a soul. The Chesapeake Bay Bridge that connects Maryland with the Delmarva Peninsula is long and very high, and Willard declared to us that he went out and bought a six-pack of beer, set it next to him on the front seat of his car and drove back and forth across the that bridge fortifying himself with booze until he lost his fear of heights. We hoped Willard was kidding, but that's how he swore he'd overcome it. We all agreed we were glad we weren't driving the other way across the bridge that night.

At NBC's request, Willard moved to New York City and stayed for several years to do his weather from the studio with the rest of us, but he always missed the Virginia farm he shared with his wife Mary until she passed away a few years ago. Willard loved being home on the farm so much, he even suggested that if the *Today* producers would paint the national weather map on the side of his barn he could do the weather every morning right there on the place. If they'd agreed, he'd probably have gone on the air in overalls and a frayed straw hat, pointing a pitchfork at the map. When his sensible wife got wind of that flight of fancy, though, she called a halt. "Willard has the rest of the world as his playground, but the farm is private, and it will *not* be the location for a television show."

In the make-up room before the show, especially on Mondays after the weekend, Willard always had a story to tell. He came in one Monday morning complaining bitterly. "I threw my back out something awful over the weekend."

"How'd you do that, Willard?"

"You see, my tax man told me I'd have to do something to get some tax breaks, and the best thing would be to buy some houses I could rent out. So I bought some, and after a refrigerator in one of 'em busted, I spent the weekend on my back trying to fix it."

"Good Lord, Willard," I said, "you make so much money, why on earth would you do that?" I knew he was pulling down well over $1 million per year.

He looked outraged. "D'you have any idea what electricians and plumbers make these days?"

We all broke into laughter, because we were damn sure they didn't make as much as the weatherman on *Today*. He could afford to hire platoons of repairmen, but Willard was anything but a spendthrift. We used to joke that he had the first dollar he ever made. He was a joy to work with, and his energy and humor got us through many long mornings on the show.

It's been said of Jane Pauley that she's never changed from the delightful, warm and friendly young woman she was when she left Indianapolis. Every word is true. She's been my loyal friend and confidante ever since I joined the show in 1982, and while *Today* was certainly important in her life, it was way down the list of her priorities after her husband Gary Trudeau and their children. Later I'll recount a simple kindness from her to me that I'll never forget.

For this Tennessee boy those *Today* show years were heady ones. I confess that I was surprised and excited to be recognized at airports and restaurants, stopped on the street from time to time by people who wanted to comment on the news or ask for an autograph. What a far cry from the dangerous streets of Beirut.

One evening I was walking along 59th Street by the Plaza Hotel when a man buttonholed me and insisted I was sportscaster Dick Enberg. Although there is some resemblance between us, in spite of my vigorous denials this stranger threatened to bust me one unless I admitted I was Enberg. At that point I walked briskly away, and fortunately he was in no shape to give chase and carry out his threat.

Former president Jimmy Carter and I crossed paths again when he was working as a carpenter in Lower Manhattan helping to renovate a building for Habitat for Humanity. I was subbing for Bryant on *Today* and as I interviewed Carter on the program he urged me, on-air to come down and join him and Mrs. Carter on the job. He was so persistent that the next day I brought jeans and an old shirt to work and joined the volunteers after the show. At noon as we gathered at a church across the street, Carter explained the lunch plans, much to my amusement, to me and his fellow workers, most of them Baptists from Georgia: "We'll all walk to a kosher restaurant a few blocks away, and when we get there and get seated, do *not* order a glass of milk and a ham sandwich!"

At the puzzled looks on the faces of his volunteers, the former president with his years of experience campaigning in Jewish communities around the country launched into a lengthy discussion of kosher cuisine and dietary rules—more than any of us wanted or needed to know. At last as we reached the restaurant, a Secret Service agent grabbed me by the arm: "No press allowed." The former president's wife Rosalyn saw what was happening and interceded for me. "Stop, John's not a reporter today. He's working for Habitat for Humanity. Let him through."

*

The *Today* show has what's called a co-op period—five minutes out of each half hour when affiliated stations cut away from the network to broadcast local news reports. Because some smaller stations don't make use of this newsbreak, the *Today* show cast usually fills that time with informal chats about the day's news or other topics. It was during one of these co-op periods that Bryant asked me, "What would you like to be doing if you weren't doing this?"

That was easy. "You know how much I love fishing. I've always wanted to run a charter fishing boat."

In no time came a deluge of letters and emails from viewers wanting to sell me their boats, marinas and fishing camps! The response was so overwhelming that it made me reconsider my dream job—if so many people wanted to get out of that business it must not be all that I had imagined.

One year around the holidays we decided to use the co-op period to exchange Christmas presents and drew names ahead of time. I drew Jane's and was wondering what to give her when I spotted, in a Fifth Avenue store window, a hunk of chocolate the size and shape of a woman's leg. Jane adored that delicious substance, and I knew the instant I saw it she'd love the chocolate leg. So that was what she got at gift-giving time, and we all had a good laugh. Since I'd presented it to her on the air, I figured NBC would reimburse me the $300 it cost. When NBC refused, I managed to pad my next expense account to make up for it, and the accountants never discovered the leg.

*

The *Today* show road trips were great fun—Rome, Paris, the Orient Express, every imaginable exotic locale. Fun, that is, for everyone but me, because I was left behind to mind the shop.

Something that happened when the show originated from Rio de Janeiro sealed my fate. The live broadcast had barely begun when a storm knocked out the communications satellite, and all at once the nightmare that keeps network television producers from sleeping became a reality. In our New York control room producer Scott Goldstein started rolling commercials on the air hard and fast as he shouted to me at the news desk: "Be ready to vamp to fill air time until we can get the satellite back!" It was awful. I have no idea what I said, but at least fifteen minutes seemed to drag by before the satellite came back up. From that day to this, the show keeps backup videotapes of interviews and features at the ready in New York with the news anchor on stand-by in the studio, should the satellite fail.

Whenever the show was on the road, Jane and Bryant would often throw it back to me for the news in New York with the line, "John, we wish you were here." It became such a joke that Steve Friedman decided it would be fun to have me show up in Miami to join the rest of the cast aboard the cruise ship Norway. As he often did when I was away, my colleague Bob Jamison filled in for me at the news desk.

Off to join the fun and games, despite my limited experience with scuba diving I appeared that Friday morning on the ship's deck in a rubber suit with two dive tanks strapped to my back. The problem arose when I realized, as I slipped into the ship's pool for a scuba-diving exhibition, that the production crew had put too few weights on my dive belt. Rather than gliding along the bottom of the pool, I floundered around on the surface like a beached sea turtle. That day's comic diversion with me as the goat sent me back to the New York studio never to go on the road again.

In spite of everyone's best efforts weird things did happen on *Today*. Again, I was subbing for Bryant and kicked off an interview with puppeteer-ventriloquist Shari Lewis when she suddenly stretched out her hand to settle her puppet Lamb Chop on my shoulder. For the rest of that interview with Shari, all my questions to her were answered by Lamb Chop, still perched on my shoulder, in his squeaky falsetto voice. It was cute at first but quickly became tedious and awkward. As I struggled to finish the interview, producer Marty Ryan, sensing my discomfort, playfully baited me through my earpiece: "So this is the distinguished NBC News Correspondent John Palmer!"

My discomfort in dealing with such light subjects had to be evident, but as time went on any such challenge stretched and broadened me. After all, this was the *Today* show, not the evening news, and I came to understand that having a little fun on the air was natural and absolutely a good thing—no threat whatever to one's credibility.

We rehearsed only one part of the *Today* show—the two-minute opening—to ensure that all mics and video switches were operating properly. In that warm-up, Jane or Bryant would voice-over a videotape of some newsworthy event, discuss upcoming program segments, then introduce me at the news desk. On one such morning, however, the clock moved up on 7 a.m. leaving no time to rehearse, so they went ahead with the show opening live. I must have been distracted, because when Bryant said, "Now let's go to John Palmer for the latest news," I, thinking we were doing the usual rehearsal, just said, "Howdy do" then sat there mute. Five seconds of dead air ensued, and it was not until I spotted our floor director Jim Straka frantically waving his arms and pointing both hands at me that I managed to pull myself together to actually deliver the news.

I felt slightly less sheepish about my goof after I recalled the same thing happening to my colleague and friend Emery King. At the time Emery had been on the White House lawn ready to deliver his report, with Connie Chung subbing for Jane. When Connie introduced Emery with a question about President Reagan's reaction to some foreign policy development, Emery, thinking it was just a rehearsal, said, "How should I know, Connie?" He, too, quickly recovered, said, "I'm sorry," and delivered his report. Ah, the fun of live television.

As I said, weird things could happen on our show. Another morning's news had as its lead story the crash of a commercial airliner in Libya. There were survivors, including the pilot, who'd been interviewed in his hospital room shortly after the crash. I was already on the air when our control room producer told me via my earpiece that a videotape of the pilot describing the crash had just arrived via satellite. I led into the tape, and up on the monitor popped the image of the pilot lying in bed and describing his crash landing.

What no one had told us was that the pilot must have wanted to remain incognito, because he pulled the bedsheet over his face and kept it there throughout his remarks. Bizarre was hardly the word. Over at the anchor desk Bryant, ever the jokester, pulled out his handkerchief and put it over his face as I struggled to keep my composure. Jane promptly did the same, and the rest of the studio crew followed suit. It was hilarious, and I would have joined in the laughter had I not known that the pilot's interview might end at any second, when an appropriately grave expression would be called for from me. All I could do to keep from bursting into guffaws was to dig my hand into the edge of the news desk and bite the inside of my cheeks. Later, when I appeared with Jay Leno on the *Tonight* show I took the opportunity to relate the event with a handkerchief over my own face. Yes, I'd learned to loosen up.

We never knew when our entire cast and studio might break up in uncontrollable laughter, as when weatherman Joe Witte asked Bryant on the air, "Do you ever paint your balls red and play golf in the snow?" For weeks afterward we chortled about that one.

12

EVEN GOOD THINGS MUST END

IN 1986, FOUR years after I joined the *Today* show, the program moved up into first place, grossing more than $200 million a year, and remained the most popular early-morning program for the next three and a half years. By the time my contract had only a couple more months to run, my agent Ralph Mann got in touch with NBC News President Michael Gartner to open negotiations on my behalf, only to be turned away with the words, "Not now." I found that strange but dismissed it, thinking there must be a backlog of contract negotiations. After all, we thought we were at the top of our game.

Then in late August 1989 NBC Chairman Bob Wright and his wife Suzanne threw a lavish Sunday afternoon garden party for 100 or so guests at their Connecticut estate, including senior producers and on-air broadcasters from the news and sports divisions. With Nancy by my side, I was there decked out in my blue blazer, open shirt and white pants, a few weeks short of marking my seventh year as news anchor for the *Today* show.

The network was flying high with superb ratings, and we were celebrating prospects of even greater success in the coming television season. At first the atmosphere of the event was congenial and fun, for we all knew an invitation to that party meant you were a valued member of the NBC family. General Electric's Chairman Jack Welch even fetched me a beer.

We hadn't been there long when I sensed that something was wrong. Dick Ebersol, president of NBC Sports, had just been inexplicably named executive in charge of *Today*, and I noticed he seemed to be avoiding me while doting on Deborah Norville, one of the network's newest on-air talents. A strikingly beautiful 29-year-old blonde, Deborah was then anchoring *NBC News at Sunrise*. It wasn't just my imagination, because the bad vibes I felt that afternoon soon turned out to be correct.

The week after the garden party Gartner called asking to see me—more bad vibes. I took the elevator up to his office, sure something big was up. When I walked in, he was behind his desk, peering over the reading glasses perched on his nose, and motioned for me to take a seat. He then got up, walked over, shook my hand, and sat down beside me.

"I like the job you're doing on the *Today* show, John."

More than wary, I just said, "Thanks."

"Beyond that, you were a terrific White House correspondent and a terrific overseas correspondent for us."

Again, I thanked him. "Now, where's the but?"

Then the boom fell. Gartner stared back at me for a moment

before he came out with the brutal truth. "We'd like someone else to do the news on the *Today* show."

I was numb, totally speechless, hardly able to take in his next remark.

"You've been doing the news on the *Today* show forever. Aren't you looking for a change?"

Finally I found words in a reply my dad had used on a similar occasion years before. "Well, it's your candy store. Who's lined up to take my job?"

"There's a feeling here," Gartner said, "that we'd like Deborah Norville to do the news on *Today*. Understand, John, you did nothing wrong. It's just that we think more of our morning viewers would rather get their news from a woman than from a man."

Stone-faced and silent, I listened as he went on.

"We want you to stay with us, so give some thought to what you'd like to do next with NBC News. Would you like to go overseas again? You name it, and we can make it happen. And until you decide what you really want, you can take over Deborah's job as anchor of *NBC News at Sunrise*."

Then Gartner confirmed what I suspected—that it had been somebody else's decision. "Look, I know the news business, and Dick Ebersol knows television. He wants to make some changes."

Tempted to argue with that old saw, "If it ain't broke, don't fix it," I knew saying anything else was futile. Instead I simply stood up, shook his hand and left.

Back in my office I closed the door to call Nancy and, with tears in my eyes, told her the news. She was stunned too, but right away my number-one fan bounced back. "Don't worry," she said. "We'll be fine."

That was hard, very, very hard. I loved doing the news on the *Today* show. Despite the early hours and other inconveniences, I found it thoroughly satisfying and had hoped to stay with the show for several more years.

A few days after I got the painful news, my friend Jane Pauley really showed her colors. I was leaving the make-up room to head down the hall to my temporary assignment anchoring *NBC News at Sunrise* when Jane called to me, "Wait, John. Let's walk together." She told me that after spending mornings with me for seven years, she would miss my presence on the show and miss me even more as a friend. Then she came out with a shocker: "I wanted you to know, I am leaving the show too."

I thought she was kidding until I saw her eyes well up. She told me that she and her husband, Gary, had talked it over, because the atmosphere had changed and she no longer found doing the program fun. She made it clear that after so many successful years with *Today* she didn't need the tension that was already apparent. All she wanted was to tear up her multimillion-dollar contract and go home to her family.

The suits at NBC couldn't understand that, least of all Gartner and Ebersol, who were sure it was just a ploy—Jane holding out for more money. They finally saw the light when Tom Brokaw told them, "Look, guys, Jane is dead serious." After weeks of negotiation Jane did leave *Today*, staying on with the network to co-anchor the successful *Dateline NBC*. So much for Ebersol's telling her she wasn't ready for prime time. A few weeks later Deborah took maternity leave and never returned to the *Today* show.

I had seen Ebersol at the garden party, but I'd never spoken with the man, and I noticed that any time he saw me in the hall at work he quickly took a different route. Then one morning as I was clearing out my office a knock came at my door. It was Ebersol. "Mind if I come in?"

"No, but you can see I don't have any furniture."

He shrugged. "A packing box will do. I just want you to know, John, that your situation is my number-one priority and will be until your future is resolved to your satisfaction."

That was the first and last time we ever spoke.

Not surprisingly, Jane's departure triggered a plunge in the

Today ratings. But soon after Katie Couric became co-host the show reached new highs that continued when Meredith Vieira took Katie's place. The secret of success? More news and less fluff.

The seven years I spent on the show were among the happiest of my life, and in spite of the sudden ending to my tenure on *Today* I left with a great fondness for the program and its cast and crew, carrying away with me a wonderful store of memories.

⁂

In the unsettled days following my departure from *Today* and, more significantly, Jane Pauley's announcement that she too would be leaving the top-rated morning television news program, NBC News President Michael Gartner approached me again. This time he offered me the job of principal news anchor at the NBC-owned television station in Miami. To sweeten the deal, he said the news division would also name me Latin American correspondent, which meant a fatter paycheck.

When Gartner said, "There's too much blood on the floor already over this whole *Today* show mess," I felt a distinct wind at my back encouraging me to quietly get out of town and head south. And I nearly did. Nancy and I visited Miami, found a lovely house and checked out schools for our three daughters.

Then, just as I was about to sign a new contract, King World Productions in New York, syndicators of such television hits as *The Oprah Winfrey Show*, *Wheel of Fortune*, and *Concentration*, approached me with an offer to anchor their new program *Instant Recall*. I jumped at the opportunity, first because it was a news program, and also because anchoring in New York meant our family could stay in our home in Rye. The television program looked back at major events and news stories of the preceding 25 years. It gave me my own half-hour television program syndicated to stations across the country and the opportunity to interview dozens of well-known Americans of national and international prominence;

in essence, pretty much anybody I wanted to bring on. Those I did interview included former secretaries of state Henry Kissinger and Dean Rusk, polio-vaccine developer Dr. Jonas Salk, test pilot Chuck Yeager and many more outstanding personalities.

Chuck Yeager, one of those unforgettable interview subjects, was a West Virginian who had flown many missions in Europe during World War II before being shot down over France. In 1947, after the war, he flew the Bell X-15 rocket research aircraft at speeds in excess of 670 mph, thus breaking the sound barrier—the first pilot to do so. When I interviewed him at a hotel in Sacramento in December of 1990 he came in wearing a leather jacket and said as he sat down: "John, I apologize for being late. You see, my wife has been suffering in the final stages of cancer, and all the family gathered at her bedside today and made the decision to pull the plug. That's why I was didn't get here sooner."

My God, I thought, as much as this man loved his wife, and I knew that he did—they'd had a long and wonderful marriage, and during his days as a pilot he'd had "Glamorous Glennis" stenciled on the nose of one of his planes—in one way he had to have had ice water running through his veins, to come to an interview about his exploits as a test pilot at such an emotionally charged time.

Go ahead we did, though, and he spoke modestly about his aviation adventures and misadventures, such as having to eject from one of the experimental planes at such a height that the air was too thin to support his parachute canopy. He'd needed to free-fall down to denser air before pulling the ripcord. Not only was his clothing torn from his body, so was a layer of skin. Afterward, he told me, when he landed in the desert out west he separated himself from his parachute and struggled to a highway, looking like "a pink man from Mars," where a car finally stopped to pick him up. The guy's bravery was unbelievable.

A primary subject of Tom Wolfe's book *The Right Stuff*, Yeager is the most courageous man I ever met. I believe one of the great disappointments of Chuck Yeager's life is that he was never chosen as an astronaut. NASA wanted the first eight original astronauts all to be smooth, college-educated, well spoken. And though Chuck hadn't gone to college, he was a brave man and a great test pilot, with every qualification to make the grade as an astronaut.

Another memorable *Instant Recall* interview was with Dr. Jonas Salk, developer of the polio vaccine that saved millions of people from one of the most dreaded diseases of the 20th century. Someone too young to have lived through the awful poliomyelitis epidemics can't comprehend the terror that disease instilled in families everywhere. It killed tens of thousands of children worldwide, left many more invalids who would spend the remainder of their lives in an iron lung so they could breathe, and crippled untold numbers of other adults. Franklin D. Roosevelt was one of its victims, as we 1940s youngsters knew so well.

No disease drew as much attention or struck with the same terror as polio. It ravaged muscles, paralyzed chests and in many instances killed its victims. I had a schoolmate who was condemned to wear leather-and-steel leg braces, while others were lucky enough to escape with only an atrophied limb. In the summer of 1951, when I was sixteen years old, there were 58,000 poliomyelitis cases in the United States, thousands more around the world. Such was the fear of this plague that when Wytheville, Virginia, 92 miles away, suffered a major polio outbreak with 189 cases and nearly two dozen deaths, our own town closed its swimming pools and movie theaters. In one of those Wytheville families, five of eight children fell ill.

What rejoicing there was, then, at the announcement on April 12, 1955, that Dr. Jonas Salk had developed a vaccine to prevent polio. Church bells pealed, car horns blared. Science had defeated the enemy that had struck down so many.

Thus it was with these powerful childhood memories that I began my interview with Dr. Salk, near his laboratory in southern California, some 35 years after he and his research team were hailed as national heroes. He, too, was a man of great courage.

When nationwide field trials of the new vaccine began in 1954, ultimately involving nearly two million children, it was Jonas Salk who administered the first vaccine injections himself. He told me why.

"If these first batches made from dead strains of the polio virus turned out to be bad, and the children came down with polio, I wanted to be the one to live with that the rest of my life, not some innocent nurse."

After our interview I'd returned to my room with just time enough to change clothes and grab my suitcase for a dash to the airport when the phone rang. I answered with an irritable "Hello!"

"John, this is Jonas Salk. I'm calling from the house phone downstairs, because I just heard that the main freeway to the airport is blocked by a bad accident. If you have a pencil and paper I'll give you a route through back roads that will get you there in time."

Busy as he was, Dr. Salk still had time to help others, even if merely to avoid a traffic delay. This admirable man was searching for an AIDS vaccine—still trying to help others—when he died in 1995 at the age of 80.

*

As I look back over my 40-plus years in broadcasting, having covered hundreds of political changes, hurricanes, wars, murders, race riots, Indian revolts, assassinations, strikes and a multitude of other notable events, I still regret having missed the opportunity to cover one historic event. On the night of Nov. 9, 1989, I was filled with envy to see my colleague and friend, Tom Brokaw, stand in front of the Berlin Wall as it came down. What a moment in history! There Tom was, reporting live on the network, as East Germans tore down the wall that had separated East and West Berlin for three decades. And so, like millions of others throughout the world, I watched the fall of Communism and end of the Cold War on television, wishing I could have been there myself.

To my dismay, *Instant Recall* lasted for just one season. The show had a budget of around $13 million, and although that first year we took in about $11 million in revenue, King World Productions was used to making huge profits and anticipated that our second-year profitability wouldn't justify their time and effort. The program was well received by viewers, but every program brings out the occasional critic.

After I did a piece on baseball great Joe DiMaggio, broadcaster Bill O'Reilly, who was then host of King World's tabloid program *Inside Edition*, suggested that my DiMaggio piece needed a lot more Marilyn Monroe. "More tits and ass," he said. "That sells!" Fortunately for me, from the outset my attorney Bob Barnett had negotiated a contract that specifically stated that if *Instant Recall* were cancelled I could not be assigned to anchor any other King World program, and that included *Inside Edition*. At that point I realized I wouldn't be a good fit for me or for them.

Once again my future looked uncertain until a few months later when I heard from my friend Bill Chesleigh, a former news producer with NBC News who was now executive producer at Christian Science Monitor Television in Boston. Bill prompted me to join their fledgling television operation, which I was glad to do. While I anchored their main evening program focusing on international news, we didn't shy away from domestic medical stories either. We knew that some of these stories, such as our reports on AIDS and treatments available for it, did not sit well with some members of the denomination who believed deeply in the healing powers of Christian Science. Our editor David Cook, himself a Christian Scientist and a superb journalist, shielded the news team from pressure.

It was a sad day when after only a few months on the air the church elders concluded that operating the channel was too expensive to justify. When they pulled the plug I felt like a rider who'd just had another fine horse shot out from under him. The Monitor honored my no-cut contract, as I knew it would, and transferred me to Washington where I spent many productive months working for Monitor Radio.

Then, at wife Nancy's suggestion, I called Tim Russert, Washington Bureau Chief for NBC News, and asked about rejoining the network.

"Is this the same John Palmer who walked away from the network several years ago?" he impishly inquired. I confessed that it was. A week later, as promised, he returned my call and said NBC News would be pleased to have me return. So I spent the next eight years back at NBC as a news correspondent covering the White House for the network and for MSNBC.

*

When I came back to the White House in 1993 with William Jefferson Clinton as president, my reporting duties took on a distinctly livelier tone. Although Ronald Reagan got irked with the press from time to time, I think he genuinely liked members of the press—maybe the only president who actually did. His Hollywood career had undoubtedly taught him the value of good publicity, but I think the truth about Reagan was that he just liked people in general. Whether Clinton liked us or not, he was not standoffish like Jimmy Carter, and he impressed us as a pretty approachable guy. We knew he liked people, too, and he always enjoyed having an audience.

We were all very tired when we boarded an Air Force One flight back from California and quite glad to have time for a drink and a movie or to work on our stories. When President Clinton came back from his cabin up front he was wearing a workshirt, boots and jeans, which he often wore on the plane. He appropriated the roll-away suitcase of Todd Purdam, the White House correspondent for *The New York Times*, plopped it down in the aisle, and sat on it. At that time, Clinton was pretty hefty, carrying about 220 pounds or so. It was obvious he wanted to talk, so Press Secretary Mike McCurry told us, "Guys, let's make this a brief discussion, short and informal and off the record."

We objected to making it off the record, but they both insisted it would just be a casual chat. Over time, as we watched Todd's suitcase get more and more squashed, it became clear that the "brief discussion" world go on for hours. The president held forth almost all the way across the country. At the time, the president was contemplating military action under NATO in Bosnia to stop the ethnic cleansing. We already knew that he'd read extensively in Thomas Jefferson's writings. Now he told us about what he'd learned of Abraham Lincoln's struggle to gain enough popular support to be re-elected, in the midst of the War Between the States with slain Federal soldiers being brought back every day to Pittsburgh, Cleveland, Boston—bodies of sons, husbands, fathers, brothers.

Clinton clearly thought Lincoln's situation paralleled the one he would face if he sent troops into Bosnia for what could be a long and potentially bloody fight and wondered how he'd explain such a decision and its consequences to the American people. He'd already done some polling that suggested sending troops to Bosnia would be unpopular, because our country's ox was not being gored. Others' oxes were being gored, however, and Clinton saw it as a moral matter in which the U.S. had to stand as a moral authority in the world.

In his readings, he said, he'd discovered that Lincoln had been able to "nest the Civil War in the psyche of the American people," framing it in the context that while the struggle might make the lives of his own generation no better, the lives of the next generation of Americans would certainly be better. Lincoln's premise was that, as a nation united rather than a country divided by civil war, the people would work to grow strong and prosper for the sake of future generations. Clinton knew he'd have a hard case to make for going to Bosnia and was searching for some way to sell it to the

American people, although I didn't think the Lincoln analogy was likely to cut much ice.

The president was talking about that and also about a lot of other things. At the time, I was reading a book by General Colin Powell and had it on the seat beside me. He noticed it and said, "John, how's that book?"

I said I found it very interesting.

He said, "I've just finished it myself, and I think it's a good book. He makes some good points, and I agree with him that in any military conflict you must go in with overwhelming force if you don't want to lose the fight."

He talked on and on as we watched Todd's suitcase get progressively more compacted. McCurry would interrupt from time to time, saying, "Mr. President, these journalists cannot live by word alone. It's been a long day for them, and a little food and drink would be appreciated."

Clinton totally ignored the interruptions and went on talking. It was interesting to hear what he had to say, and we were taking notes and rolling tape recorders, because even though it was supposedly off the record, if there was a morsel of news, we had to pluck it out and argue about putting it on the record. We sat up and listened more acutely when the president said at one point, "You know, I think this country is in a funk."

Whoa! That reminded us of the forbidden word "malaise" from Carter's time.

Somebody said, "Do you really mean that?" If the president of the United States said the country was in a funk, it would be well worth reporting.

"Yeah, I do. It is in a funk. You know what a funk is, not bad, not terrible, like a low-grade fever, maybe. You don't feel great. You're in a funk. Generally that's where I think the country is right now."

One of the reporters said, "I'd like to go on record with that, Mr. President, if that's all right with you."

McCurry shook his head. "No, no. This is off the record." Eventually, with a nod from Clinton, McCurry relented.

The president talked about many other things that day besides Bosnia—the merits of dog ownership, the dangers of nuclear proliferation—you name it, he seemed to touch on it. And we couldn't report on a word.

It was a very long trip, with a seemingly tireless president coming back to our cabin to address us at such extraordinary length. He didn't often do that, just usually came back to shoot the bull with us for a little while before retiring to his forward cabin. When he was wound up to talk, we were always a captive audience ready to listen.

An absolutely amazing thing took place on the south lawn of the White House on Sept. 13, 1993—all the more amazing to me after my experiences in the Middle East. Yitzhak Rabin, the prime minister of Israel, and PLO leader Yasser Arafat came together there and shook hands. That handshake—the first ever in public between the two former archenemies—marked the signing of a Declaration of Principles for peace between the Arabs and the Israelis. In his remarks to the assembled crowd that day, Rabin said, "We who have fought against you the Palestinians, we say to you today in a loud and clear voice, enough of blood and tears, enough."

In his turn, Arafat declared, "The difficult decision we reached together was one that required great courage." But several years later Arafat's courage must have failed when he rejected a Clinton-brokered arrangement that would have returned to the Palestinians most of the land captured during their wars with Israel. It takes more courage to make peace than to continue a state of war, and so it was with Arafat.

And Rabin, like Sadat, ultimately paid with his life for his commitment to peace.

*

Covering the Clinton White House brought us in touch with major world-changing events, yet often we also had to report on stories of far less stately import. One thing that had changed greatly by the time the Clintons came to the White House was the press's refusal to hush up presidential sexual adventures. During John F. Kennedy's presidency rumors aplenty flew about his liaisons, but the press gave him a pass on that topic. By the time Bill Clinton took office the gloves were off, and his extramarital activities became fodder for the national press. For a time Gennifer Flowers was a hot news item, then later his other female interests were lumped together as Clinton's "bimbo eruptions."

Like other reporters assigned to the White House beat, I looked forward to covering stories of national and global importance, historic events that would help to shape the future of our country and the world. Thus, it came as a distinct shock when, for two agonizing years of the Clinton administration, the main story from the White House concerned a sleazy sex scandal between the president of the United States and a young White House intern. It was an uncomfortable time for all concerned. Sure, we got on the air a lot, but that didn't make up for the discomfort we all felt in having to deal with that story day after day.

At first, during the time the scandal was unfolding, none of us knew about the sexual liaisons between Bill Clinton and Monica Lewinsky. People often ask me if I knew about it while the affair was going on, and I can honestly say I didn't until it became public knowledge. Looking back later, I realized I'd had a chat with him moments after he'd left Monica in his private office, but I certainly didn't know it at the time, nor even know who she was.

Normally when the president walks from the Mansion to the Oval Office the White House press corps never sees him. He uses the covered colonnade alongside the Rose Garden and enters a set of French doors to his office, shielded from the Press Room the whole way by a wall. No one except the Secret Service agents, who walk with him, ever knows his comings or goings.

The Rose Garden is usually private unless there's a ceremony or a press briefing there, but on the day of the White House garden party when invited guests have access to the garden it would be awkward for the president to walk along that colonnade. Regardless of how much Bill Clinton loved talking to people, even he would choose a different route that day. In the press area there's a room where TV crewmembers sometimes play cards, with a door to an alley that leads straight across to the Mansion. So on that Saturday morning of the garden party the president came through that door into the crew lunchroom. He was dressed casually in Levi's, cowboy boots and a blue workshirt.

The card players greeted him eagerly. "Oh, Mr. President, come sit down with us for a hand or two."

He smiled. "Maybe I will when I come back. Right now I've got some work to do." So he walked purposefully down the hall into the Oval Office. We didn't see him again until about 4:30 p.m., when I noticed a Secret Service agent standing outside our booth—the usual indication that the president is on his way. When I saw the agent chatting with someone in the Associated Press booth, I didn't want the AP getting some piece of news I might miss, so I went out and stood beside the agent to find out if anything unusual was happening.

In a minute the president came along, said, "Hey, John," and started walking back with me in the direction of the NBC booth.

I knew that Mrs. Clinton had made some comments about him on her return from a trip to South America the night before, so I said, "I understand your wife's been traveling and was talking about you last night."

He looked interested. "Really? What'd she say?"

"I just saw a wire story on it. Stop by the booth here and I'll print it out."

He came in with me as I went over to the printer and pressed keys to start the printing. "It's her birthday, you know," he said. "I need to go upstairs because there's going to be a little party for her."

As it happened, this was also the very day when an Arkansas woman named Paula Jones had said publicly she could prove that the president had made inappropriate sexual advances at her by describing the president's unusual private member, which she'd personally seen at close range. Suddenly I remembered, terrified that her comments might also show up on the printout. Clinton kept moving closer to the machine, which was already churning out paper, as I did some fancy footwork to keep him from getting there first. What if the penis comment came up along with whatever Mrs. Clinton had said?

He was reaching for the paper when I jumped four feet ahead. "Wait, Mr. President, I'll get it!"

Annoyed, he said, "You know, I'm not helpless. I might be president of the United States, but I know who to retrieve a printout from this machine."

I held up both palms. "I know, but just a minute. Let me get it, because there's some other stuff in there too." I grabbed the paper myself, scanned it quickly, and passed it over when I saw that the penis story hadn't been printed.

When Special Prosecutor Kenneth Starr came out with his report, I discovered that that particular Saturday was one of the times when Lewinsky had come to the White House by way of the North Gate for an assignation with the president, and when Clinton came through the press area and we had that chat he had just come from being with her in the West Wing.

After the Lewinsky revelations came out and Al Gore was campaigning, he and his wife Tipper didn't want Clinton to play much of a part in their barnstorming. They used him occasionally, as at one rally in Harlem, to try to capture African-American votes. Clinton was very popular with this constituency, but Gore, and especially his wife, worried that the president's philandering would hurt Gore's chances. Tipper Gore had very little use for Clinton after the scandal, and I'm sure she influenced her husband on the subject. I don't think Al Gore had known much about Clinton's carryings-on. He certainly didn't know about Monica, because no one did. People knew Clinton had been a "bad boy" with several girlfriends when he was in Arkansas and I doubt that Hillary Rodham had been under any illusions about the man she was about to marry. Like many women, perhaps she figured he'd reform after they were married and she had him under her control.

In the aftermath of this scandal, President Clinton was impeached by the House of Representatives on Dec. 19, 1998, and acquitted by the Senate on Feb. 12, 1999—the charges being perjury and obstruction of justice. Mr. Clinton claimed the impeachment proceedings were largely political, and indeed, no Democratic representative voted to impeach, while he was acquitted in the Senate with 50 votes each way.

*

It was some time later, when I was packing for a trip to Amelia Island, Florida, to cover President Clinton at a Democratic fundraiser when Mike McCurry suggested I bring my golf clubs along, "just in case." So I had an idea that I might be invited to play golf with the president. Sure enough, I'd just settled into the hotel when an assistant to the president called. "John, plan to meet the president on the first tee tomorrow at 12:30, and don't forget your clubs."

I was excited, for few reporters ever get such a presidential invitation. Clinton plays a lot of golf, but rarely with reporters, and my previous experience of presidential golf outings had been limited to watching him tee off at country clubs all over the place.

Like everyone else who covers the White House regularly I'd heard stories about the unusual number of mulligans President Clinton took—hitting a second ball if the first one doesn't go where you want it to. The Professional Golf Association doesn't think much of the practice, so I wondered whether the First Golfer would play the PGA way.

When I called Nancy the night before the big match I told her how nervous I was, particularly about the first tee where my press-corps colleagues would be watching and taking pictures. We both know that I'm not the greatest golfer in the world. "Don't worry about it," she said. "Just play golf and have fun."

When 12:30 came I was on the first tee, ready to go. After the Secret Service examined my golf bag, I joined two of the president's friends who were to make up our foursome—a businessman from Maryland and a California entrepreneur. Then we waited three-quarters of an hour. I didn't expect the president to be on time, because he rarely was, and while we waited we took the opportunity for a few practice swings. We finally knew he'd soon be joining us after groups of Secret Service agents in golf carts rode our way wearing sunglasses and what looked like bulletproof fishing vests that concealed their sidearms.

All smiles, Clinton greeted us with the suggestion that since he hadn't had a chance to warm up, each of us should hit 10 balls off the first tee before starting play. Now, normally using the first tee as a driving range would cost any golfer his club membership, but not here. We were playing with the First Golfer. After we'd practiced to his satisfaction he stepped back and motioned for me. "John, why don't you hit first?"

I tried to ignore the sinking feeling in my stomach and strode confidently forward to take my stance and tee off. My drive traveled 150 yards out and to the left, hit the trunk of a large oak 30 feet off the ground, and ricocheted into the middle of the fairway.

"Got a little help from nature there," the president muttered, and after the others took their turns and Clinton smashed his ball down the center to within a few feet of the green we were off, accompanied by a dozen Secret Service agents and the club pro.

The long tee shots seemed to be the best part of his game. Bill Clinton takes his golf game very seriously, analyzing every shot. After he sliced the ball into a large pond he whirled around and called out to the pro, "What happened? Did I pull the ball or what?" Later, after the pro gave him what he thought was bad advice about a putt, he was quick to point it out. "You were wrong about that, weren't you?" He wasn't kidding. Time and again he asked the pro about distances to the cup, the pitch of the green, sophisticated questions about strategy. I reckoned he brought the same analytic skills to his golf game as he did to decisions about enlarging NATO, welfare reform and other weighty issues he dealt with every day.

In addition to being highly analytical, Clinton is also a risk-taker. In the same way he loved to "shoot the moon" while playing Hearts aboard Air Force One, or engage in amorous dalliances that might lead to trouble, he enjoyed challenges on the golf course. At one point he tried to take a short cut on a dogleg to the left by hitting his ball over a high stand of trees 250 yards down the fairway, and he almost made it. Almost.

Whenever he made a good tee shot or chipped the ball onto the green near the pin he was quick to congratulate himself: "That was well hit," he'd say, or "Right on!" A poor shot brought "We've got to fix that," and he'd drop another ball or two onto the turf and hit away to correct the problem. Never did he use the term "mulligan" after a bad shot. It was always, "Let's just hit another'n." In his mind, that wasn't cheating, it was trying to fix what didn't work. And there was certainly no rush that day, because the hole ahead of us and the one behind us had been cleared for security.

Time and again during our game the president seemed to go out of his way to put people around him at ease. On a half dozen occasions he strolled off the fairway to greet people in backyards bordering the course and clearly enjoyed meeting them, just as if he were on the campaign trail. At one point we came upon a woman with a Dalmatian dog, and he listened while I spoke with her about the problems with that breed. After we moved on he asked me, "How do you know so much about that kind of dog?'

"Because we had a Dalmatian, and he had the same problems hers has. He had fits, and had one brown eye and one blue eye. You know your friend is the cause of this, don't you?"

"What friend? Who are you talking about?"

"Michael Eisner. You know, *101 Dalmatians*. As soon as that movie came out, people set up puppy mills to breed Dalmatians. Then it came out on DVD and the same thing happened all over again.

These breeders have sisters mating brothers, and inbreeding brings on problems."

He looked thoughtful, even bothered. "I did not know that. I did not know that." He said it a third time. "I didn't know that." Clearly he was very troubled by what I told him. I wanted to say, "You can't know everything! Lots of people must know things you don't know," but of course I couldn't. He felt very strongly that Dalmatian inbreeding was something he should have known about.

At one point when he saw me heading into the woods in search of a ball he shouted, "John, John, get out of there! There're snakes in those woods, they warned me." And when he saw that I was having trouble driving on one hole he suggested I take a wider stance for better balance, which got me honors on the next three holes. He analyzed everything about the game that day, even the conversation that went along with it.

My game with President Clinton ended as it began, with a little help from nature—or maybe the Secret Service. On the ninth hole my drive hit the roof of one of the agents' golf carts and careened onto the apron of the green, evoking a wry smile from the commander-in-chief. After we posed for a final picture the president headed for the back nine and a new foursome.

That golf game happened long after Paula Jones's allegations that included mention of Clinton's distinctive genital feature, and I was telling a colleague about our golf outing afterward and chanced to mention that the president had stopped along the way to take a whiz in the woods.

My friend grinned. "Did you check out that distinctive characteristic Ms. Jones mentioned?"

"If I'd moved around in front of him to check on it, that would have been more than a little awkward."

During the Clintons' vacation on St. Thomas in the Virgin Islands, Bruce Lindsay, the president's close friend and personal advisor, who rarely spoke with reporters, invited me to join him for dinner one evening. Even though I'd already eaten and was ready for bed,

I jumped at the chance to spend some time with him. "Meet me in the lobby in fifteen minutes," he said. I got dressed and went downstairs, waited, then asked the desk clerk if he'd seen Bruce Lindsay. He told me he'd gone with several other journalists to a fish restaurant about a half-mile away, just outside the hotel compound. I walked there as quickly as I could and when I saw the line of official cars in front of the restaurant, I surmised that Lindsay quietly set up a dinner with the president. The ground floor of the restaurant was dark, so I went around to a side staircase and started up when a Secret Service agent stopped me to ask where I was going. After I told him Bruce Lindsay had invited me to dinner, he motioned for me to go on upstairs. The dimly lit room was empty except for the President and Mrs. Clinton, who were sitting at a large table in the center of the room, holding hands and deep in conversation.

I felt like an intruder, and I could tell they hadn't seen me, so I sat with a secret service agents on the other side of the room. Finally, Lindsay arrived with several other journalists and motioned for me to join them at the president's table. He greeted each of us warmly, saying, "I hope you all brought some money, because I don't have a dime," and laughed. He must not have been kidding, because later we all chipped in to pay for the dinner.

The most interesting thing that came out of our dinner table talk was the president's revelation of how he communicated with a small group of old friends. He told us about a secret ZIP code that he'd given out to about 15 selected friends, and that the White House staff knew that any mail with that ZIP code was to be opened only by the president. That same small group had access to his personal email address.

"Those are the people I really trust and want to hear from," he said. "When I'm in town, my chief of staff usually sets aside an hour after lunch every day to take calls and read emails and personal letters."

He told us about a classmate he used to play basketball with in high school in Arkansas and mentioned that if he had played poorly on the court, his friend would confront him in the locker room and would tell him, "Bill, you really played like shit today." The president went on, "If I do something now that my Arkansas friend thinks isn't good, he'll write me a letter and say 'You really played like shit today.' Every president needs people to do that for him, tell him the truth."

*

We stayed there talking for about two hours, and it was a fascinating conversation for me. He also spoke about how hard it is to stay in touch with what's real. "Everywhere I go I try to meet people. If I go to the golf course, I try to chat with people about what's on their minds, but for some reason most of them just clam up and won't say what they're really thinking, nothing more than, 'Hello, Mr. President.'"

Sometimes they didn't even get that right, either, because when I took my own usually with-it sister to a White House evening she came through the line, met President Clinton and got so flustered she said, "Hello, Mr. Kennedy," to which the president responded, "Why, thank you!"

It was a different situation when Clinton invited a group of us reporters to join him for dinner at a restaurant in the old city of Antigua in the Guatemalan mountains. The others there besides me were Bill Nichols of *USA Today*, Karen Tumulty of *Time*, Ken Walsh of *U.S. News & World Report*, Ann Compton of ABC News, Bill Plante of CBS News, John Broder of *The New York Times*, and Jim Angle of Fox News. Bruce Lindsay joined us there as well. That dinner lasted about three hours. Again the president clearly wanted to talk, and we wanted to listen. But constraints were placed on us before a word was said, with Lindsay telling us the whole conversation was off the record. In other words, no part of it was to be published or broadcast. That's a moot point now, as most of what was said that night has already been leaked.

When John Broder asked him if it would be possible for him to remove the stain of his impeachment during his remaining two years in office, the president said, "I don't agree with the premise of your question. There is no stain." Clinton went even further to give us another of those whoa! moments when he said, "I wear my impeachment as a *badge of honor*," "I did nothing illegal, nothing ethically or morally wrong . . . although I do regret that I misled the American people." Hold the fort, we were all thinking, this is news! If he saw it as a badge of honor, he had to be the only one in the country who did.

He also said that in defending himself against charges made by Ken Starr, the special prosecutor, he had racked up $20 million in legal bills. Bills which he paid off after leaving the White House.

That wide-ranging conversation covered many other topics: Hillary's possible run for the Senate, King Hussein's funeral, Boris Yeltsin's health, the Republican leadership in the House and plenty more. On the topic of Hillary's senatorial ambitions her husband said that after an exploratory visit to New York she came home saying now she understood what it's like "when your ass is out there on the limb." He said that gave him a good laugh.

When I mentioned the first lady's reputation for not liking the press, the president interrupted: "You mean more than me?" He contended that her feelings stemmed from the 1992 campaign, when she felt that the press had not dealt fairly with them. Bill Plante suggested that the New York media might be even meaner than the Washington press corps, to which Clinton replied that his wife could handle it, because the accusations of the press over the past year had inoculated him and his wife against further attacks. He went on to say that if Hillary ran for the Senate and was elected, he envisioned her as a "national senator," dealing with national issues rather than just issues that affect the voters of New York. At that point there was no mention of her later campaign for the presidency.

The evening's most entertaining disclosure was Clinton's telling us that at 8:30 one Saturday morning a call came to the family quarters from the Secret Service to say that Sen. Strom Thurmond was at the White House gate with his daughter and a friend and wanted a tour of the White House.

"You know, most Friday nights we're really tired," the president said, "and we like to sleep in a bit on Saturday morning, but I told them to let Strom and his party in, and gave them a tour of the entire mansion, including the family quarters." Apparently Sen. Thurmond took literally the idea that the White House belongs to all Americans..

Thurmond had enjoyed himself so much, he and his companions stayed until noon.

"You know, he may be old, but he's in great physical shape," Clinton said. "He has good genes, exercises regularly, eats five very small meals a day, never anything larger than an egg at one sitting."

13

UNTIL THE WORLD CHANGED FOREVER

Covering the White House full-time means a lot of traveling, visiting towns and cities across the U.S. and around the world, but exotic travel to such faraway countries as China, Australia, Thailand and Chile can be exhausting as well as exhilarating. For the most part, I found being on the road with the president offered a great and welcome change of pace from life in the cramped quarters of the White House press room.

These trips required astonishing investments of time, effort and money, such as the one I took with President Clinton to Australia in 1996. The White House estimates that every hour Air Force One is in the air costs the taxpayers about $56,800, and there's always a second plane for back-up in case of mechanical problems. Clinton was in Illinois once when Air Force One taxied off a runway to become stuck in the mud. Minutes later an identical presidential jetliner arrived to pick up where the first one left off. The traveling presidential fleet also includes huge cargo planes to carry helicopters and bulletproof limousines for the president's use, plus an entourage that numbers in the hundreds—Secret Service agents, presidential aides, advisers, medical personnel, cooks, secretaries, stenographers and a host of others.

For White House reporters, the White House Travel Office is a vital, yet little known, operation. It dates back to Andrew Jackson's administration and handles travel arrangements for the White House press corps, with costs billed to their respective news organizations. The office charters the press plane that accompanies Air Force One on presidential trips and handles reporters' luggage. That's a real boon, because on long trips with several overnight stops, the travel office sees to it that our luggage gets to our hotel rooms, is picked up the next morning and follows us throughout the trip.

That particular office became front-page news during the first few months of Clinton's administration, in a scandal that became known as Travelgate. It first surfaced in May 1993, when several long-time travel office employees were fired. The White House claimed that the action was the result of financial improprieties, although critics said the firings, reportedly urged by first lady Hillary Rodham Clinton, were ordered so that friends of the Clintons could take over the lucrative travel operation. The critics were right. After numerous investigations, five of the fired employees were reinstated with back pay, while two others retired.

In addition to a wealth of travel experiences with various presidents throughout the United States, visits to exotic places was another of the perks of my White House career, such as going to Barbados with the Reagans. Later there was a fascinating trip to

Australia and New Zealand with Clinton that included diving on the Great Barrier Reef and for some, bungee jumping from a railroad trestle. At Port Douglas in Queensland we discovered a novel bar that had submerged bar stools, so you could swim over and have a drink while sitting in water up to your waist.

As for the bungee-jumping site in New Zealand, that was one of two options offered for our free time—a wine tasting was the other. I can't imagine now that I gave any thought to actually jumping myself, although I opted to see what it was all about. The moment we got there I knew I wasn't about to let somebody tie my knees together and lash me to a rubber cord so I could jump off that trestle headfirst. Merely walking out onto the trestle made me nervous. .

I asked about an ominous sign reading THIS IS NO TIME TO LIE ABOUT YOUR WEIGHT, to be told they measured how far the cord would stretch according to how much you weighed. Down at the very bottom of that gorge ran a stream that might have been the size of the Mississippi for all I knew, but we were so high above it that it looked like a tiny silver thread. Even though helpers waited in a boat down below to retrieve thc bungee jumpers, I could barely imagine the terror of plummeting headfirst through the air, at the mercy of gravity and that tiny rope.

Several off-duty Secret Service agents decided to jump, and so did Gene Sperling, the president's chief economic adviser at the time. We were surprised that he took the gamble, because he didn't seem the type. After he jumped and made his way back up we rushed over to ask him what it was like.

Still pale and shaking, Sperling said, "I have a terrible fear of heights and thought this would cure it."

"Well, did it? What was it like?"

"I felt like the general surrounded by enemy troops coming up the hill to kill him. When it seemed he wouldn't survive for long, he told his aide, 'Bring me my red shirt.' The aide said, 'Why, general?' And he replied, "If I am shot, that would demoralize my men to see me bleed. So, bring me that red shirt.'"

He was still trembling as he went on with his story. "The aide brought the red shirt, with things looking worse and worse. At that the general turned to his aide again. 'Now bring me my brown pants.'"

When I heard that, I knew without a doubt that bungee jumping wasn't for me.

*

In terms of temperament, most of the time Clinton was in full control of himself, but there were exceptions. Before Ruth Bader Ginsberg won appointment to the Supreme Court she was at the White House to give a talk in the Rose Garden. Her remarks touched on what it was like growing up in a poor Jewish household and the trials and tribulations of being a Jewish woman at Harvard striving for a law degree yet not being allowed to use the library. She gave the most eloquent speech imaginable, all about what she'd been through to reach the eminence she'd achieved. When she finished there was hardly a dry eye in the crowd.

Then Brit Hume, then a White House correspondent, said, "Mr. President, sir, why all the zigzagging on this nomination before you settled on this nominee?"

I'd never seen President Clinton lose control, but he lost it then. His face froze, then turned beet-red. "Brit, for you to ask a question like that after what you've just heard, after what we've all just heard in this garden, for you to ask a question like that I have no answer." He then escorted Ms. Ginsberg out of the Rose Garden and disappeared back in the White House.

Next day we were all assembled in the briefing room waiting for the press secretary when we were surprised to see the president walk in. With a smile, he said, "Before we start. Brit, I think you had a question." "Yes, Mr. President," Brit said, "I have a question for you, but it's not the same one as yesterday."

"That's all right," Clinton said. "Fire away."

Over at one side of the press room sat presidential advisor David Gergen, nodding to the president as if to say, that was great, just the way we planned it. Clinton was well aware he shouldn't have lost his cool. And while Brit had asked him a pretty rough question at a delicate moment, it was a legitimate one, because the president he had in fact had trouble settling on his court nominee. That was Clinton's way of making up with Brit. After he answered Brit's question that morning he said, "There's another thing, Brit. You've just come back from your honeymoon, and I guess I'm a little jealous, because we never got to have a honeymoon." It was an adept piece of pacification, well thought out in advance and carried out with aplomb.

That's how Bill Clinton was, a people-pleaser most of the time, but he has a hot temper and with provocation could get very angry. His aides shared that when it happens it's a storm that sends people running for cover, but it's only a storm, and next day you're back with him where you were before. One top-ranking aide told me he really did not want to face Clinton if he got mad enough to start pointing that finger and yelling, "I TOLD YOU, NEVER EVER . . ." and sometimes the finger would almost touch your nose.

I stayed with the Clintons all the way through the campaign that brought George W. Bush into office, traveling around with him until, as he said, "the last dog has died." Regardless of his impeachment and the infamous last-minute pardons, I thought Clinton did many good things during his term in office. Presidents always get blamed if the economy turns bad on their watch, and they should get the praise if the economy is good. Regardless of the reasons, the economy was good during the Clinton presidency, the best in several generations.

Once again, at 12 noon on Jan. 20, 2001, I saw the quiet, impressive transfer of power at the White House as Clinton left, for his so-called "long goodbye" with a leave-taking at Andrews Air Force Base just outside Washington. It was a replay of that great lesson in democracy, seeing Bush's people coming in and the Clinton people going out in a peaceful transition. From television sets all around the White House we could hear the new president, George W. Bush, delivering his inaugural address at the Capitol before coming to the White House to review the inaugural parade and take charge of the government.

I hadn't covered George W. Bush during his campaign for the presidency, nor did I report on his father's time in the White House since I was with the *Today* show in New York during those years. I had met the elder Bush when he was vice president under Reagan, and I got to know him somewhat better after President Reagan was shot in March of 1981, when he took up the recuperating president's schedule. While President Reagan was hospitalized and spending time later recuperating at the executive mansion, the White House press corps switched over to cover Vice President Bush until the president was back at the helm.

So now I would be covering George W. Bush, a man I didn't know and had never met. My White House colleagues at the time included David Bloom and Claire Shipman, who had covered the younger Bush on the campaign trail. After the new president took office, he invited several of us who didn't know him personally to meet in the Roosevelt Room. Joined by about a dozen other reporters, we entered the conference room, took our seats and then stood when the president entered to introduce ourselves. I said, "Hello, Mr. President, my name is John Palmer with NBC News."

He'd been very well briefed. "Well, whom do you think I've watched for years on the *Today* show?" he said. I didn't mind that a bit, of course, and he had a few personal remarks for each of the reporters in the room. The message was, "You don't have to tell me who you are, I know who you are." Good politics.

During our session, his knowledge on a great variety of issues was impressive, everything from nuclear throw-weights to the environment, to immigration issues, medical issues and the economy.

We went around the table taking turns asking him questions, and he was quite charming, well prepared. He was never caught blind-sided, never didn't know or have the facts about any particular issue. But one unuttered question hung like a cloud over that table. None of us had asked it, but it was on everyone's mind—the belief, by many people, that George W. Bush was not intellectually up to the job, that he lacked the mental capacity to serve as commander-in-chief of the United States.

Finally when the turn fell to Wendell Golder of Fox News, Wendell said, "Mr. President, some of your critics say that you are simply not up to the job of being president of the United States, that you lack the intellectual capacity."

At that I felt a tightening in my belly, proud that Wendell had had the guts to ask the question that was on everyone's mind and thankful that I didn't have to ask it. Here we were, in this very impressive room honoring Theodore and Franklin Roosevelt, and the new president of the United States had just been asked whether he had the intellectual capacity for the job.

Wendell broke the silence by saying, "Mr. President, are your critics wrong?"

President Bush thought for a good many seconds before he looked down the table, then a half-smile flickered over his face. "Are my critics wrong? Golly, I sure hope so!"

Everybody chuckled, the tension broken, and I thought he handled it well. I admired Wendell for asking it and I was impressed by the way new president fielded the question. We all shook hands at the meeting's end, and I came out with a different feeling about George W. Bush than I'd had during the campaign. I went back to my colleagues in the NBC News booth to tell them all about it. "You know, I was really impressed by the president's knowledge of the issues. There wasn't a subject we brought up that he wasn't prepared to address," I said.

One of my colleagues asked, "John, how long were you in there?"

"About an hour."

"Well, if you'd had two hours with him, you would have plumbed the depth of his knowledge. You'd find that the bottom of the well would come pretty quickly. He has a good veneer of knowledge across the spectrum of various issues, but if you took the time to do it you could easily get to the bottom of it."

Nevertheless, I came away feeling that he had been treated unfairly by those who doubted his ability.

A couple of times after that at news conferences I asked the new president a question or two, but covering his presidency was very different than what we'd known during the previous eight years with Bill Clinton. No president likes leaks, but this one was eminently successful in stopping them. The White House quickly became a much more closed, insular place. His staffers were asked to fill out a telephone list of all the people they talked to, and if they talked to a reporter, their superiors often wanted to know what was said. That was so intimidating that rather than have to fill out that form and report to their bosses, many White House staffers simply stopped returning phone calls.

Ari Fleischer was press secretary at the time, and while he did a competent job, he wasn't part of the president's inner circle as some of his predecessors had been. With the big communication clampdown and so little information being disseminated, the job got to be extremely frustrating for me, and a considerable element of "been there, done that" played into my feelings. With another year of my contract to go, I'd covered Carter's last two years, Reagan's first two, pretty much the whole of the Clinton administration, and now at the beginning of George W. Bush's first term I decided to go to my boss, Tim Russert, and lay my cards on the table.

"Tim, I'd like to go over the wall," I told him. That was our term for getting out of the White House. I'd done it once before, then come back to the White House for a while, and with time marching on, I had other things I wanted to do—some lecturing, some writing, spending more time with my family—and I told Tim all of that.

He understood completely, so that in the fall of 2001 at the age of 66 ½, I decided to retire. Tim asked me to stay on for a couple of months until the first of the year, which I did. Because NBC has no mandatory retirement age I could have stayed on as long as I wanted to, had I still found the assignment challenging or interesting.

So for a while I worked weekends, going on the air every Saturday and Sunday for *NBC Nightly News* from the White House, and worked three days a week for MSNBC. That was a little frustrating as well, because I would often just go out and talk with a show anchor about a particular story, doing a lot of ad-libbing. It seemed to me the anchors often came to the White House just to fill time when there wasn't any real news breaking there.

Real news did break, though, on Sept. 11 of that year. It was my day off as White House correspondent, so early that I hadn't even turned on my television at home. When my brother-in-law Bob Doyle called to say a plane had crashed into the World Trade Center tower, Nancy and I turned on the television in time to see the second plane hit the second tower. Horrified, I called in to NBC's Washington Bureau right away, but all the lines were tied up, so I got dressed, put on a suit and tie and made the six-minute drive to the bureau.

Once in the newsroom I was asked to call all my sources at the White House and anywhere else to try to find out what the hell was going on. President Bush was in Florida speaking to a group of students at their school, and most people whom I called were just as confused as I. On the other hand, my contacts in the intelligence community were unanimous in their opinion: "Terrorism. It has to be terrorism." Several mentioned Osama bin Laden by name.

I phoned Nancy and urged her to go to our daughters' school to pick the two of them up. She was already on the way. At the time students there weren't allowed to have cell phones, although now they are. Nancy drove anxiously to the school to find the frightened students waiting in front of the main building for their concerned parents to pick them up. When she headed toward home she encountered so much traffic leaving the capitol that the usual seven-minute trip took her an hour.

About the time she made it back home I was dispatched to the Pentagon, where I spent the next two days and nights. On my way there I could see smoke billowing into the air as I drove to a gasoline station a few hundred yards from the crash site which had been designated as an assembly point for reporters and television crews. From that vantage point we could see the gaping hole in the southwest side of the building where the plane had hit, with flames visible on either side of the hole and coming from the building's eaves. Victims, many badly burned, were being carried out of the building. Priests arrived to give the last rites to those near death or already dead. As I looked around I saw the tops of several trees sheared off, marking the path of the low-flying plane as it aimed at and then slammed into the Pentagon.

Sobered and shaken by what I was seeing, we all knew that new era of terrorism had begun with this unimaginable strike at the very symbol of our country's military might. If it was this bad in Washington, I could only imagine the scenes of horror in New York City around the collapsed World Trade Center towers. For anyone of my generation, the Japanese attack on Pearl Harbor came to mind immediately, yet when that attack happened 60 years before, Pearl Harbor had seemed so far removed from our homes and the places where we worked. Now terror had struck in our very midst, and a nation's hearts and minds would never be the same.

Family seemed more precious than ever in the days that followed, as we learned of all those desperate cellphone calls from the towers to family members: "I love you," over and over again, were the last words of so many. Ever since, many of us always end phone calls to family and close friends with those very same words.

*

When the end of the year came I knew it was time to wind up my career with NBC, and I never really looked back. To this day I never think, Gee, I wish I hadn't left when I did, nor do I wish that I'd stayed on. Another chapter of my working life was ending, and it was time to turn that final page. They say that the past is the best predictor of the future. Had I remembered that maxim I'd have known that the world of television journalism still had plenty more for me to do.

14

FISHING—THE ULTIMATE CATCH

LIKE FINE WINE or a good cigar, fishing is an acquired taste and, in my case at least, offers its practitioner innumerable rewards. It calls for skill, a love of nature, and, most of all, patience.

The unbridled joy of anticipation arises well before the fisherman sets out for a favorite stream, river, lake, bay, or beach. While the actual experience may not live up to those expectations, it will have been time well spent. An old saying goes something like this: "In allotting each man his time on earth, God never counts the days spent fishing." True or not, angling offers plenty of rewards in itself:

solitude, time to think, reflect, and perhaps dream, all the while enjoying the wonders of nature. Catching a fish is just a bonus.

My father and I took up the sport at the same time, when I was eight years old and he 47. Dad had just lost his mother, who lived next door to us and had been his opponent at chess most evenings after supper. To fill the void left by her death, he turned to fishing and initiated me as his willing companion. We bought rods, reels and lures, picked the brains of experienced fishermen and spent many twilit evenings thereafter prowling the riverbank in pursuit of bass, carp and whatever else swam in the South Fork of the Holston flowing through my East Tennessee hometown.

As our interest and skills grew we moved our activities 50 miles from home to TVA's Cherokee Lake and bought a 14-foot fishing boat with a 5-HP Johnson outboard motor, and after we graduated to a larger boat and a 25-HP motor, good-weather months found us fishing at the lake for bass and crappie most every weekend.

Oh, the memories from those happy days! Dad taught me to drive his stick shift Ford on our way home from those expeditions, which added to my anticipation of those outings. However it came about, I quickly came down with a lifetime case of the fishing bug.

What youngster could forget hooking an eight-pound bass while trolling? I thought I'd snared a log and handed Dad my rod, but when a huge largemouth jumped and gave the line a mighty jerk, Dad handed the rod back to give me the joy of landing the biggest bass I had ever caught. Dad had a taxidermist mount that unlucky fish, which adorned a wall in my bedroom for years afterward.

We were forever experimenting with fishing techniques—some helpful, some less so. Our most outlandish scheme was probably the one we hoped would help us locate and track an entire school of fish. As soon as we caught the first one, we'd attach a fishing line to its mouth and tie a small balloon to the other end. Our theory was that the floating balloon would lead us to a whole flotilla of fish as soon as our bellwether rejoined his peers. To our disappointment, it never worked.

Then there was that unfortunate time when, in the interest of sanitation, I set fire to some toilet paper in the woods. The resulting blaze quickly spread and soon engulfed a thick pine forest. Dad brought our fishing trip to an abrupt halt and drove me to the nearest forest ranger station where, under his watchful eye, I confessed to causing all that black smoke rising in the western sky.

Another of life's lessons came later that summer in South Carolina while our family was vacationing at Myrtle Beach. Dad enjoyed surfcasting for hours even when there seemed to be no fish in the sea, and he was waist-deep in the water when I waded out to join him, mustering up my most nonchalant voice. "How's it going?"

Dad turned to answer and noticed a crowd gathered on the beach. "Say, son, what's going on up there?"

I hoped I sounded casual. "Oh, some kids were playing softball, and one of 'em got hit with the bat."

Dad's suspicious gaze settled on me. "Did you have anything to do with it?"

Busted. "Well, I was the batter, but the catcher was standing too close. It was an accident."

Accident or not, Dad made me spend my remaining vacation days in that boy's hotel room, reading him stories while the egg-sized bump on his forehead slowly disappeared.

During my teen years our father-son team branched further out—surfcasting along South Carolina's beaches for pompano and mullet; trolling for northern trout and muskies in Canada; angling for marlin, sailfish and king mackerel offshore in the Atlantic; and stalking bonefish in the West Indies.

Once we were fishing for marlin off the coast of Mexico when we spied dozens of those magnificent fish, some six feet long, stacked like cordwood on a dock. Blackened by the sun and robbed of their beautiful silvery blue, they were fit only to be ground up for dog food. For both Dad and me that was a turning point. The thrill of big-game fishing faded, and we abandoned it for a more satisfying pursuit that called for greater skill—going after smaller fish with light tackle. That disillusionment also marked the start of our mutual adherence to catch-and-release fishing, a policy I've tried to follow ever since. A fish is too precious to catch just once!

*

In the mid-1960s, while working at NBC News in Chicago, I saw a movie short about a Canadian fly-in fishing camp on Cormorant Lake north of Winnipeg. It was one of those places fishermen dream about—an out-of-the-way, virgin lake reachable only by floatplane, where Indians paddle out in their birch-bark canoes to ferry you and your luggage to a rustic fishing lodge. I could almost feel the bliss of arriving there, knowing that we'd spend all day every day during the week that followed angling for Walleyes and Northerns and relishing the triumphs of the day every evening.

When I phoned Dad at home in Tennessee to tell him about it he caught my enthusiasm. "You make all the arrangements and I'll pick up the tab."

That's how it happened. Three weeks later we were off to the wilds of northern Canada by plane, train and, finally, floatplane. Dad and I had just crammed ourselves into the two tiny seats of a single-engine plane when our young pilot announced proudly that he'd be 16 on his next birthday. At that Dad and I started muttering to each other about the fix we were in. The lad, overhearing us, tried to reassure us by boasting that he already had two years of flying experience under his belt.

Dad wasn't satisfied. "What about your fuel gauge? I see the needle's sitting on empty."

"Oh, that," our adolescent pilot said. "Don't pay no attention to that, it's been broke as long as I can remember. Anyway, I filled her up just last week, and even if we was to run out of gas I'd just put her down on one of these lakes and radio my dad to fly in with a can of gasoline."

We dared not ask whether the radio still worked.

Day One of our fishing on Cormorant Lake was a great success. Charlie, our genial guide, put us onto some big fish and served us a delicious shore lunch that featured some of our catch. Back at the lodge that evening we were thanking Charlie for promoting our success when he told us sadly that he couldn't come back the next day.

"My little girl's sick, and I have to come up with some money to buy her medicine."

Dad said, "How old's your little girl?"

"Ten months old," Charlie said, serious as a judge.

At that Dad opened his wallet and handed Charlie a $20 bill. "Use this to buy your medicine, and if the baby's okay, be here again in the morning to guide us."

Beaming, Charlie promised to be back at 6 a.m. sharp for another day on the lake. But when morning dawned Charlie was nowhere to be found.

The lodge's manager saw Dad's troubled face and strolled over. "What's the problem, Mr. Palmer?"

"We expected Charlie again today, but he hasn't showed."

"In that case," the manager said, "you must have violated one of the cardinal rules of guide-fishing."

Dad was a stickler for doing things right. "Oh? What rule is that?"

The manager smiled. "Never tip your guide until the last day, and above all never do it up here in the wilds."

"But Charlie told me he needed money for his sick baby's medicine!"

"Oh, the old sick child story? Well, some of the other guides saw Charlie staggering around last night with a whiskey bottle in his hand. That's where your tip went."

Two days later Charlie came back to guide us again and managed to stay away from alcohol for the rest of the week, or at least till after Dad handed over his second and final tip.

*

Before we discovered Cormorant Lake we'd already been fishing at the Bahama island of Bimini several times. Only a few miles long and less than a mile wide, Bimini offers unique fishing opportunities—shallow flats ideal for bonefishing on its eastern side, while on the west, the seabed drops off hundreds of feet. Ideal for deep-sea fishing.

The reality is that Bimini's entire economy depends upon fishing. During winter months when fishermen flock to the island, its population of black-and-yellow hound dogs appears healthy and well fed, but during the long, hot summer months when the fishing crowd seeks out cooler climates those dogs are scrawny—a graphic illustration of trickle-down economics.

During what would prove to be our last stay at Bimini's Big Game Fishing Club, Dad and I were playing chess after supper on the patio outside our ground-floor room when a local steel band came by asking if there was a song we'd like to hear. I looked to Dad, who suggested one of his favorites, "Yellow Bird." The band launched into the song, and when it ended Dad thanked the leader and offered the man a dollar. At that, to Dad's astonishment, the band's leader took the dollar bill, tore it into shreds, and blew the pieces back into dad's face.

Sure, the tip was a bit light, even for the 1960s, but we knew then and there that the island had changed. Over the years we'd encountered a spirit of friendliness and willingness aimed at encouraging tourism. Things were different now that Miami television regularly aired coverage of H. Rap Brown and other militant civil-rights leaders, inciting street protests and other violent demonstrations all across the States. I'd already seen enough in the Midwest to make their anger very real to me, and that was our last trip to Bimini.

A couple of years later I was on a deep-sea fishing trip far off the coast of Key West near Cuban waters with my friend Phil Caputo, former Marine and author of *A Rumor of War* and other bestsellers, when a U.S. Navy helicopter swooped low over our boat and hovered there for several minutes. More experienced than I at fishing in the Florida Straits, Phil waved to the pilot as he reassured me.

"Don't worry, they're just checking to see if we're smugglers or fishermen. Our lines in the water will show them why we're here."

During my Chicago years, even though the fishing in Lake Michigan wasn't great, two friends and I owned a used 24-foot cabin cruiser named the *Sea-Deuce*, and any time I could get out onto the water I was there. Once we were on our way across the lake with night falling when a heavy fog suddenly engulfed us. We couldn't figure out why the trip was taking us so much longer than we'd expected, but something had to be wrong. I was searching for answers when I noticed a beer can somebody had set next to the compass, throwing all readings off by 30 degrees.

Right away we shut down both engines and began ringing the fog bell to let other boats know we were there when a strange sound came floating across the water—barking dogs. We dropped anchor on the spot and waited for the fog to lift. When clearing came with dawn we saw how dangerously close we'd come to the rocky Michigan shoreline and, fortunately for us, a dog kennel.

*

During my Beirut sojourn for NBC News, I witnessed a type of fishing even more bizarre than Dad's and my strangest experiments. I was swimming at a seaside beach club one Sunday when a colossal underwater explosion rocked the area so violently I thought my eardrums had burst. It wasn't gunfire, that much I knew. As terrified bathers all around me scrambled out of the water also holding their ears, a couple of fishermen in a nearby boat hurriedly gathered up stunned fish that had floated to the surface. The lifeguards went swiftly into action, dove into the water, swam to the fishing boat and dragged the two fishermen to shore where they received a sound beating. After that word got around pretty fast that fishing with dynamite near the beach club was strictly taboo.

*

My eight years as news anchor on NBC's *Today* show were some of the best in angling terms, because my work schedule of 4 a.m. to noon allowed considerable time for afternoon and early-evening forays on Long Island Sound. We lived near the shore for a time, and with my buddy Greg Massa I spent many hours on my 24-foot Grady White boat. Our oldest daughter, Molly, was catching the fishing bug too—by age six she was good at handling the lines and boathook at the dock. Molly was also good at spotting seagulls diving for bait fish out in the Sound—a sure sign of bluefish in the area, sometimes so many of them that we'd catch a dozen four- to eight-pounders in an hour's time.

Pound for pound, I consider blues the best fighting fish there is. Bluefish are as agile as an all-star shortstop, imbued with the fighting spirit of a prize bull, and they've been known to strike a lure on a full stomach just for spite. The record blue caught in America by rod and reel, off a pier at Cape Hatteras in 1972, weighed 31 pounds 12 ounces. Unfortunately bluefish are far more fun to catch than to eat, because they have a gamy taste and should be eaten as soon as possible once they're caught. And yet, strangely enough, few things taste better after a day of fishing than smoked bluefish accompanied by a cold beer.

I can't deny that, as author John Hershey noted in his book *Blues*, the length and weight of a fish often expand with the telling, driven by "the mysterious force of nature that pushes people's hands apart when they're trying to tell how big the fish was that got away." Hershey goes further to quote a Maine fishing guide: "The only difference between a hunter and a fisherman is that the fisherman expects to be branded a liar and therefore exercises some control over his imagination."

All fishermen, including me, have stories about the one that got away, but how about the dozen that got away? Near the end of a successful day's fishing with Dad I added our latest catch to 11 others on the stringer, then tossed the whole lot into the lake, forgetting I hadn't reattached the stringer to the boat. Dad was not pleased.

Since I'm confessing all, I'll admit to another fishing horror story from Belize. Most fishermen, including me, learn early on that the best way to keep a bass or bluefish from spitting out the hook is to keep a tight line. With tarpon fishing, though, you must do exactly the opposite. At the instant a tarpon strikes you must give him slack, because that particular fish's mouth is so bone-hard inside that a tight line will surely pop the lure out. Tarpon fishermen have a phrase for it: "Bow to the King." Despite the screams from my guide I failed to follow that rule on not one, not two, but three consecutive strikes. My guide hardly spoke to me the rest of the day.

*

Every June for more than 20 years, my wife Nancy and I have attended the John Havlicek Celebrity Fishing Tournament on Nantucket and Martha's Vineyard off the Massachusetts coast. Over its lifetime this tournament, run by John and his wife Beth, has raised hundreds of thousands of dollars to help children with birth defects.

I first met John Havlicek at Redbone Celebrity Fishing Tournament in the Florida Keys. The basketball Hall-of-Famer was there with other celebrities, including baseball great Joe DiMaggio and sportscaster Curt Gowdy. Other frequent celebrity guests included actor Jim Sikking, baseball great Ted Williams and scores of other sports stars, famous entertainers and fishing celebrities—an impressive group.

On my first morning we stood on the dock ready to leave for a day's fishing when I recognized DiMaggio himself at my side. Gowdy was there too, and he spoke up. "John, you know Joe, don't you?"

I suppressed a gulp. "No, I haven't had that pleasure."

At that Gowdy walked away, leaving Joe and me in an awkward silence. To break the ice, I asked DiMaggio about the previous night's clambake on the beach, which I'd missed because of a late flight.

"It was great," Joltin' Joe said, "if you like bugs and sand in your food and can't see what you're eating because a 30-knot wind blew out all the torches." To put it mildly, he was not in a good mood.

Just then Gowdy, puffing away on a cigar, pulled up to the dock in his boat. "Get in, Joe," he said.

DiMaggio growled, "Not on your life, not until you douse that cigar."

"Hey, Joe," Gowdy came back, "How many times did I see you in the Yankee dugout with a cigarette in your mouth? There were days I thought the dugout was on fire!"

"I was a lot younger and dumber then," DiMaggio said. "Now put out the damn cigar."

I knew Joe could still call the plays when I heard the hiss of Gowdy's stogie hitting the water.

*

Although tournament fishing to raise money for charity is fine, I no longer take part in fishing tournaments where the object is simply to win cash prizes or merchandise. The temptation can be enormous, because some professional tournaments now offer tens of thousands of dollars in prize money. At one such tournament in New Rochelle, New York, the prizes were so valuable that at least one entrant hoped to win it the easy way. His "winning" catch was disqualified after a suspicious judge cut open the fish's belly and found it frozen. Apparently, the angler had caught the prize fish days before and kept it in his freezer until tournament day.

Tournament fishing does add competitiveness to the sport, but much of it is about money, like the shark-fishing tournament held every July at Oak Bluffs, also on Martha's Vineyard. As the local newspaper pointed out, its organizers are exploiting the public's fear of and fascination with sharks, unjustly heightened by Peter Benchley's novel *Jaws* and its later film adaptation. Benchley, to his credit, spent the last years of his life fighting to reverse the damage his novel had done, but the numbers of most shark species have plummeted by at least half over the past decade. The $1,400 entry fee for the Oak Bluffs shark tournament produces more than $300,000 in prize money for the winners, along with their grotesque trophies—dead sharks hung up for public display. With such pressure as that, survival of that particular species doesn't appear to stand a chance.

Fishing everywhere is big business, and like any sport involving big money, it carries with it the danger of exploitation. We're not talking about cane poles and worms here, because according to the American Sportfishing Association the U.S. has about 44 million fishermen, and we spend millions of dollars a year on the sport.

*

Spencer Palmer, my dad, best friend and fishing companion, died in 1979 when I was forty-three—only four years younger than Dad when he first took me fishing. On assignment for NBC News in London when the sad news came, I wasn't ready to let my father go, but since failing health meant his own fishing days were long past I took consolation in his special legacy to me—the joys of a sport that will be mine, if I'm lucky, for the rest of my life. He had taught me how to cast a surface lure for bass in lake waters, then the art of throwing a fly into a fast-flowing stream and still later how to listen over the roar of a charter-boat engine for the outrigger's zinging sound that signals Fish On. And over and above a love of fishing, he left me with many valuable lessons about life.

*

For the past 25 years my friend Greg Massa, with the gracious approval of his wife and mine, has joined me for numerous fishing trips to Canada, Florida, Virginia, Montana and Oregon, and closer to home we've fished for bass in the Potomac in Washington, D.C. In later years I've enjoyed similar trips with two fine, young fishermen—Doug Romaine and Tommy Krauth.

Nowhere has the fishing been better, more exciting, or more challenging than on the Bighorn River in Montana, which boasts thousands of trout per mile—a figure put forth by wildlife officials who periodically shock sections of the river with electricity, then count the temporarily stunned fish that float to the surface.

On my excursions to the Bighorn I stay at the Eagle Nest Lodge on the Crow Indian Reservation with John and Rebecca Shirley, whose hospitality makes the place a second home for their dozen or so guests. Not only do their fly-fishing guides impart their skills to visiting anglers, they also serve up a great shore lunch.

Bryant Gumbel, my friend and former *Today* show host, used to argue with me that fishing was a hobby, not a sport since, he claimed, it required no physical stamina or skill. I countered that it is undoubtedly a sport that requires not only skill but patience. His opinion would change if he ever managed to hook a big steelhead trout with a tiny fly on five-pound test line. Steve Chaconas, another friend and top bass-fishing guide, makes the case for me: "Fishing is a *skill* [my italics]. The only luck in fishing is not falling out of the boat."

*

Several years after Jimmy Carter left the White House, he and I spent a day together at his secluded vacation cabin hard by a trout stream in the North Georgia mountains. He'd written a book about his love of fishing and the outdoors, and as an ardent fisherman myself, I jumped at the chance to shoot a television interview with him on the subject.

My crew hooked us up with wireless microphones as we waded the stream and cast trout flies into a deep pool, under the watchful eyes of two Secret Service agents who followed along the bank. I'd barely begun the interview when Carter hooked a big brown trout, and at the moment he landed his fishy prize I blurted out, "Mr. President! If you'd been that lucky in Washington you might have had a second term."

My comment met with dead silence and that familiar cold, steely glare. I'd overstepped my bounds, for even though many months had passed the pain of defeat was clearly still very much with the former president. To his credit he continued the interview with no mention of my rude remark.

Many U.S. presidents have found solace by spending time in a trout stream. Former President Herbert Hoover, an avid fisherman, put it this way: "I have discovered the reason why presidents take to fishing—the silent sport. Next to prayer, fishing is the most personal relationship of man. Fishing seems to be the sole avenue left to presidents through which they may escape to their own thoughts and find relief from the pneumatic hammer of constant personal contacts. Moreover, it is a constant reminder of the democracy of life, of humanity and of human frailty—for all men are equal before fishes. And it is desirable that the president of the United States should be periodically reminded of this fundamental fact—that the forces of nature discriminate for no man."

For me, fishing is much more than an enjoyable way to spend a day. It gives me time and space to reflect, away from the pressures of television news. It offers delightful pauses in my life to reorder priorities and goals. It has a spirituality that brings me, at once, closer to God and to nature. It feeds all the senses: the sight of a trout taking a dry fly and breaking water with a huge splash, the sound of a screaming reel as a big fish makes a run, the feel of a tug on your line when a fish takes the bait, the watermelon-like smell from the oil slick left when blues slash through a school of bait fish and, finally, the joy of releasing your catch to swim and live again.

More than 300 years ago Izaak Walton mused, "You will find angling to be like the true virtue of humility, which has a calmness of spirit and a world of other blessings attending upon it."

Brother Izaak said it all.

15

FAMILY, UN-RETIREMENT, AND JOURNALISM TODAY

SO IT WAS contentedly that at age 66½ I retired from NBC News after forty years, looking forward to spending more time with Nan and our three daughters, reading and writing, playing a little golf, even traveling some. You might think I'd have had my fill of travel, but always being the reporter with the suitcase by the door is a hard habit to break. In retirement I discovered one thing pretty quickly—you can't play golf every day, or at least I can't. Plenty of people do that and seem to enjoy it, so whenever I want a game I know avid golfers who are always ready to play.

At first, invitations to speak or emcee charity events and my involvement with nonprofit organizations filled some of my time, but the fact remains that I've always been fascinated with the news. Retired or not, I was still up early every morning, reading the newspaper and surfing the Internet. During those first few retirement years I probably watched more news and read more news than ever before, because I had the time to do it. And it was certainly nice to be at home for more of the family's events, for my daughters' special milestones, free to enjoy leisure time with Nancy.

My experiment with retirement turned out to be rather short lived, however, ending in August of 2006 when veteran producer Jay Garfinkel offered me the opportunity to anchor several programs for Retirement Living Television, a new cable venture launched by visionary retirement-community scion John Erickson. Given a fresh chance to use my habit of keeping up with current events and continuing to use skills built up in a long television career, I decided to resume an active role in news and public affairs.

Today I can honestly say that few things in my broadcasting career have given me more personal satisfaction than hosting RLTV's various presentations. *The Informed Citizen* is a political program, while *The Prudent Adviser*, which I did with former *NBC Dateline* correspondent Lea Thompson, deals with finance, and my interview program *Encore with John Palmer* has featured a wide range of guests including Alan Greenspan, the late Art Buchwald, Tom Brokaw, Oliver North, Mike McCurry, Walter Isaacson, Bob Schieffer, Helen Thomas, Sam Donaldson, Tim Russert, Marlin Fitzwater, G. Gordon Liddy, General Richard Myers, Letitia Baldridge, Admiral Stansfield Turner, Norman Minetta, Dorothy Height, Lee Hamilton, Bill and Janet Cohen, Mario Cuomo, Ed Koch, Geraldine Ferraro, Bryant Gumbel, and movie and television stars of my generation including Phyllis Diller, Rose Marie, Ed Asner, Jim Sikking and Sally Kellerman.

One of my more entertaining interviews had as its subject veteran commentators Marvin and Bernard Kalb. These brothers have a sort of act together, coming on like Abbott and Costello, which can be highly amusing. My first experience of their routine happened at Harvard, where the School of Business and School of Education sponsored a joint forum in political science for teachers from around the country. Marvin headed it up, and I participated in it for three or four years. He'd bring Bernie on and they'd do their shtick about the news together, almost like Jewish vaudeville. So I was ready for them when they showed up for my program.

We'd started the interview when Bernie's phone went off. RING ... RING ... it played some tune or other. He reached for the phone and said, "HELLO!" Bernie has a very loud voice. "HELLO! YES ... DEAR, I'M ON A LIVE TELEVISION PROGRAM. ... NO, THE PAINTERS ARE SUPPOSED TO DO THE *BACK* ROOM UPSTAIRS FIRST."

When I looked to the floor director for a cue he was signaling me not to stop, so I let Bernie go on and on with his conversation about the painters, although I said, "Marvin, I guess we ought to take a pause here and wait till Bernie finishes."

Bernie was still holding forth, loud as could be: "YES, WHAT? ... OKAY, BUT I CANNOT TALK NOW! I'LL CALL YOU BACK! SHEESH!" He stuck the phone back in his pocket, and we kept the whole thing in the show because it was fun.

Retirement Living Television is geared to people 55 and older. We deal with big issues such as stem-cell research and other timely health topics, immigration, U.S. foreign policy, senior lifestyles, financial issues and politics as well as dozens of other subjects that directly affect the lives of senior Americans. We don't do shuffleboard shows! In many people's minds I may be something of a poster boy for RLTV, having officially retired then deciding, like many other seniors, that I'd rather be busy and engaged with life. Nancy said she detected a decidedly new spring in my step when I get up every morning, and after television news legend Walter Cronkite joined RLTV in the fall of 2007, no longer was I the oldest kid on the block.

*

Now, a word about television journalism today. Since I now carry the label "veteran" news broadcaster—I think that's a euphemism for "getting on up there"—I'm frequently asked what I think about television news as practiced today, and how it has changed over the years.

When I began in broadcast news at WSB-TV in Atlanta in 1960, we shot black-and-white film with huge Auricon cameras that weighed about a hundred pounds. And something new, called "videotape," had just been introduced. We used to think, as the song from *Oklahoma* has it, "Everything's up to date in Kansas City. We've gone about as far as we can go."

But then came color television with color videotape; small unobtrusive microphones, cameras and recorders; satellites; computers; cellphones; and websites. Unfortunately, reporters haven't always kept up with these technological advances. Nowadays when covering, say, a fire, the crew, under intense pressure to "go live," is set up and ready to do just that before the reporter has a chance to get the facts or find out what's really going on.

Then, too, the blending of news and entertainment straddles a line that has become increasingly blurred. Stories focused on celebrities and sensational crimes are often featured on the networks' evening news programs at the expense of far more important events. Now with three cable news channels—CNN, MSNBC and Fox—the blurring has become even more pronounced. Stories about scandals routinely take precedence over more meaningful events, and while Fox News has a clear conservative agenda, MSNBC has moved to the other end of the political spectrum. In a weird way, those two news channels, taken together, actually come close to achieving the "fair and balanced" approach Fox News claims for itself.

Then there is the tendency by cable news channels to give great importance to trivial events. The late distinguished news broadcaster David Brinkley put it well when he said, "The one function that TV news performs very well is that when there is no news, we give it the same emphasis as if there were."

Several years ago Adam Cohen wrote an excellent essay for *The New York Times* about what Thoreau might think of today's 24/7 news cycle. As the following excerpt reveals, Thoreau's observations are as cogent now as when he wrote them.

Thoreau would be disturbed by today's endless flood of celebrity bulletins and made-for-cable-TV courtroom face-offs, not because he thought gossip was inherently wrong, but because of what it was distracting America from. He missed the opportunity to deplore the fact that people who can rattle off the details of the voting in *American Idol* know little about the presidential campaign, and that the Laci Peterson killing got more attention than North Korea's nuclear program. He anticipated long before the 24-hour news cycle and cellphones that in modern America, the problem might well be not too little access to information, but too much.

*

In the 1960s, the average length of a political candidate's sound bite on television newscasts was 42 seconds. Now it's a mere eight. David Brinkley, noting this trend toward brevity, summed it up nicely himself: "If Moses came down from the mountain today with the Ten Commandments, television news would report it something like this: 'A man, who calls himself Moses, came down from the mountain today with a 10-point plan for human survival. Tonight, we have time to tell you about two of the most important ones.'"

There is no such thing as an objective point of view. No matter how hard reporters try to maintain that ideal, we are influenced by our society, our culture and the experiences we had growing up. Yet ethics and objectivity are strong influences on news reporters, and when we step over the line, good new organizations have editors in place to backstop. Even so, at times reporters are obliged to take a stand. In response to criticism regarding her reporting of clear evidence of genocide during the siege of Sarajevo, Christiane Amanpour, chief international correspondent of CNN, explained it this way: "There are some situations one simply cannot be neutral about, because when you are neutral [in those situations] you are an accomplice. Objectivity doesn't mean treating all sides equally. It means giving each side a hearing."

Veteran White House correspondent Helen Thomas has a saying all reporters should remember: "If your mother tells you she loves you, check it out." One of the hardest-working reporters I have even known, Helen covered the White House since the Kennedy administration. She, along with the late Frances Lewine, White House correspondent for the Associated Press who covered six presidents, led the fight against discrimination against women in the journalism profession.

Frances, too, had a memorable work ethic, telling the *Washington Post* shortly before she died at the age of 86: "I don't understand people who quit. We have the best jobs in the world. I have a front-row seat to history. What are you going to do that's possibly better than this?" In the fall of 2007 when Frances accepted an award from the University of Missouri's School of Journalism, she said, "In times like these, when the credibility of our nation and our president often comes into question, it is the reporter on the scene that can raise issues and put the spotlight on problems so the nation can address them." That tradition of excellence in White House Coverage has been continued by such reporters and writers as AP correspondent Terry Hunt, one of the best in the business.

And throughout the profession fine young reporters are doing great work, many of them in broadcast news. Richard Engel, has distinguished himself with outstanding original reporting overseas for NBC News. He speaks and reads Arabic fluently, as well as being fluent in Italian and Spanish and his bravery and insight covering armed conflict make him a standout. Kate Snow is another excellent young reporter and anchor who is as much at home covering politics and domestic issues as she is reporting from overseas. ABC News Correspondent David Wright, who has reported from 40 countries, covering major news events in the Middle East, Europe, Africa, India and here in the States, has won numerous awards for his coverage of the Darfur genocide in Sudan.

Lee Cowan, now with CBS's *Sunday Morning*, is one of the best writers and story tellers on the air and is an integral part of what may well be the finest news broadcasts on television. And I'm not just saying that because he's my son-in-law.

*

Coupled with such experienced broadcast journalists as Andrea Mitchell, Pete Williams, Lisa Myers, Charlie Gibson, Christiane Amanpour, Judy Woodruff and Bob Schieffer, among others, these younger reporters offer television news viewers a rich choice.

NBC News Correspondent David Bloom would certainly be among these outstanding younger reporters, had his life not been cut tragically short. David was traveling with the 3rd Infantry Division during the U.S. invasion of Iraq when he suddenly suffered a deep-vein thrombosis and died of the resulting pulmonary embolism. He is remembered for creating his "Bloom Mobile," an Army tank retrofitted with live television and satellite transmission equipment so he could broadcast continuous reports as U.S. troops made their way across the desert to Baghdad.

David and I worked side-by-side for two years at the White House, where I appreciated his tireless and dogged reporting when he was on the trail of a good story. A passionate family man, David Bloom is survived by his wife Melanie and their three daughters. One can only imagine the great things he would have accomplished in broadcast news had he lived. Appropriately, in 2006 the Radio and Television Association established the David Bloom Award to honor excellence in enterprising reporters, naming as the first recipient *ABC World News Tonight* co-anchor Bob Woodruff, another outstanding journalist, who was seriously wounded in Iraq.

*

Despite the revelations that some Americans don't know the name of the president of the United States, and despite the flaws of broadcast and cable news (of which there are more than a few) the American people are better informed today than ever before. I'm proud of the role we in television news have played in American society to inform and bring perspective to events. But as the internet siphons more and more viewers away from both newspaper and network news, if broadcast news is to continue to be a serious, meaningful source of information for the public, broadcasters must do a better job of exercising responsibility and care as to what they put on the air and how they present it. For as Edward R. Murrow observed years ago, "Television can illuminate and, yes, it can even inspire. But, it can do so, only to the extent that humans are willing to use it to those ends. Otherwise, it is merely wires and lights in a box."

After almost half a century as a television news reporter and anchor, I'm amazed to see our country still struggling with many of the same issues and problems that we faced in the 1960s, such as race relations, healthcare and education. And of course there will always be new concerns. The fear of nuclear war with the Soviet Union, so much a part of my growing-up years after World War II, has been succeeded by the menace of international terrorism. Among today's other cogent issues are our national debate over immigration, fueled by the influx of millions of illegal immigrants and the continuing dispute over global warming in the face of clear evidence that it threatens our planet. These are all issues that can and will be resolved, provided that free and vigorous journalism keeps them before the public eye.

News broadcasting has given me a fun, exciting and most satisfying career. In what other profession would I have met and come to know four presidents of the United States, or such scientists as Dr. Jonas Salk and such world leaders as Egypt's Anwar Sadat? In one lifetime, most people can't expect to have more than two or three careers, if that; but journalists can sample what it is like to be a business entrepreneur, a politician, an astronaut, a movie star, a pope, a farmer, a flood victim or an inmate on Death Row. You name it, we report on it. And reporters do meet the most fascinating people. On a personal level, I would never have met my wife Nancy had we not been assigned to work together on a news story. I wouldn't have traveled throughout the world as a foreign correspondent, nor lived in the Middle East and in France, nor would I have covered the White House for a dozen years or anchored the *Today* show news.

When I think of all those who helped me along the way the list quickly grows long.

My dad, by his example, taught me valuable lessons about life, including a healthy work ethic epitomized in one of his favorite sayings: "Make the most difficult thing you have to do each day your first order of business."

My mom passed along a sense of humor and appreciation for the value of community service.

My late sister Audrey, who loved sports and life itself, left this earth far too early, but not before setting an example that I still haven't matched.

My sister Pat, by her own initiative of joining the Peace Corps at the age of 70, still holds up a worthy model of giving back.

Today my branch of the Palmer family has become something of a journalistic clan. My wife Nancy is a screen and magazine writer as well as an event producer. Our two older daughters are in California. Molly, the eldest, is a producer with the *Today* show, while middle daughter Carter is a casting associate for reality television programs. Our youngest, Hope, is right here in the NBC Washington Bureau working as a researcher for *Today*.

As I reflect on my career, I think of all the "ifs" that could have given me a far different life. Suppose Nancy Necessary Pridemore hadn't been my high school debate coach nor encouraged me to go to Northwestern University to pursue broadcast journalism. Suppose family friend and teacher Lib Dudney hadn't offered constant encouragement. Suppose News Director Martin Karant at my hometown radio station hadn't taken a chance by giving me my first broadcasting job. Suppose I hadn't signed up for Professor Richard Leopold's Northwestern University course "The Diplomatic History of the United States," which kindled a lifelong interest in world events. Suppose such news professionals as WSB-TV's News Director Ray Moore and NBC News executives Reuven Frank, Richard Wald, Ed Planer, Irv Margolis, Sid Davis, Tim Russert, Steve Friedman and Rebecca Bell hadn't taken an interest in my career and helped me along the way. I truly feel that I am standing on the shoulders of every one of these mentors who saw something special in me and did what he or she could to nurture it.

My book editor, Betsy Tice White, a friend since junior-high days in Tennessee, gave me the opportunity to reflect on my career by insisting that I write this book. Without her help, encouragement, and yes, occasional nagging, I would never have put it all down on paper. For this I will always be grateful, as I am for the deeper friendship and trust that has developed between us during the course of the work. Way back when we shared the fun of acting in high school class plays, who knew it would lead to this amazing result?

And as for my career in broadcast news, given the chance, would I do it all over again? You bet I would, doing my very best to enjoy it even more the second time around.

PHOTO GALLERY

1986–2012

Palmer Family portrait with Carter, 4; Molly 6; and Hope, 3 months, Rye, New York, 1988

John's other family on the set of *Today*, 1989

John relaxing about the cruise ship *Norway*, Miami, 1986

Interviewing aviator Chuck Yeager for *Instant Recall*, 1990

Interviewing President Clinton in flight under Press Secretary Mike McCurry's (standing) watchful eye, 1998

Greeting First Lady Hillary Clinton at White House Christmas Party, circa 1999

John as a boy fishing at Cherokee Lake, Tennessee, circa 1945

Fishing trip with Spencer Palmer, John's father, in the Bahamas, circa 1955

Once a fisherman, always a fisherman, Martha's Vineyard, 2005

John and Nancy celebrate his 75th Birthday, Sept. 10, 2010

Molly Palmer marries CBS *Sunday Morning*'s Lee Cowan, April 14, 2012

With First Lady Michelle Obama at White House Christmas Party, 2012

REMEMBERING JOHN

A Reflection by Tom Brokaw

John Palmer was a charter member of the second generation of network correspondents, a Tennessee boy who grew up wanting to take his place in the ranks with Chet Huntley and David Brinkley, Walter Cronkite, and Ed Murrow.

And so he did, covering the world from Chicago to the Middle East, from the White House to the anchor chair on NBC's *Today* show, as well as natural disasters and presidential elections.

The story of this gifted and ego-free colleague takes the reader behind the scenes with telling anecdotes and instructive insights.

His dream came true and now he's shared it with all of us.

—TOM BROKAW,
Special Correspondent, NBC News

BONUS GALLERY

Career
Memorabilia
Publicity

In Jerusalum, circa 1975

Interviewing King Hussein of Jordan, 1975

On the scene in Africa, circa 1976

John mocking himself as wartime reporter, circa 1977

Reporting from the Middle East, 1977

On assignment overseas, circa 1977

White House Correspondents Sam Donaldson (ABC), Bill Plante (CBS) and John Palmer(NBC), circa 1981

Having a laugh during a commercial break on *Today*, circa 1982

Today publicity shoot at Rockefeller Plaza, (L–R) Bryant Gumbel, Willard Scott, John Palmer, and Jane Pauley, 1983

Reporting on the *Challenger* Shuttle disaster, 1986

Scuba diving on the cruise ship *Norway*, 1986

Reporting from Washington, circa 1991

Golfing with President Clinton, Amelia Island, 1999

Interviewing actor Ed Asner for RLTV's *Encore with John Palmer*, 2010

B29-1-13-1147-S-8

EASTEN STNS

CENTEL STNS

WESTEL STNS

ATTENTION ALL STATIONS

NBC NEWS ROUTINE & EXCERPT SERVICE

SHOW OPENS

BRINKLEY LEAD & FILM: SENATE APPROVES BOBBY KENNEDY, RIBICOFF, GOLDBERG

TWO MINUTES

HUNTLEY: LAOS WRAP-UP FORTY FIVE SECONDS

LAOS FILM: U.S. PLANES IN LAOS FORTY SECONDS

HUNTLEY: U.N-CONGO WRAP-UP FIFTY SECONDS

TEXACO COMCL ONE MINUTE

ATLANTA FILM: JUDGE SAYS TWO NEGRO STUDENTS MUST BE READMITTED TO

GEORGIA UNIV; FILM OF PETITIONS, INTVUS WITH STUDENTS PRO AND CON

TWO MINUTES THIRTY SECONDS

HUNTLEY: AIR FORCE CLAIMS SIX WORLD SPEED RECORDS FOR B-58 TEN SECONDS

BRINKLEY: IKE'S LAST CABINET MEETING & MISCELLANEOUS POLITIX TWO

MINUTES

HUNTLEY PAD: KHRUSH KNOCKS SOVIET PIG PRODUCTION; GENERAL NEWS

ROUND-UP STOCK MKT REPORT ONE MINUTE

TEXACO COMMCL ONE MINUTE FIFTEEN SECONDS

HUNTLEY & FILM: NEW MANNIKINS MADE TO RESEMBLE KENNEDYS FORTY SECONDS

HUNTLEY CLOSER: THIRTY SECONDS

ENDS

NBC NEWS

Civil rights news bulletin, Atlanta, 1961

"THE QUITTER:
PORTRAIT OF A
HIGH SCHOOL
DROP-OUT"

WITH
JOHN PALMER

REPEATED BY POPULAR DEMAND

HERE'S WHAT THEY SAID ABOUT THE SHOW:

"It might be a good idea if teachers and all the high school students in this area would urge their classes to view the documentary on television and report on it."
Paul Jones, Atlanta Constitution.

"I have met 'The Quitter' hundreds of times and you have accurately portrayed his dilemma with all its frustrations and helplessness."
Judge Sam S. Harben,
Hall County Juvenile Court.

"I think your documentary shows clearly several areas where adults may begin to attack the problem."
Mrs. William S. Shelfer,
Georgia Congress—PTA.

YOU CAN'T AFFORD TO MISS THIS PROGRAM!

WSB-TV TONIGHT AT 7:00 Channel 2

This Ad Will Appear In The Atlanta Constitution and
The Atlanta Journal On May 21 -- The Date This
Program Will Be Seen.

Ad for WSB-TV Channel 2 documentary, 1962

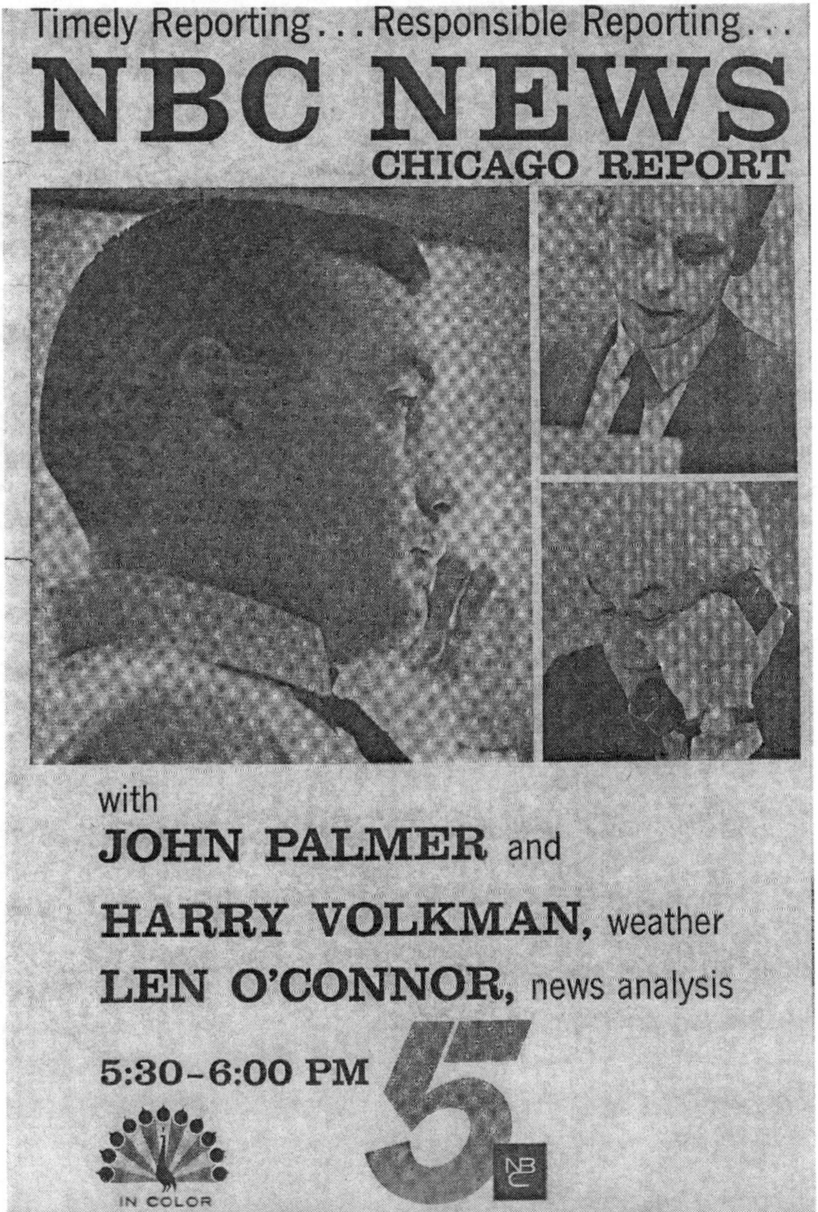

Timely Reporting . . . Responsible Reporting . . .

NBC NEWS

CHICAGO REPORT

with

JOHN PALMER and

HARRY VOLKMAN, weather

LEN O'CONNOR, news analysis

5:30–6:00 PM

IN COLOR

WMAQ NBC Chicago ad, circa 1965

WNBC NY local ad featuring John, page one, 1970

Covering all areas of the news spectrum . . . "The Sixth Hour News" with anchorman Lew Wood, city reporter Gabe Pressman, sportscaster Kyle Rote and Science Editor Dr. Frank Field, whose weather radar-scope reports complete the news picture on New York's first full hour local and world report. On "The Eleventh Hour News" Jim Hartz details the day's events, with Bob Teague and John Palmer handling the Saturday and Sunday editions.

No wonder it all adds up on NBC. With expert news coverage by the award-winning team of Chet Huntley and David Brinkley (7 pm, Mon-Fri, 6:30 pm, Sat). And the largest global news gathering organization in broadcast journalism. And television's most distinguished corps of correspondents whose ranks include John Chancellor, Frank McGee ("The Frank McGee Report"), Bill Monroe ("Congressional Report") and Sander Vanocur ("First Tuesday").

WNBC NY local ad featuring on-air personalities, page 2, 1970

BULLETIN (AP)

(NEW YORK) --N-B-C NEWS REPORTS AN ATTEMPT TO RESCUE THE AMERICAN HOSTAGES IN IRAN WAS ABORTED FRIDAY WHEN EIGHT CREW MEMBERS OF A U-S AIRCRAFT WERE KILLED AND TWO OTHERS INJURED IN A CRASH IN A REMOTE DESERT AREA OF IRAN.

THE NETWORK QUOTES WHITE HOUSE OFFICIALS AS SAYING THE PLANE WAS GLIDING OVER THE DESERT WHEN IT CRASHED.

NBC SAYS PRESIDENT CARTER IS TAKING RESPONSIBILITY FOR THE CRASH.

FURTHER DETAILS ARE NOT IMMEDIATELY AVAILABLE.

AP-RM-0425 0121EST

THE ASSOCIATED PRESS REPORTS
MY BIG WHITE HOUSE SCOOP
1980

AP bulletin of John's report on Iran Hostage rescue attempt, 1980

Luncheon

Cold Lobster
Sauce Rémoulade
Golden Twists

Medaillons of Veal
Garden Vegetables

Coconut Ice Cream
in Hibiscus Shell
Petits Fours

Demitasse

Beaulieu Vineyard
Pinot Chardonnay

Simi Rosé
Cabernet Sauvignon

Korbel Natural Champagne

The White House
Tuesday, April 22, 1980

Menu from White House Luncheon (aka John & Nancy's first date), 1980

President Reagan's explanation for not responding to question from John Palmer, West Texas, 1981

(ADVANCE FOR AMS, MONDAY, AUGUST 10, TO GO WITH TOM JORY STORY SLUGGED: TV TALK) (NY22-August 7)--CANDIDATES FOR "TODAY" HOST POST--Tom Brokaw will leave NBC-TV's "Today" show in the spring to co-anchor the "Nightly News" with Roger Mudd. When Brokaw goes on vacation Monday, NBC will give four correspondents a shot at the job. The correspondents are, from left: Bob Jamieson, John Palmer, Bob Kur and Chris Wallace. "It's not like we're running an audition," says Steve Friedman, the program's executive director."But we do want to see how these four guys will do in all phases of the job-doing the news, interviews and so on."(AP Laserphoto) (1h52010ho)1981 (all photos recent undated file photos)

"Candidates for *Today* Host" AP anchor comparison, 1981

TV SCENE

MAY 17 - 24

Will John Palmer cruise?

Or will the 'Today' show's intrepid anchor be left high and dry when the rest of the crew sets sail? Vince Staten seeks some answers on Page 3.

Staff illustration by Ben Ramsey

TV Scene magazine article, 1989

JOHN PALMER ACKNOWLEDGEMENT

Much of what went into this book has been drawn from boxes filled with old scripts, hundreds of press passes, notebooks, letters, videotapes, pictures and salvaged personal memories.

My parents encouraged me to pursue my interest in news and broadcasting, even though they didn't quite understand why I was so fired up about this newfangled thing called television. So, better late than never—Thanks, Mom and Dad.

I hope I've remembered most of those special people whose influence put me on the road to success and helped to keep me there in the pages that went before. Still, I can't fail to say thanks again to such television news executives as Ray Moore, Hal Suit, Bill Corley, Ed Planer, Sid Davis, Bob Mulholland, Bill Small, Reuven Frank, Richard Wald, Tom Pettit, Sy Pearlman, Irv Margolis, Russ Tornabene, Bill Chesleigh, Les Crystal, Steve Friedman, Marty Ryan, Tim Russert, Steve Capus, Jim Dick, David Cook, and Jay Garfinkel.

Then there are friends such as Chris and Kevin Madden whose introduction to agent Jonathan Lazear brought the gift of help with the structure of my book. Frequent golf partner Paul Hersh kept asking me how the book was coming, implanting guilt and sending me off the course and back to the computer. AP's Washington Deputy Bureau Chief Terry Hunt and his wife, Jeanie, dear friends, were always supportive.

Author's editor Betsy Tice White, a friend since junior high days in Tennessee, gave me the opportunity to reflect on my career by insisting that I write this book. Without her help, encouragement and yes, occasional nagging, I would never have put it down on paper. Betsy helped this television news reporter who spent a career shaping word to the ear learn to write for the reader's eye. Without her talents and persistence I would never have finished this effort, which stretched over three and a half years. For this I will always be grateful, as I am for the deeper friendship and trust that has developed between us during the course of the work.

Finally, words are just not adequate to thank my wife and best friend, Nancy Doyle Palmer and our daughters Molly, Carter and Hope and my son-in-law Lee Cowan, along with my sister Patricia, for their never-failing love, support and encouragement. Thank you, one and all.

JOHN PALMER

NANCY PALMER ACKNOWLEDGEMENT

John worked on this memoir for several years and then put it aside. A few days before he passed away on August 3rd, 2013, at George Washington Hospital our oldest daughter Molly thought to bring the manuscript to him in the intensive care unit and we all took turns reading chapters aloud to him. For the rest of my life I will remember his face as he listened to each story told here, smiling, gazing off to that other place, sometimes with tears streaming down his face, often chiming in with each punch line or lesson learned.

This is his story, his voice, his life.

We are very grateful to the people who helped make this wonderful book and this beautiful man come back to us again. Thanks to our NBC family—Tom Brokaw, Brian Williams, Deborah Turness, Cheryl Gould and Alexandra Wallace and to publisher Michael Fabiano and e-book producer Peter Costanzo for making John's dream come true.

Because John Palmer was our dream come true.

With love and gratitude,

NANCY PALMER
MOLLY PALMER COWAN
LEE COWAN
CARTER PALMER
HOPE PALMER

CPSIA information can be obtained at www.ICGtesting.com
Printed in the USA
LVOW10s2323240615

443784LV00026B/667/P